PRAISE FOR *BRAVE GIRL EATING*

"Brown tells the story of her family's battle with anorexia, the 'demon' that suddenly possesses her bright, pretty daughter, Kitty. Brown carefully amasses facts about anorexia and the effects of starvation in between bouts at the dinner table as Kitty refuses to eat and, occasionally, hides her food. At the crux of Brown's affecting and informative memoir is the idea that anorexia can happen to any family and that it can be defeated through determination and love, even though Brown recognizes that permanent success can be elusive." —*Booklist*

"As a woman who once knew the grip of a life-controlling eating disorder, I held my breath reading Harriet Brown's story. As a mother of daughters, I wept for her. Then cheered."
  —Joyce Maynard, author of *Labor Day*

"What sets this book apart is the author's incorporation of clinical research findings from the field of eating disorders into the story of one family's struggle . . . [A] compelling story of family strength and an inspiring story for all of us committed to treating individuals with eating disorders."
  —Evelyn Attia, MD, Director, Center for Eating Disorders,
  Columbia University Medical Center, Weill Cornell Medical College

BODY *of* TRUTH

Also by Harriet Brown

Brave Girl Eating: A Family's Struggle with Anorexia

Edited by Harriet Brown

*Feed Me!: Writers Dish About Food, Eating,
Weight, and Body Image*

*Mr. Wrong: Real-Life Stories
About the Men We Used to Love*

BODY *of* TRUTH

How Science, History, and Culture
Drive Our Obsession with Weight—
and What We Can Do About It

HARRIET BROWN

Da Capo
∞
LIFE
LONG

A Member of the Perseus Books Group

Set in 11 point Fairfield LT Standard by the Perseus Books Group

Cataloging-in-Publication data for this book is available from the Library of Congress.

First Da Capo Press edition 2015
ISBN: 978-0-7382-1769-7 (hardcover)
ISBN: 978-0-7382-1770-3 (e-book)

Published by Da Capo Press
A Member of the Perseus Books Group
www.dacapopress.com

Note: The information in this book is true and complete to the best of our knowledge. This book is intended only as an informative guide for those wishing to know more about health issues. In no way is this book intended to replace, countermand, or conflict with the advice given to you by your own physician. The ultimate decision concerning care should be made between you and your doctor. We strongly recommend you follow his or her advice. Information in this book is general and is offered with no guarantees on the part of the author or Da Capo Press. The author and publisher disclaim all liability in connection with the use of this book.

Da Capo Press books are available at special discounts for bulk purchases in the United States by corporations, institutions, and other organizations. For more information, please contact the Special Markets Department at the Perseus Books Group, 2300 Chestnut Street, Suite 200, Philadelphia, PA, 19103, or call (800) 810-4145, ext. 5000, or e-mail special.markets@perseusbooks.com.

10 9 8 7 6 5 4 3 2 1

*This book is dedicated, with love,
to all the women in my life, but especially
to my daughters
and to Ellyn Satter*

"I called you crazy. I called you a bitch.
But I never called you fat."

—Lance Armstrong,
to the wife of a former teammate

CONTENTS

ACKNOWLEDGMENTS

Thanks to Rebecca Garden, Pamela Reilly, Erik Ness, and Stephanie Fetta for reading chapters along the way and giving me excellent feedback.

Thanks as always to Miriam Altshuler, who truly midwifed this book into being. She believed in it from the start and insisted I get it right. I hope I have.

Thanks to my amazing editor, Renée Sedliar, who is a woman of uncommon perception, insight, and foresight, and to the whole team at Da Capo.

And finally thanks to Jamie, who puts up with my worst qualities and brings out my best ones.

INTRODUCTION

How My Life Changed with One Sentence

On a sticky summer evening back in the 1990s, I sit in a chair in a therapist's office and cry. My body, I tell her, is too fleshy, too hungry, too uncontained. It doesn't look like the bodies I see five hundred times a day* online, on TV, in magazines, and on billboards. It doesn't look the way it's supposed to, the way I want it to. There have been years when it did, when I weighed and measured and wrote down everything I ate, worked out twice a day, pummeled my body into shape. Inevitably, though, it reverts to its natural state. Like now, when it's thirty or forty pounds heavier than I want it to be. Than it should be.

I'm here because I want someone to fix me. Specifically, to tell me how to regain control of my body (and, yes, the brain that goes with it). This therapist runs a ten-week program that's supposed to help people with eating issues. I hope she's going to teach me how to control my appetite again, something I was better at in my

---

*In 2007, a marketing research firm estimated that people living in cities saw up to five thousand ads a day; some advertising executives and commentators question that number. Considering the continuing proliferation of ads over the last eight years, five hundred ads a day seems a conservative estimate.

twenties. Now, more than a decade later, after three pregnancies and a whole lot of living, I just can't seem to do it anymore. So I sit in the chair, leaking tears of self-pity, and wait for the therapist to break out the Kleenex and reassure me that yes, it's OK, she'll help me lose weight, we will take care of this together.

She does hand me a box of tissues. But she doesn't murmur soothingly. Instead, she leans back in her chair and looks at me. This woman in her fifties with spiky dark hair, a soft stomach, and stocky legs bridges the space between us with an expression I can't quite read. Pity? Sorrow? Judgment? Sweat slides down the back of my neck as I wait for her to save me. A long moment goes by, and then she says something unimaginable, something that will change my life, though I don't know it yet.

"What if you were OK with your body the way it is right now?" she asks.

I stare at her. What I *want* to say is "Are you fucking nuts?" I mean, that's why I'm here, because I'm *not* OK with it. Does she want me to have a heart attack or stroke or get diabetes because I'm too fat? Does she know how much time I've wasted crying in front of the mirror? Does she think I want to *look like her* for the rest of my life?

Of *course* I've never considered the possibility of being OK with this body. This unacceptable body. And I'm not *going* to consider it. That would be letting myself go, as my grandmother used to say, shaking her head, about any woman who'd gained a few pounds. Even as a child I knew what she meant: they'd stopped caring about themselves, and they'd stopped *taking* care of themselves. And now they deserved exactly what they got from my grandmother and every other woman in their social circle—censure, gossip, and pity.

I will never let myself go. I will never, ever, *ever* be the sloppy, lazy, dull, fat friend or mother or relative people like my grandmother shake their heads about.

This therapist must understand how hard it is to be a woman in this time and place and not have the right kind of body. After all, she's not exactly thin herself. She must have experienced the nasty comments and patronizing remarks directed at any woman who's considered too big. She must have felt the same shame at having a body that won't behave, can't be reined in, and doesn't look the way it should. How can she possibly ask me such a question?

I consider leaving now, mid-session, and never coming back. But something keeps me in the chair. I have the sense that if I walk out, I'll be missing something big, something important. So I sit and I rock and I stutter through the rest of the session. I don't ask any questions because I don't want to hear that I'm unfixable, that I'd better get used to living this way for the rest of my almost-certainly-shortened life. By the time I get home I'm furious with her for suggesting that I'm the kind of person who would let go of the thing I want most in the world. I might be fat; I'm not a quitter.

But her words stay with me. They haunt me as I brush my teeth and talk to my daughters and put dinner on the table. I'm in my late thirties, and it's actually never occurred to me before that some people might be OK with not being thin. Some *women*. It's as if her words revealed a huge blind spot in my vision, one I didn't know I had.

So over the next few weeks, without meaning or wanting to, I do consider them. Actually, I think about them night and day. I think about what it would be like to live in this body for the rest of my life. I also start panic-dieting, though not very successfully, swearing off carbs, then cutting out desserts, then declaring myself strictly vegan. It's all futile and ridiculous, because I can't keep up any of these new regimens for more than a day. I find myself jolting awake at night, drenched in sweat, adrenaline burning through my veins, the words *I'm fat I'm fat I'm fat* beating time in my head. I'm smart, disciplined, hardworking. By any standards I'm a successful woman. And I just can't do this anymore.

WE'RE IN THE midst of an epidemic, one that's destroying both the quality and the longevity of our lives. It affects not just us but our children, and likely their children, too. And while this epidemic has been around a while, it's growing at an alarming rate, not just here but around the world. You'd be hard-pressed to find a twenty-first-century culture that *didn't* struggle with it.

I'm not talking about overweight or obesity. I'm talking about our *obsession* with weight, our never-ending quest for thinness, our relentless angst about our bodies. Even the most self-assured of us get caught up in body anxiety: 97 percent of young women surveyed by *Glamour* magazine in 2011 said they felt hatred toward their bodies at least once a day and often much more. Ninety-seven percent—that's pretty much everyone. Another eight out of ten women say they're unhappy with their reflection.

I've interviewed hundreds of women about weight and body image over the last few years, and every one of them says she has struggled with body hatred, or continues to struggle, to one degree or another. Too many of us waste our time, our emotional energy, our very sanity trying to meet the ever-more-rigid rules about what size and shape our bodies are supposed to be. Even for women who get it, who know intellectually that the quest to be thin is ultimately both fruitless and pointless, it's unbelievably tough to challenge the cultural norms around weight.

The barrage of prescriptive messages starts early. Several studies have shown that three- and four-year-olds are afraid of getting fat, and no wonder: They're primed to absorb and internalize the lessons we teach them, which in this case means shame about their bodies and self-loathing. Even if they don't hear it at home, they get it from TV shows, books, teachers, doctors, games, and other children. Even the most confident women struggle to navigate a daily gauntlet of images and messages warning us of the psychological, social, and physical perils of not meeting society's unattainable body ideals. And this isn't just a women's issue, either; men and boys are increasingly caught up in their own variation of body anxiety (in fact, 18 percent of men say they feel fat every day)[1]: Women want to be thin; men want to be buff. Women want thigh gaps; men want six-packs.

This obsession isn't new, of course; my friends and I spent many miserable hours in front of the mirror as teens in the 1970s. What *is* new is how encompassing the issue has become. It comes at us from all directions—from the media, from doctors and medical professionals, from school administrators, from politicians, from *environmentalists*, for pity's sake. Practically every modern problem from the recession to climate change has at some point been blamed on fat. We're told that we're undisciplined, gluttonous, lazy, that our children will be the first modern generation whose lives will be shorter than their parents' because of obesity. That weight issues rack up an extra $66 billion a year in health-care costs, contribute to global warming, strain the world's food resources as much as an extra five hundred million people living on the planet.

Obsessing about weight has become a ritual and a refrain, punctuating and shaping every relationship, including our relationships with ourselves. It's become social currency not just for women but for teens and even children. My younger daughter was fifteen when she told me (with a great deal of exasperation at my naïveté), "Mom, fat-bashing is how girls bond with each other. I *have* to say bad things about my body if I want to have any friends." And saying those "bad things" to others reinforces our own inner critics, the ones that pick apart every outfit, that assess every inch of flesh, every blemish, every choice we make. We're so used to that constant inner judgment, we don't even think to question it.

The words we use to talk about our bodies have changed, too. We're no longer plump or chubby, stocky or stout or husky; now we're overweight or obese, words that connote facts and figures, illness rather than aesthetics. You're considered overweight with a BMI over 25 and obese with a BMI over 30. (According to the American Medical Association, with a BMI over 30 you're also diseased.) These words influence the way other people— including our doctors—relate to us. And, most devastatingly, they change the way we think about ourselves and others. The word *overweight,* for instance, suggests there's one acceptable weight, and everything above that is too much. It's "over" what it should be. The word *obesity* has become a diagnosis rather than a description, shorthand for a boatload of undesirable qualities: gluttony, lack of self-discipline, laziness, sloppiness, grotesqueness.

If you're reading this and thinking *wait a minute, that's not what's going on,* cast your mind back to the last TV news story or web article you saw about obesity. I bet it was illustrated with photos of extremely heavy people shown from the neck down, no faces, plodding along or overflowing a chair or scarfing down French fries or ice cream—what British psychotherapist Charlotte Cooper has described as "headless fatty" images.[2] It's tough to empathize with or relate to a faceless, fleshy blob, which is, of course, the point. (And maybe, too, there's also an element of "It's too embarrassing to show someone this fat, so we'll hide her identity." Which is equally offensive.)

I prefer the word *fat,* which is based in description rather than judgment. We have fat on our bodies, all of us; you can't be alive without it. More than half your brain is made of fatty acids;[3] without enough fat, your brain deteriorates, leaving you vulnerable to ailments from depression and anxiety to fatigue and cognitive decline.

But some people fear the word almost as much as the condition. At Syracuse University, where I'm a professor, I created a class on body diversity, in part because I've watched my students struggle with body issues over the years. They practically fall out of their chairs the first time I use the word in class. To call someone *fat* in this culture is beyond offensive; it's unforgiveable. Even Lance Armstrong wouldn't do it.

What was once a source of personal anxiety and distress has morphed into an ongoing public dialogue. Just ten years ago, a Google search for the word "obesity" returned about 217,000 hits. A similar search in just the first six months of 2014 turned up nearly twenty-seven million hits. Not that Google searches represent a scientific standard, but they do reflect a culture's preoccupations—in this case, the reality that we're more freaked out than ever about how much we weigh and what our bodies look like. Many of us believe, as the Duchess of Windsor so famously said, that we can *never* be thin enough—and that if we're not thin, we can never be successful, desirable, lovable, or worthwhile, either.

In fall 2013, former *Good Morning America* host Joan Lunden joked on the *Today Show* that one of the benefits of having triple negative breast cancer, and going through several rounds of aggressive chemotherapy, was losing weight. I know this was gallows humor, meant to help defuse a terribly painful situation. But no one would have laughed if there wasn't some truth to the idea that thinness is prized even if it comes from battling a potentially fatal illness.

The way we talk about weight has become a kind of code. "I need to lose five pounds!" we complain to a friend, meaning *Tell me I'm OK the way I am,* meaning *I don't think I'm better than you are,* meaning *I feel inadequate.* "I just can't find a way to lose this weight," we say in despair, meaning *I can't find love, or work, or success, and it's all because of this one enormous thing wrong with me.*

Every January, for instance, when the whole country engages in its annual post–New Year's self-flagellation, the media run countless stories on resolutions and diets, bikini bodies and love handles. And those stories make us feel worse, not better. They reinforce the idea that we're supposed to have Michelle Obama's arms, Jennifer Aniston's stomach, Joe Manganiello's six-pack, but they offer no useful resources.

If all this body angst made people healthier and happier, maybe we could argue that the end justified the means. But it doesn't. Instead, many of us spend a lot of our waking hours on a hamster wheel of self-loathing. We're screwed up about food, too; one recent survey found 75 percent of American women report disordered eating behaviors.[4] I believe it. I've heard my students boast about eating only once a day, seen grown women stare at a piece of bread with a heartbreaking mixture of fear and longing. We bounce between depriving ourselves and then "eating with disinhibition," a fancy way to say overeating.

And we're paying the price. Many prices, actually. When we focus on the size of Hillary Clinton's ankles rather than on her voting record, we miss the chance to make a meaningful political choice. When we can't skip a day working out at the gym, we sacrifice the chance to get a graduate degree, learn a language, acquire career skills, develop relationships, do volunteer work—to spend that time more productively in so many other ways. When we nag our children about their weight or what they eat, we're telling them they're not good enough and damaging our authentic relationships with them.

Over the years I've seen my body as an enemy to be conquered, deprived, and beaten into submission—that is, into the smallest possible shape and size. Occasionally I felt proud of its strength and curviness. But more often I saw it as a symbol of my personal weakness and shame, an outward manifestation of my inadequacies and failures. Catching sight of myself in a mirror—an experience I tried to avoid—could send me into a dark place for hours. I spent years wallowing in self-hatred because of the size of my thighs. My weight went up and down over those decades, from the low side of "normal" to mildly obese, but my level of despair and self-loathing stayed sky-high.

The worst part was that I knew better. I'd read Simone de Beauvoir, Gloria Steinem, Naomi Wolf. I understood intellectually that the more freedoms and power women achieve, the more insistent and damaging the social pressures that squeeze us (and, increasingly, men) into a certain shape, size, and attitude.

But when it came to my own body, everything I *knew* evaporated and what I *felt* became overwhelming. So while I understood that in reality I was a reasonable-looking woman, with a loving husband, beloved daughters, and good friends, I still felt freakish and ugly. I felt like I took up way too much space; I imagined myself lumbering rather than walking, bulging where I should be taut. I got so used to thinking of myself as enormous that sometimes I was surprised when I caught sight of myself in a mirror and thought, for a second, *She looks normal.* I could argue a friend off a ledge of body hatred, but I couldn't feel good about my own body. Some days I wished I could just wear a plastic bag and be done with it.

Each of us thinks our obsession with weight and body image is ours alone. We blame ourselves for not being thin enough, sexy enough, shaped just the right way. We believe we're supposed to fit the standards of the day. And if we're not in the 1 percent of the population born with the body du jour, we feel it's our fault. We believe we can get there if only we eat less, eat differently, work out more, go vegan, throw up what we eat, give up gluten, take laxatives, fast, give up sugar, fill in the blank.

But the reality couldn't possibly get any clearer: *This is not a personal issue.* This is not about your weakness or my laziness or her lack of self-discipline. This obsession is bigger than all of us. It's become epidemic, endemic, and pandemic. It comes from all around us, but it's dug its way deep under our skins, and it festers there. It's a pain that involves our deepest sense of who we are in the world. We experience the world through our bodies, our skin and neurons and nerves. Other people see us only and always in the context of our flesh and bone and blood. How can you feel good about your essential self when you hate what contains it?

You can't, as it turns out. That's how I wound up in the therapist's chair, staring at her in disbelief, wondering if she'd lost her mind. And that's how I started on a journey that's put me into a completely different place. Along the way, my relationship with food started to shift, and so did my physical sense of myself.

It took years for my perspective to evolve, years of thinking and knowing before the feelings began to change. While I still occasionally react to food as if it were an enemy to be conquered, most of the time now I focus on what feels good—physically and mentally—rather than on weight. I eat well and enjoy what I eat. I take long walks and go for bike rides because doing those things makes me feel good, not because they burn calories.

And I see the beginnings of change in other people, too. There's evidence that fewer American women are dieting now than in previous years.[5] We're starting to talk about *health* rather than *weight*—at least occasionally. We pay lip service to the fact that bodies naturally come in all shapes and sizes even if many of us don't believe it, especially when it comes to ourselves. I think we're smart enough to be confused by the half-truths and misconceptions, to know there's a lot we don't yet understand about weight and health, about how metabolism works and why "calories in, calories out" may not always hold true. We're beginning to separate facts from fictions and, each of us, make decisions about what's best for our health.

Because contrary to what you hear in the media, the relationship between weight and health isn't simple or straightforward. It's terrifically complex, as multidimensional and complicated and elegant as the human body itself. We automatically conflate fat with being unhealthy, and praise thinness as a model of health. But in reality, that's *never* been the whole truth, or even most of it. People naturally come in a range of shapes and sizes. We might be short or tall, lanky or curvy, athletic or clumsy. We might feel wretched at a weight the doctor says is fine and comfortable at a weight society deplores. We might be actively engaged in taking care of ourselves or not. There's no one-size-fits-all approach (so to speak). We each have our own physical and emotional realities, which, along with all the social and cultural baggage we carry, shape our experiences and reactions.

I still have occasional moments when I look in the mirror and feel a little zing of panic, when I find myself thinking *I won't ever eat any more bread! Or sugar! Or fat!* Luckily, I've learned to deflect and redirect the inner monologue that still sometimes runs on a continuous loop in my head, commenting viciously about the size of my thighs, my waist, my chins, my appetite.

I know I'm not the only one who's fed up with this obsession, who's tired of seeing weeks and years of my life go down the drain of self-loathing and self-denial. Over the last decade I've interviewed hundreds of women about how they feel about their bodies. I came away from those conversations with a profound sense of sadness at the real suffering this obsession creates and perpetuates. And eventually I got mad. Mad enough to spend years immersed in the research so I didn't *have* to believe everything I read, so I could understand the facts for myself. Mad enough to talk to many of the scientists who study obesity and eating disorders, to ask them the tough questions and know enough to contextualize their answers.

What I've learned from this process has been shocking and enlightening, enraging and empowering. It has forever changed the way I look at myself and others, how I think about weight and health and food. There's no question that we need a different kind of conversation, one rooted in science and evidence and reality rather than blame and fantasies, our own and others'. This book, I hope, will help move us in that new direction.

When I give lectures on this subject, audiences often react with disbelief—at first. Our intellectual perspectives and emotional comfort zone around weight and body size have developed over years, and are reinforced constantly by much of what we see and hear. It takes time to understand things differently. And it can be scary to shift the paradigm; many of us have a lot invested in seeing things the way we've always seen them.

Some of what you're about to read here may feel shocking to you, too. But I believe each of us deserves to hear the whole story. I encourage you to keep an open mind and, ultimately, come to your own conclusions.

A FEW WORDS ABOUT RESEARCH

Much of what you're about to read comes from or is based on scientific research and literature. I'm not a trained scientist or statistician, but over the years I've developed a basic understanding of research methods and results. I've also consulted with many experts who are trained in the sciences and statistics to help me understand and check my conclusions about what I've read. Any mistakes here are mine and mine alone.

In the process of writing this book, I've learned about both the power of research and its limitations. Those of us without a scientific background tend to accept what we read when it comes with the stamp of approval of a published research study. So what are we supposed to think when we read about two studies, both conducted by experienced professionals, that reach completely opposite conclusions? How do we judge between them or interpret them in a way that makes sense for our own lives?

That's part of what I've tried to do in this book—offer a guide through some of the confusing research on weight, health, fitness, and longevity. For instance, methodology—how researchers structure the study and analyze the data—can dramatically alter a study's findings, for better or worse. So understanding methodology can be an important (though rather unsexy) part of thinking critically about a particular study.

Conflicts of interest, too, can and do shape research conclusions, both blatantly and invisibly, though researchers are quick to deny this. And as I've learned, the more subtle, behind-the-scenes conflicts of interest often wind up having the deepest and longest-lasting influence on research. I want readers to be able to make up their own minds after learning how such mechanisms work.

Finally, there's a lot we just don't know yet. Some of the contradictory findings on weight reflect our incomplete understanding of highly complex mechanisms and systems. But complexity doesn't come across very well in headlines and sound bites. The nuances of the research on weight and health often get lost in the rhetoric.

I've come to believe that the key to understanding research, on this or any other health-related topic, is to think critically and be willing to question everything. It's unlikely that any one study will suddenly give us the definitive answer on anything. Knowledge accrues, in part, through the replication of scientific findings. So hang on to your skepticism and think of research as an important element but not the only one in this journey.

Chapter 1

Four Big Fat Lies About Weight and Health

"There are many core ideas within the science of body weight and health and the mediating role played by exercise and diet which are simply assumed to be true."

—Michael Gard and Jan Wright,
from *The Obesity Epidemic:
Science, Morality, and Ideology*

We were sitting in my backyard, a handful of women from the neighborhood. We were eating cake, as it happened, a lemon poppy seed cake I'd made that morning, and drinking iced tea, and talking about our lives. And so it was inevitable that the conversation came around to weight—the weight we wanted to lose, the weight we'd gained, the weight other women had lost or gained, or lost *and* gained. A typical conversation, in other words.

One neighbor mentioned a popular TV show featuring an actress who would be too large to, say, walk the runway. "I can't stand watching anything she's in," the neighbor commented. "I'm afraid she's going to have a heart attack any minute. She's just so *unhealthy*. Doesn't she know she could drop dead? Doesn't she know what she's doing to herself?"

There was no chance the actress would keel over mid-episode, of course, since the show was taped. So what was my neighbor getting at? I puzzled over this for a few minutes and eventually realized that she wasn't actually worried about the actress's health. She couldn't be because in fact she didn't *know* anything about the actress's health. So what she was actually talking about was the actress's looks, not her health. My neighbor thought the actress was unattractive because of her weight, but she was too politically correct to come out and say that. Critiquing health in the context of weight, on the other hand, is perfectly acceptable in polite company. In fact, it's almost required in some circles. As health—or at least the *perception* of health—has become a social and moral imperative, judging other people's health status has become not just accepted but expected.

In his 1994 book *The Death of Humane Medicine and the Rise of Coercive Healthism,* Czech doctor Petr Skrabanek defines *healthism* as a worldview that judges human behaviors by how we *think* they affect health. Notice that emphasis on belief rather than reality. Behaviors we *believe* make people healthier—exercise, for instance—carry a sense of moral virtue; we say we're "being good" when we take the stairs instead of the elevator, eat salad (without dressing!) for lunch, spend an hour at the gym. Behaviors we think make people less healthy are seen as unacceptable. We're "bad" when we eat a slice of cake or binge-watch *Orange Is the New Black*. Restaurant owners know this; it's why they name desserts sinful cheesecake or chocolate decadence, cleverly acknowledging and deflecting the moral judgment around eating them.

A lot of what we believe about weight and health comes from assumptions of healthism, starting with one of our most cherished truths: *Fat is unhealthy*. It's a statement that's so general, so broad, and also so deeply ingrained, it's hard to pin down precisely what it means. It's just something everyone knows, right?

It's hard, in this culture, to question that statement—to even imagine a world where that might not be true. That long-ago day in my therapist's office, I couldn't even consider the possibility that maybe being overweight or even obese wasn't as unhealthy as I thought. I'd spent years worrying about how my weight might affect my health, especially after one doctor sat me down and told me if I were her sister, she'd put me on a diet *that very minute* and *make* me lose weight. "If you don't," she warned, "you'll wind up with heart disease or diabetes or high blood pressure, or all three."

She didn't have to convince me; I already believed it. I already worried about whether I was (as my grandmother often commented about others) eating myself into an early grave. I already imagined my arteries clogging each time I ate a shred of fat—actually, each time I ate anything. By the time I got home from the doctor's office that day, panic was making me hyperventilate, which made me think I was having the threatened heart attack right then and there.

Compared with some of the stories I've heard from other people since then, her tactics were actually pretty mild. She didn't, for example, refuse to treat me until I'd lost weight, or write "noncompliant" on my medical chart, or try to sell me a carton of

Medifast or a Weight Watchers membership. But she did make it perfectly clear that I would never be healthy until I lost weight. (And she did insist on putting me on statins, which caused extreme muscle pain; I had to stop taking them.) Ironically (but predictably), her well-meant lecture had the opposite effect from what she'd intended. I went into such an anxious tailspin over the next few weeks that I wound up stress-eating and gaining weight.

It took a family catastrophe to make me even start to question what I thought I knew: my then-fourteen-year-old daughter developed anorexia. As I sat hour after hour in silent shock beside her bed in the ICU, the formula I'd lived with all my life without question—fat=bad, thin=good—seemed horribly skewed. Suddenly there *was* such a thing as too thin, and it was right in front of me, in the matchstick thinness of her arms and legs, the almost pornographic arches of her ribs, the knobs of her vertebrae.

My feelings about food were turned upside down, too. In the months that followed I became an expert in making calorie-dense concoctions, to deliver the nutrition my daughter needed in the smallest possible footprint. Foods like butter and nuts and ice cream, long banned from my kitchen and my diet, now filled the shelves and freezer and featured prominently at each meal. My husband and I ate what she ate to help her get past her fears about fat, to model for her that this was how normal people ate. I knew I couldn't show any ambivalence about what we were eating; my daughter is extremely empathic, especially when it comes to my feelings. So I had to not just eat what she was eating, not just pretend it was normal, but actually believe it was. I couldn't do it for my own sake, but I could do it for her.

Over the next year, as my daughter put on weight and wrestled with recovery, I grappled with my own feelings about food and weight in a new way. My former fear foods were now saving my daughter's life, and, maybe, protecting my younger daughter from the same disease. Each pound my oldest gained represented not a problem to be solved but a victory over the demon that held her hostage. Now when I saw a young woman who wouldn't be considered thin, my automatic thought was *She's lucky* (though, to be clear, it's entirely possible to be overweight or obese and suffer from anorexia or other eating disorders). Now when I hit the grocery store, I scrutinized labels looking for the highest-calorie foods rather than the lowest. My daughter and I even laughed about it one night, as we noticed the horrified looks from other shoppers observing our quest for more calories.

But maybe the biggest push to change came from watching other people respond to my daughter. Especially middle-aged women. More than once, when she was sick, they literally approached her in the street to praise her beauty, admire her gaunt figure, even ask her—a fourteen-year-old girl who looked like she was dying—for diet tips. Even friends who knew how ill she was commented admiringly on how gorgeous, how svelte she was. It was as if they couldn't help themselves. And if I hadn't seen with my own eyes how much my daughter suffered and how ill she truly was, maybe I would have found her thinness glamorous and beautiful, too.

As she put on weight, those comments dried up. To my eyes she looked infinitely better with every pound; her eyes were shining and she actually smiled. To the rest of the world, apparently, only ribs you could count, sunken cheeks, and a hollow look were worth praise.

I learned a lot from my daughter's anorexia. I learned about the neurobiology of hunger and appetite, how our "choices" around food and eating are influenced by physiology. People with anorexia nearly always have a family history of eating disorders, anxiety, or both. They also tend toward certain personality traits, inborn characteristics like perfectionism that don't typically change over the course of a person's lifetime. I learned that, in fact, both my own struggles with food and my daughter's illness likely derived from our shared genetics and the way our brains are wired rather than from anything either of us had said or done or experienced.

Most tellingly, I learned how pervasive and deeply entrenched our culture's preference for thinness has become. We all know this, of course; we've read countless magazine stories about it, we've taken college courses on it, we talk about it with our friends and families. But until you experience it personally on some level, it's hard to fathom just how automatic it's become.

For example: one of my best friends grew up tall and thin, never worrying about her weight. In middle age she gradually put on about 30 pounds. Last year she lost the weight, not because she set out to diet but because she changed the way she ate for health reasons. She was shocked at the number and kind of comments that suddenly came her way. "I began feeling that how I look is of supreme importance to other people," she told me. "And then it struck me that we shouldn't be focusing on the physical image we project at all." She'd been listening to me think and talk about the issue for years, but it took her own experience to make her aware of both how common and how destructive such judgments are. "Honestly, until that moment, the subliminal thoughts I had sometimes about myself and others still had an echo of my mother's idea that being overweight means 'having no self-control,'" she said. "Now I don't think that will be true."

A HUGE PART of being OK with my body was connected with health. Could I be healthy at this weight and at this point in my life? According to the BMI chart, I was mildly obese, a phrase that haunted me. And of course "everybody knows" you can't be obese and be healthy.

But what does *health* actually mean? It's a fuzzy concept, a word so general, so vague, that it's virtually meaningless. Is health the simple absence of illness? That didn't feel right; we talk about health as a positive condition, not just the lack of a negative one. Is health the state of feeling good, energetic, happy? Is it a physical state, or does it include mental and emotional well-being, too?

I couldn't answer any of these questions. Neither could anyone else, it turned out, though plenty of people have tried, starting with the World Health Organization (WHO), arguably the world's experts on this subject. In 1948, WHO issued a statement defining health as "a state of complete physical, mental, and social well-being and not merely the absence of disease or infirmity." That seems more aspirational than realistic; by that standard, I don't know anyone who would qualify as healthy.

Other experts have tried to refine that definition. Alistair Tulloch, a now-retired British MD, posed the question in a 2005 article in the *British Journal of General Practice*. He suggested that since we live in a world full of accidents, infections, disease, poverty, poor working conditions, and a host of other adversarial forces, health measures our ability to adapt to and function normally in such a hostile environment. It's an interesting idea, but it suffers from the same vagueness that afflicts the word *health*: Who's to say what "normal" functioning is or what "successful adaptation" looks like?

Around the same time Tulloch was grappling with the concept, Swiss pharmacology professor Johannes Bircher took a stab at the problem with this statement: "Health is a dynamic state of well-being characterized by a physical, mental, and social potential, which satisfies the demands of a life commensurate with age, culture, and personal responsibility."

That covers a lot of bases; too many, really, like the WHO definition. And it doesn't bring us closer to a common vocabulary. It doesn't speak to the fact that what's healthy for me might not be what's healthy for you because we have not just different physical and mental needs but different expectations, too. For instance, I've struggled with a chronic anxiety disorder since I was ten. Thanks to exercise, meditation, and better living through chemistry, I experience way fewer symptoms than I used to. I function a lot better than I did in my twenties, but maybe not as well as someone without an anxiety disorder. Does that make me mentally unhealthy?

I don't care either way; I don't need to slap a label on my mental health. But it does matter to me, you, and everyone when, say, we open a magazine or a website and see the headline "Can you really be fat and healthy?" Because the answer depends on what we mean by "healthy." Are we talking about medical health? Psychological health? Heart health? Nutritional health?

Medical definitions, which often dominate the conversation, tend to focus on measurable characteristics like cholesterol or glucose levels. Depending on age, gender, genetics, and other factors, one person's ideal range might be too high or too low for someone else. Even medical health is a constantly moving target, one we're not likely to come to consensus about any time soon.

But let's get back to the magazine or the website, to the automatic sense of dread we get when we read a headline that asks whether we can be overweight and healthy. Most of us aren't parsing the literal definition of health; we're worrying about *our* health, *our* weight. And the message we get over and over is that we can't be healthy—whatever that means—and also be overweight or obese.

So what do we actually know about the relationship between health and weight? I've talked to hundreds of experts, looked at more than a thousand studies, and immersed myself in the research over the last five years to investigate this very question. (And there's a lot of it; I've been told by numerous researchers that the easiest way to get a study funded now is to include the word "obesity" in the proposal. Even better, cite "childhood obesity.") What I've found is that much of what we think we know either isn't true or doesn't mean what we think it means, starting with these four often-repeated "facts" about weight and health.

1. Americans are getting fatter and fatter—at this rate nearly half of us will be obese by 2030!*

We measure overweight and obesity these days using body mass index, or BMI, a ratio of height to weight. Doctors and scientists like BMI because it's convenient and noninvasive; you just plug in the measurements and voila! You've got an easily quantifiable way to characterize, compare, and contrast. The problem with BMI is that it's not an accurate measurement or predictor

---

*Per projections from "The State of Obesity: Better Policies for a Healthier America," Trust for America's Health, www.healthyamericans.org/report/115/.

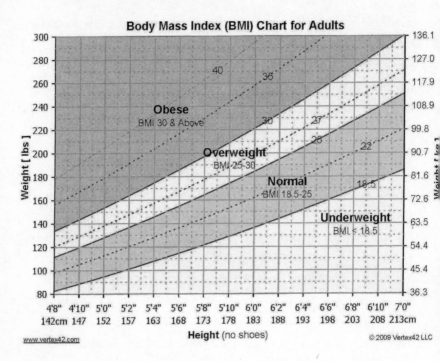

Body Mass Index Chart from Vertex42.com. Reprinted with permission.

of health, especially for people who are shorter or more muscular than average. It doesn't take into account the amount of muscle or fat in a body, or how strong (i.e., heavy) a person's bones are. It says nothing about a person's future risk of disease or death, and it was never intended to. Its creator, Belgian mathematician Adolphe Quetelet, came up with BMI in the 1830s as a way of looking at trends in populations, not in people. But in the late 1970s, researchers began using it precisely as Quetelet hadn't intended, to categorize individuals' weight and health status. It's been the medical model go-to ever since.

Using the BMI categories, the most recent reports from the Centers for Disease Control and Prevention (CDC) classify 34 percent of adult Americans as overweight and another 35 percent as obese. About 2 percent of adults are considered underweight; the rest fall into the "normal" category.

The number of overweight and obese Americans* has certainly risen since the mid-twentieth century, with the biggest jump happening between 1980 and 2000. The first researcher to call attention to the change was Katherine Flegal, an epidemiologist at the CDC's National Center for Health Statistics in Hyattsville, Maryland, which compiles statistics on everything from fertility to mortality. Flegal, who grew up in Berkeley, California, wears her hair short and spiky, and looks at least ten years younger than seventy, has spent her career analyzing all sorts of medical data. According to her research, between 1960 and 1991 the percentage of Americans who were overweight rose from 25 to 33 percent.

It's hard to get a precise handle on how those numbers compare with today's, though, because the definitions changed abruptly between then and now. Before 1998, the BMI chart had only three weight categories: "underweight," or below 18.5 on the chart, which included 2 percent of Americans; "normal," from 18.5 to 27.3 (the cutoff for men was higher) on the chart, which applied to 40 percent of Americans; and "overweight," anything above 27.3 (or 27.8 for men), which covered 58 percent of

---

*Europeans got heavier, too, in the same time period; according to the World Health Organization, 30 to 70 percent of European adults are overweight (that's a pretty big range), and 10 to 30 percent are obese. See www.euro.who.int/en/health-topics/noncommunicable-diseases/obesity/data-and-statistics for more information.

the population. Those cutoffs were revised downward in 1998 to where they are now,, and a category for "obesity" was added. So comparing pre-1998 BMI statistics to post-1998 stats is like comparing pre-steroids home run records to those made in the age of performance-enhancement drugs. In other words, more or less pointless.

Still, we do know a few things. The average American is in fact heavier (by about twenty pounds) and taller (by about an inch) than we were in 1960. And dire predictions notwithstanding, the rates of overweight and obesity leveled off around 2000. We're not actually getting heavier and heavier; our collective weight has pretty much plateaued.

Why did our weight go up? Plenty of experts have theories, including what I think of as the Big Three: We eat too much. We eat the wrong kinds of foods. We exercise too little. There's likely some truth in all those statements (for everyone, not just for those on the heavier end of the weight spectrum). But other factors have contributed to the rise as well: Many of us are poorer than we used to be, and poverty is strongly correlated with both how much you weigh and your likelihood of developing certain diseases, like type 2 diabetes.[1] We also live with rising levels of chemical contaminants, and researchers are finding more and clearer correlations between exposure to those contaminants, levels of obesity, and levels of diabetes. The main culprits are the so-called persistent organic pollutants—pesticides, PCBs, and other compounds that build up in our food, water, and bodies[2]—and endocrine-disrupting chemicals (EDCs) like bisphenol A (also known as BPA). For instance, a 2011 study from researchers at the University of California–Irvine found that early exposure to EDCs, which are found abundantly in plastics, canned food, agricultural fungicides, and elsewhere, made mice fat.[3] And a number of studies have confirmed links between the prevalence of diabetes and our exposure to persistent organic pollutants and EDCs.[4]

More of us take psychotropic medications, too: one in five Americans, and more than a quarter of all American women, according to a 2011 report.[5] Drugs treating anxiety, depression, bipolar disorder, personality disorders, psychoses, and other mental-health conditions are known to cause weight gain, especially when taken over a period of time.[6] I've experienced this myself. The first time I went on an SSRI for anxiety, I gained forty pounds over three years. When I went off the medication, I dropped twenty-five pounds within a month, and the rest soon after. Going back on the drugs was a difficult decision for a lot of reasons, and weight gain was one of them. I remember thinking *Which is worse, being fat or being crazy?* I chose to take the medication again. This time around I didn't gain as much, but I still gained some, and I'm guessing that weight will stay with me as long as I take the SSRIs. Which is likely to be for the rest of my life.

Some nutrition experts think the low-fat craze of the 1980s contributed, too. Marion Nestle, a professor of nutrition and food studies at New York University, told *Frontline* a few years back that the emphasis on cutting fat out of foods led to many Americans eating more carbohydrates, which in turn triggered the weight gain.[7] (More on that in Chapter 3.) And new research suggests that our long love affair with artificial sweeteners like aspartame, saccharine, and sucralose contributes to weight gain by interfering with the "good" bacteria in our guts, and thus altering our metabolisms.[8]

Whatever the causes, the rise in our average weight has translated to small gains for some and precipitous gains for a few.

"About 20 percent of the population is much heavier than it was, but the majority of the population isn't much heavier," explains Linda Bacon, a researcher and professor of nutrition at City College of San Francisco. She suspects that the percentage of people who have gained significant amounts of weight are more vulnerable to whatever combination of factors caused the shift in the first place. But we're certainly not all destined to become obese, says Bacon.

Humans aren't the only species that's heavier. Animals are, too. And while human-related changes in diet and activity levels might explain some of that increase, especially among pets and zoo animals, it doesn't explain the changes for lab animals, for instance, whose diet and activity levels are closely monitored and documented. Their higher weights can't be blamed on overeating, sedentary lifestyles, or any of the other causes often mentioned in connection with humans. A 2010 study published in the *Proceedings of the Royal Society* theorizes a different set of factors at work, including, potentially, environmental toxins, viruses, and epigenetic factors we don't yet understand.

2. Obesity can take a decade or more off your life.

After charting the prevalence of overweight and obesity, epidemiologist Katherine Flegal began to wonder what her findings meant for Americans' health. Were more people going to die earlier because they were heavier? To answer that question, she and her colleagues set out to map the relationship between BMI categories and mortality. They *expected* to find a linear relationship:

the higher a person's BMI, the greater his or her risk of dying prematurely.

But that's not what they found. Instead, Flegal and her colleagues discovered what statisticians call a U-shaped curve, with the bottom of the curve—the lowest risk of death—falling around 25 to 26 on the BMI chart, making the risk of early death lowest for those now labeled overweight. People considered "mildly obese" had roughly the same risk of dying as those in the "normal" category. Death rates went up for those on either end of the scale—underweight and severely obese—but not by much.

"The differences we're talking about overall are pretty tiny," explains Flegal. (Researcher Reubin Andres, who was director of the US National Institute on Aging back in the 1980s, had suggested a similar U-shaped curve, though his was linked more closely with age: the older you are, the less "risky" it is to be heavier.)

As soon as Flegal's analysis appeared in the *Journal of the American Medical Association,* the excrement hit the air conditioning. Other researchers claimed her work was shoddy, that she'd left out important data. They said there was no way her results could be accurate. S. Jay Olshansky, a professor of epidemiology at the University of Illinois–Chicago, responded with a journal article arguing that rising obesity rates would shorten lives by two to five years.

That statistic got a lot of attention and helped establish the idea that, as countless media outlets went on to report, for the first time in history a generation of children would have shorter life-spans than their parents. And that prediction is still floating around today, despite the fact that it's been utterly and thoroughly debunked. As one of Olshansky's coauthors, University of Alabama–Birmingham biostatistician David B. Allison, sheep-ishly told a reporter from *Scientific American,* "These are just back-of-the-envelope plausible scenarios. We never meant for them to be portrayed as precise."

This type of end-justifies-the-means truth-bending is com-mon in the world of obesity research. Last year, for instance, the National Obesity Forum, an influential lobbying group in the United Kingdom that works on behalf of a long list of pharma-ceutical companies, admitted to lying—actually *admitted* it—in its latest report. The authors had warned that obesity in Britain was continuing to rise, and that an earlier prediction that half the population would be obese by 2050 was "optimistic and could be exceeded by 2050."[9] In actuality, rates of obesity in the United Kingdom, as in the United States, have plateaued or diminished slightly. The group knowingly misrepresented the facts "to reach a wider public," confessed spokesman Tam Fry.[10]

Reports like these, which are grounded in opinion and clear agendas rather than fact, feed an increasingly hostile and confus-ing public conversation around weight. And it's hard to under-stand where they're coming from. I mean, shouldn't we be *glad* to hear that a few extra pounds—or more than a few—might not be so bad for you? Might, in fact, even be good for you under certain circumstances?

Given the ongoing backlash, Katherine Flegal decided to clear up the relationship between weight and mortality once and for all. She and her colleagues spent several years meticulously col-lecting every study they could find with data on weight and mor-tality—ninety-seven in all. They pooled the data, broke it down in every possible statistical configuration, and published their meta-analysis in early 2013. The results were exactly the same as results from the earlier analysis: being overweight does not increase a person's risk of dying prematurely, and being mildly obese increases it only slightly.

Flegal's painstaking methodology didn't prevent the uproar this time, either. John Wass, an endocrinologist and vice president of the Royal College of Physicians, told the BBC, "Huge pieces of evidence go against this. Countless other studies point in the other direction," a claim he failed to substantiate. Tam Fry, the above-mentioned spokesperson for the National Obesity Forum in the United Kingdom, commented, "It's a horrific message to put out. We shouldn't take it for granted that we can cancel the gym, that we can eat ourselves to death with black forest gateaux."

Which, of course, isn't what Flegal's meta-analysis says at all. It simply maps correlations—in this case, associations between the risk of dying early and BMI. It doesn't speculate on how to interpret these correlations or why they might hold true. In fact, Flegal takes pains to point out that she never recommends policy or puts out "messaging"; she simply crunches numbers and presents data.

And in any case, surely there's some middle ground between stuffing ourselves with cake and starving? "Seek moderation in all things," wrote Aristotle 2,500 years ago, advice that has stood the test of time. Demonizing cake—or sugar, or fat, or carbs— typically leads us to bounce between depriving ourselves (sugar is evil and must be avoided!) and bingeing (I ate a crumb of cake so I might as well eat the whole thing!).

One of Flegal's biggest critics has been Walter Willett, a Harvard scientist and nutritionist. After the 2013 meta-analysis came out, Willett told National Public Radio, "This study is really a pile of rubbish, and no one should waste their time reading it."

A month later, he organized a symposium at Harvard with the sole purpose of attacking Flegal's work. One of his main critiques was that Flegal's team hadn't accounted for the confounding effects of smoking. Since people who smoke tend to both be thinner and die earlier than nonsmokers, researchers have to compensate statistically for those effects. One way to do that is to run the data both with and without smokers. Flegal says she did just that and the numbers were virtually identical. And most were very close to a relative risk of 1, meaning that each group (here, smokers and nonsmokers) had the same probability of experiencing a particular outcome—in this case, dying prematurely.

But it's also true that if you fiddle with statistics enough, you can make them play any tune you want. When I asked Willett to explain his critique of Flegal's work, he declined to comment, referring me instead to a 2010 study he worked on that found mortality risks lowest among people with "normal" BMIs. That study, it turns out, deleted not only anyone who had ever smoked but also anyone with a history of cancer or heart disease, ultimately eliminating nearly 80 percent of the deaths in the data. Which no doubt explains why Willett's findings were so different from Katherine Flegal's.

In his excellent book *Naked Statistics,* economics professor Charles Whelan explains why, as Mark Twain once commented, "There are three kinds of lies: lies, damned lies, and statistics." While statistics are rooted in math, and math is an exact science, Whelan points out that statistics are often used to describe complex, multidimensional phenomena, and they can approach those descriptions from all sorts of perspectives.

To put it another way, most people think of statistics as black-and-white, either–or statements: *Either* being heavier shortens your life *or* it doesn't. But life doesn't work that way, and neither do statistics, which usually describe coexisting truths—what we might think of as this-and-that statements. In this case, being overweight is associated with a longer life *and* severe obesity is associated with a shorter life *and* the relative difference between them is small.

You could spin those truths any number of ways. For instance, you could say that obesity takes time off a person's life. In the broadest possible sense there might be some truth in that statement. But what it doesn't convey is that (a) it's only severe obesity that correlates with a shorter life span, (b) being overweight correlates with a *longer* life span, (c) the effects of obesity on mortality predictions are low overall, and (d) all of these relationships are correlations only; there is no established cause and effect pattern between weight and mortality. (See #3 below for more on correlations.) So even severe obesity (what's often labeled "morbid" obesity") may increase a person's chance of premature death only slightly. If at all.

That last fact is a function of risk factors, something we hear a lot about but rarely understand. In their 2005 book *The Obesity Epidemic: Science, Morality, and Ideology,* Australian professors Michael Gard and Jan Wright explain that a risk ratio needs to be large to suggest a strong association between a disease and a given variable. Their example: the risk ratio for lung cancer in middle-aged male smokers compared with nonsmokers is 9 to 10, meaning that smokers die from lung cancer at rates nine or ten times higher than nonsmokers. So smoking is considered a significant risk factor for lung cancer. By contrast, the risk ratio for heart disease in people who are overweight or obese is between 1.1 and 2, meaning their risk of developing heart disease

When Doctors Can't See Beyond Weight

Ray's daughter, Pattie, fifty-seven,
teaches sociology at a college in Las Vegas.
She shared this story after Ray's death.

My father was a mechanic. He did a lot of physical labor, and he was always a small man. When he was sixty-six, he retired and started gaining weight rapidly. When he tried to eat anything, it would make him feel so full he'd be short of breath. He told the doctor he wasn't eating but was continuing to gain weight. The doctor out-and-out didn't believe him. He said, "Here's a diet. Come back in three months."

Eventually my dad went to the hospital and they pulled twenty-seven pounds of fluid out of his abdomen. It turned out he had hemochromatosis, where your liver doesn't process iron well. It's a simple blood test to diagnose, and once they find it they can treat it and you can live a long life.

But because he was sick for a year before he was diagnosed or treated, my dad got liver disease and died eighteen months later. I feel he died of malpractice, but I couldn't *prove* he didn't overeat while he had twenty-seven pounds of fluid on him. I couldn't even get an attorney to take the case. Our society is so sure it's all about calories in, calories burned. The relationship between health and weight is so complex, and we try to make it simple. And that hurts people.

is the same as or only slightly higher than the risk for people with "normal" BMIs.

Gard and Wright also point out that we are becoming a society obsessed by risk, and by the fantasy that we have nearly infinite power to control it. "Fundamental to such notions is that by naming the risk it can be managed—that is, uncertainty can be reduced—and by understanding the lines of causality, one can act rationally to avoid it," they write. If that were true, we'd all live forever. Or at least a lot longer.

Because statistics describe relationships that often can't accurately be reduced to simple statements, writes Charles Whelan, "That leaves plenty of room for shading the truth." Which is how researchers using the exact same data can—in good faith or not—come up with such different findings. And why reading the research on weight and health can feel like being trapped in an M. C. Escher drawing, where the walls turn into ceilings and water flows upward and where, no matter which path you follow, you wind up going around and around the same closed loop.

Meanwhile, most researchers accept Katherine Flegal's findings that overweight and mild obesity confer no added risk of dying early, while underweight and severe obesity add a slight risk. For most people, it seems, weight alone is not strongly linked with mortality.

3. Being fat causes heart disease, stroke, type 2 diabetes, and other serious illnesses.

One of the big challenges in considering weight and health is how to distinguish *correlation* and *causation*. Both are ways of talking about relationships among sets of events or variables. Correlation is, essentially, an association; this happened *and* that happened. The events may be unrelated—for instance, your sister gets married and you get a new job. Or one may cause the other—you give birth to a child and your health insurance premiums go up. Or a third variable may influence both of them: people who have yellow teeth are more likely to develop lung cancer, because smoking correlates with both.

Causation, as the term suggests, refers to a cause-and-effect relationship: the gravitational pull of the moon *causes* the ocean tides. Without the moon's force, the tides literally would not flow in and out. In medicine, causation is notoriously difficult to prove, since so many variables contribute to human health. Still, some relationships are considered causal. For instance, the fact that smoking causes lung cancer. This doesn't mean everyone who smokes will get lung cancer, or that only people who smoke will get lung cancer. It does mean that for a certain percentage of the population, smoking will lead to lung cancer.

Mostly, when we talk about weight and health, we're talking about risk factors, forces that increase susceptibility to a particular disease or condition. All risk factors are not created equal, though we often talk about them as if they were. For instance, both having yellow teeth and smoking are risk factors for lung cancer, but clearly smoking carries a much higher degree of risk than tooth color, which after all can be caused by all sorts of things. So we need to be careful not to conflate risk factors with causes, unless, like smoking and lung cancer, they actually do cause a disease.

One of the underlying assumptions about health is that if only we do everything right, we'll be healthy. On some level we seem to believe, however illogically, that if we eat right, exercise enough, take care of ourselves in all the ways we're supposed to, we'll live forever. Or maybe till we're 110. But the truth is we're all going to die of something someday, and whether that *something* is accident, murder, disease, or plain old age, we can't control it. We might think we can, or hope we can, but in the end the best we're likely to do is take care of ourselves as well as possible and hope for the best. Or at least not the worst.

As Michael Gard and Jan Wright point out, it's human nature to think we can control our destinies by changing our actions. We want to believe we're in charge. "I am the master of my fate, I am the captain of my soul," as Victorian poet William Ernest Henley wrote in 1875.[11]

I've experienced this firsthand every time I pick up a package of Cheerios at the grocery store. The label on the box says "May reduce the risk of heart disease," and even though I recognize the weasel words ("may reduce the risk" rather than "will prevent you from developing"), and even though I know the FDA warned General Mills to change the wording on the label *because* it's misleading, still I get a warm fuzzy feeling every time a big yellow box goes into my cart.

In the case of weight and health, dozens of risk factors can come into play, and few if any have been proven to cause any given outcome. That's why we usually end up talking about surrogate markers like blood pressure and cholesterol levels, measurements that may be associated with true clinical endpoints like heart attacks and strokes but aren't in and of themselves diseases.

So what do we actually know about the relationship between weight and disease? We know that obesity has been correlated with heart disease, gallbladder disease, and type 2 diabetes, as well as with risk factors for those diseases. The strongest correlation is found between obesity and type 2 diabetes; one 2014 study found that people who were obese but also "metabolically healthy" (that is, their cholesterol and glucose levels were normal) were four times more likely to develop diabetes than metabolically healthy people who were not obese.[12] The question is how to interpret that correlation, since many other factors also correlate with type 2 diabetes. (Repeat after me: correlation does not equal causation.)

One aspect of the weight–health relationship that's rarely mentioned is the fact that definitions and cutoff points for many illnesses and risk factors have changed quite a bit over the last decade. For instance, diabetes used to be diagnosed when blood sugar levels hit 140 milligrams per deciliter (mg/dl); now the cutoff is 126 mg/dl. Suggested treatments include statins and blood pressure medications.[13] New disease categories like "prediabetes" and "prehypertension" have also emerged; a blood sugar level above 100 is now considered "prediabetes" and is often treated aggressively. Similarly, hypertension is diagnosed when blood pressure reaches 140/90, and now "prehypertension" begins at a reading of 120/80. There's been plenty of controversy over these widening disease categories, but whether they're valid and helpful or not, they skew the perceived medical relationship between weight and health by shifting millions of people into the "ill" category.

One of the most influential studies on heart disease is the Framingham Heart Study, founded in 1948 to identify some of the risk factors for heart disease and come up with prevention strategies. Researchers identified a group of about five thousand middle-aged men and women, all white, all living in Framingham, Massachusetts. Over the last sixty-some years, the lives and health of those men and women have been studied, measured, analyzed, and recorded. The study now includes a second and third generation of Framingham residents, the children and grandchildren of the original batch, as well as two cohorts that are more diverse, also from Framingham.

A lot of the current thinking on heart disease comes from the Framingham data and two other ongoing studies: the Nurses' Health Study, which follows about 120,000 middle-aged female nurses from eleven states, and the National Health and Nutrition Examination Surveys (known as NHANES), which studies a sample of about five thousand people from around the country. Katherine Flegal uses the NHANES data, which is considered a strongly representative sample, in her analyses.

These three large studies, as well as smaller studies, show correlations of varying degrees between overweight/obesity and health conditions including heart disease, type 2 diabetes, gallbladder disease, stroke, fatty liver disease, and risk factors for those diseases. The strongest findings link BMI and type 2 diabetes, especially for people younger than age fifty-five with BMIs over 40.

That's where the story ends for many researchers, doctors, and media outlets: with correlation. The trouble is, we still don't know much (if anything) about causation. Nor do we know what to do with this information on correlation, how to best apply it practically to improving human health. One underlying assumption is that since being obese correlates with a higher risk of heart disease or diabetes for some people, we should *all* be trying to lose weight. But the research doesn't support that, for a variety of reasons (see Chapter 2). And that assumption doesn't take into account contributing factors that might explain those correlations.

For instance, there's the chicken-and-egg question. We assume that weight gain comes first and causes diabetes and other illnesses. But what if, as surgeon and nutrition researcher Peter Attia has suggested, weight gain is actually an early *symptom* of diabetes?[14] Or what if weight gain and type 2 diabetes are both caused by an unknown third variable? Pediatric endocrinologist Robert Lustig, who's written copiously about the evils of sugar, suggests that we actually can't identify which comes first, weight gain or insulin resistance. "Behavior can alter biochemistry, but biochemistry can also alter behavior," he wrote in a 2008 editorial in *The Journal of Pediatrics*. No one truly knows which comes first, the illness or the weight gain. What we've got right now is a limited correlation, not out-and-out causation, though if you read the news or talk to your doctor about it you're unlikely to hear this perspective.

Another factor that rarely makes it into the weight–health research is physical activity. Most researchers don't even ask people whether or how much they exercise. And according to researchers like Steven Blair, who's been described in the *New York Times* as one of the country's leading experts on the health benefits of exercise, that's junk science. "I continue to get irritated at the establishment in general focusing on obesity and ignoring activity," says Blair, a professor of exercise science, epidemiology, and biostatistics at the Arnold School of Public Health at the University of South Carolina.

Blair, who's in his early seventies, resembles Kris Kringle with less hair and more attitude. In other words—in *his* words—he's short and fat. He also runs every day for an hour, making him short, fat, and physically active. In the early 2000s, Blair directed the nonprofit Cooper Institute in Dallas, a research group founded by Kenneth Cooper, MD, who coined the term *aerobics*. Over the years, Blair has produced or worked on hundreds of studies looking at how, exactly, exercise benefits health. His research has convinced him and others that physical inactivity is a much bigger health problem than overweight or obesity. "How successful can we be in getting sedentary people to become active?" he says. "That's been the focus of my life. Fitness is a powerful indicator of physical health."

Blair has done much of his work with Paul McAuley, a professor of health education at Winston-Salem University in North Carolina with a PhD in exercise physiology. McAuley spent a while in the corporate world, setting up a fitness program at Sony Pictures. Eventually he wound up back in academia, a few years after cancer epidemiologist Eugenia Calle published a study[15] that's still cited when researchers talk about how obesity is linked to early death. The key word here is *linked;* Calle's study showed a correlation between higher BMI and early death, but it didn't— it *couldn't* by definition—show causation.

Paul McAuley sees two big problems with Calle's meta-analysis. "They failed to control statistically for a major known confounder, fitness," he says. "That's invalid." Given the strong links between fitness, illness, and mortality (the "you can be fat but fit" concept), leaving out physical activity irreparably muddies the findings. Then, too, says McAuley, in the Calle analysis, higher BMI did not predict early death for African Americans. (Most of the research on weight and health has been done only in white populations.) So whatever's going on in the relationship between weight and mortality is clearly a lot more complicated than fat=death.

In 1999, Steven Blair published research showing that being physically unfit was as much or more of a risk factor for heart disease and death as diabetes, obesity, and other weight-based risk factors. Since then McAuley, Blair, and others have argued it's healthier to be fit and fat than unfit and thin, while Walter Willett and other researchers continue to insist that fitness and metabolic status can't possibly make up for the negative effects of obesity.

No Such Thing as a Fat Athlete

Liv, thirty-nine, is a social worker in Portland, Oregon.

I was a fat baby, a fat kid, a fat teen, and I've been a fat adult. Having to navigate the health-care system has been continuously a challenge. I would go to the doctor with a cold and he'd tell me, "You need to go on a diet." I'd go in with an ear infection and it would be, "You need to go on a diet."

I'm five seven and weigh 350 pounds. I play in a competitive adult kickball league and it's a lot of fun. A few summers ago I injured my knee, and when I went in the nurse practitioner said, "You weigh 350 pounds, it's going to be hard on your body." I told her it felt like more than that. I bike to work four times a week, eight miles round trip. I swim, I do yoga, I'm pretty in tune with how my body feels. She said, "Just ice, elevate, ibuprofen."

Eventually, twelve weeks after the injury, they determined I had a torn meniscus. The orthopedist said they wouldn't do surgery even though that's the only way to fix it, because they only do surgery on kids and people who actively do sports. I said, "I tore this playing kickball." I told her how active I am. She said, "We only do this for athletes." So now I can't play kickball. I was out all season and I don't foresee being able to play again. It feels like my kneecap is sliding down my shin. And I feel the real reason they won't repair it is that I'm a fat person and they don't think I'm really an athlete or someone who deserves to have the surgery done.

There's one more issue that riles people in the often contentious world of weight–health research: the so-called obesity paradox. (The name reflects the widespread assumption that obesity must be bad for health, ergo any finding that seems to contradict that assumption is paradoxical.) Study after study has shown that overweight and moderately obese patients with certain chronic ailments live longer and do better than normal-weight patients with the same health problems. And many of those problems are the ones most often blamed on obesity, like heart disease, stroke, and diabetes.

One of the earliest researchers to document the obesity paradox, Carl Lavie, says he had a hard time getting anyone to publish his first paper on heart failure. "People thought, this can't be true, there's got to be something wrong with their data," says Lavie, a cardiologist and professor at the Ochsner Heart and Vascular Institute in New Orleans.

For instance, because type 2 diabetes correlates with higher BMIs, doctors typically recommend that patients diagnosed with diabetes lose weight if they're heavy. That's what epidemiologist Mercedes Carnethon had been taught, and she had no reason to question it. She'd read about the obesity paradox in people with heart failure and end-stage kidney disease, but she'd dismissed it, figuring it reflected the fact that thinner people were losing weight because they were close to death rather than the other way around.

Then Carnethon, an associate professor at the Feinberg School of Medicine in Chicago, started hearing about an obesity paradox in diabetes. She didn't believe it at first, but a look into her own data turned up the same effect. "People who were normal-weight at the time their diabetes was identified went on to have a doubling of mortality compared with those who were overweight or obese," she says. A deep dive into the research confirmed the pattern, though no one yet understands why. Some recent hypotheses: Maybe thinner people actually develop genetic variants of these chronic illnesses that are deadlier than the usual versions. Maybe heavier people get more aggressive treatment because they're thought to be at higher risk, and so they wind up with better outcomes. Maybe body fat *distribution*, rather than weight per se, plays a role.

Or maybe the missing piece of the puzzle is something altogether different. Paul McAuley looked at hundreds of studies documenting the paradox and became convinced (unsurprisingly) that fitness was the key. In 2010, he published an article based on data from Stanford's Veterans Exercise Testing Study, an ongoing study of more than twelve thousand middle-aged male veterans whose fitness levels were documented through lab testing. McAuley's conclusion: overweight and obese men lived longer than normal-weight men *only* if they were fit.

Another factor complicating the relationship between weight and health is poverty. It's no secret that poor people, at least in the United States, are more likely to be fat than wealthier people. All sorts of factors play into this: lack of access to good food and opportunities for exercise (for instance, many kids can't play outside because they live in dangerous neighborhoods), lack of time for self-care (especially among people working two or three jobs), and stress, which also independently contributes to illness and premature death. American and Canadian research groups have found strong correlations between being poor and developing type 2 diabetes, especially among African American women, regardless of how much people weigh or their BMIs.[16]

In fact, stigma and stress probably play a much bigger role than we think. In one 2014 study of nearly ten thousand people, those who were unhappy about their weight—whether they were thin, overweight, or obese—were more likely to go on to develop type 2 diabetes, especially if their dissatisfaction went on for years.[17] Findings like these illustrate yet again the complexity of the relationship between weight and health. It just can't be reduced to a sound bite.

Unfortunately, none of this stops doctors and researchers from recommending weight loss for health reasons, even to people diagnosed with diabetes, heart failure, and other conditions where the paradox operates. I asked Mercedes Carnethon if she still counseled her diabetic patients to diet. "We'd *never* want to back away from weight-loss recommendations," Carnethon said in surprise, as if I'd suggested that the world was flat. When I pressed her on why, she said, "Evidence does generally show that being in an overweight range is less healthy." What about Katherine Flegal's work, I wondered; that suggests otherwise. There was a long pause, and then she said, "Dietary changes that support healthy cholesterol levels are still warranted." Which wasn't what I was asking at all.

THE FOURTH often-repeated lie about weight and health is that dieting makes us thinner and healthier. At the very least, we consider dieting benign, something that can't hurt us even if it doesn't really help. But the truth is, dieting is actually harmful for many of us for all sorts of reasons. And it doesn't make most of us thinner or healthier. On the contrary.

Chapter 2

The Amazing! Seventeen-Day! Flat-Belly! Grain-Brain! Biggest Loser! Raw Food! Diet

"What some call health, if purchased by perpetual anxiety about diet, isn't much better than tedious disease."
—Alexander Pope, eighteenth-century English poet

Every year in January—the height of our annual weight-loss frenzy—fifty million Americans go on a diet. That's roughly one-sixth of the entire population restricting what we eat, creating a negative energy balance (deliberately burning more fuel than we take in) with the express goal of losing weight. Many of those dieters give up after about two weeks,[1] but try again and again over the course of the year, which means, estimating conservatively, that the average forty-five-year-old American woman has been on fifty diets in her adult life.[2]

Those numbers say a lot about how we see the act of dieting. At best, it works for a while; at worst, it can't hurt. And that's true across the board—you'd be hard-pressed to find a woman in America who has never dieted. There's a social component to dieting, especially for women. Coworkers, friends, and families join Weight Watchers or do the "biggest loser" challenge together. Misery loves company, after all.

I was one of those miserable dieters for many years, starting at fifteen, when my mother and I joined Weight Watchers together, each with the goal of losing twenty pounds. I wasn't the only teenager dieting, of course; in the 1970s, the average age for girls to start dieting was fourteen. (Now, by contrast, it's eight. Eight years old.)[3] It took us four months to lose the weight, four months of Weight Watchers frozen dinners, packed lunches, and my mother's homemade "bread pudding," which contained neither bread nor pudding.*

Eighteen months later I went to college, where I rapidly gained back those twenty pounds plus another ten, and struggled with nightly bouts of uncontrollable eating. This was long before anyone used the term *binge eating,* or talked about the fact that a history of dieting predisposes people to compulsive eating. Every night I ate ready-made frosting straight out of the can, and hid the evidence at the bottom of the garbage so my roommates wouldn't see. Every morning I felt shame and despair and vowed to do better. But I stayed trapped in that vicious cycle for a long time.

As a result, I spent the next decade in a classic yo-yo pattern, swinging between extremes of deprivation and overeating. I

---

*If you've ever spent time at Weight Watchers (or even if you haven't), get hold of *The Amazing Mackerel Pudding Plan: Classic Diet Recipe Cards from the 1970s,* by Wendy McClure. Her snarky commentary on recipes like Fluffy Mackerel Pudding, Crown Roast of Frankfurters, and Cabbage Casserole Czarina (I am not making these up) makes me howl every time.

rejoined Weight Watchers at age twenty-eight to get thin enough to fit into my mother's wedding dress. (Oh, the symbolism.) This time I lost forty pounds, getting down to a weight that fell into the normal category on the BMI chart but left me weak, tired, and ever more obsessed. I weighed and measured and recorded every bite I ate. I dreamed about food, counting the minutes until my next meal or snack. I ate the same things every day without deviating because that was the only way I could know I was eating the "right" amount.

When I got pregnant three years later, I quickly gained back those forty pounds, despite weekly scoldings from the midwife. I loved being pregnant, in part because it *was* OK to gain weight, and because now when I ate, I didn't feel guilty and self-indulgent; I was feeding my baby as well as myself, and I had no ambivalence at all about that. But two more pregnancies, a miscarriage, and a severe postpartum depression treated with antidepressants left me at my heaviest ever. And each time I gained another pound, the voice in my head got a little nastier: *You're worthless and lazy and stupid. You're out of control. You're the ugliest woman in the room, the neighborhood, the world.*

I went back to Weight Watchers three or four more times, but I never lasted more than a few days. Something in my brain had shifted. I just couldn't bring myself to count calories and measure portions and weigh every bite I put in my mouth. No matter how determined I felt, how much I hated my body, I just couldn't do it anymore. I told myself I was weak, I lacked self-control, I was gluttonous, but the usual goads fell flat. I couldn't sustain the deprivation of dieting. That's what sent me into treatment, and into that relationship with the therapist that changed my life.

WE DIET FOR one of two reasons, or both: Looks and health. If (a) you're a woman, and (b) you want people to think you're attractive, you've got to be thin (or least thinnish) by the cultural standards of the day. And whether you're a woman or a man, if you're not thin you've certainly been told in many ways that your health will suffer if you don't lose weight.

So we diet. We consider it harmless at worst, and if it doesn't work, well, that's our fault for not cutting back enough or sticking hard enough to our unsatisfying meal plan, isn't it? And the solution is—you guessed it: more dieting, different dieting, stricter dieting. In 2013, Americans spent more than $60 billion on weight-loss products,[4] and that number keeps rising. A lot of bottom lines are at stake in the efforts to trim our bottoms.

Unfortunately, the evidence suggests that dieting makes people neither thinner nor healthier. Quite the opposite, actually: nearly everyone who diets winds up heavier in the long run, and many people's health suffers rather than improves, especially over time. Repeated dieting in particular causes a cascade of negative physical and psychological consequences (which we'll look at in more depth later in this chapter). In fact, dieting is a major risk factor for both binge eating[5] and obesity.[6]

Dieting *can* make people thinner for a while—six months, a year or two, maybe three. Which, coincidentally, is about how long most studies follow dieters, and how they claim success. In reality, your chance of maintaining a significant weight loss for five years or more is about the same as your chance of surviving metastatic lung cancer: 5 percent. It doesn't matter what flavor of diet you try—Paleo, Atkins, raw, vegan, high-carb, low-carb, grapefruit, Ayds (remember those chewy chemical-infused caramels?)—only 3 to 5 percent of dieters who lose a significant amount of weight keep it off. Weight-loss treatments are cash cows, in part because they *don't* work; there's always a built-in base of repeat customers.

You'd never know any of this from reading the weight-loss research, or from talking with most researchers in the field. In fact, when I asked the University of Alabama's David Allison about dieting research, he insisted that studies do show success after five years, "just less than what we'd push for." I told him I was aware of only one research project that followed dieters for five years or more, the Look AHEAD project, a ten-year study of people with type 2 diabetes. I asked Allison to point me toward other studies that followed dieters for five years or more, regardless of their findings. He couldn't come up with any.

How I Keep It Off—For Now

Debra, fifty-five, has worked in nonprofit development and is now studying to be a hospital chaplain in Kansas City, Missouri.

I had three "yo-yos" of more than 10 percent of my body weight. The first was in high school, when my mother told me I was the fattest girl in drama class and I needed to lose weight. The second was after my wedding. The third was when I was forty-two and for the first time in my life got a borderline cholesterol reading. I remember crying in the shower and pounding my thigh, mad at how fat I was.

I started walking, then running. I lost about sixty-five pounds. I became a running nut. I was maintaining the loss easily because I was a runner. Then my body failed me—my foot started to swell every time I ran and my joints weren't behaving. I started researching and had a big stinking oh shit moment when I

➛

→

realized everything I thought I knew about dieting and weight loss was a lie. I saw that only 3 percent of people could keep weight off for more than five years, and even then it was only 10 percent of their body weight. For me that would have been nothing.

What I ultimately arrived at to maintain the weight loss works for me, but I don't want it to be presented as a panacea. I eat 1,800 calories a day and I always have a running count in my head. I allow myself 200 calories a day of grain-based carbohydrates and I save 200 for a glass of wine at night. And then I exercise as a fat chick. I wear a weighted vest and ankle weights that add up to around thirty pounds. I put on an exercise video and do it at double time for fifty minutes. I also watch the news. That's how I make it tolerable and possible to do other things with my life besides weight loss. Because this is not a lifestyle. It's a job.

Maintenance takes up a lot of mental real estate, though not as much as it did in the beginning. There's the voluntary part, where I'm doing all the research. Then there's the involuntary— the intrusive thoughts, the preoccupations with food, that kind of thing.

Right now I do my crazy exercise thing on a padded carpet and I don't twist my ankles. But guess what's going to happen at some point? When I can't do the exercise videos anymore, maybe I'll try water aerobics. To do the equivalent of what I'm doing now I'll be the pruniest woman. And I am probably going to be fat again. I never want to be held up as someone who will make fat people feel bad. There's nothing that scares me more than that.

Unlike Debra, most of us believe we just have to try a little harder and the weight will come off and stay off. We must think so because we keep trying, again and again and again. Consider the market for diet books, which seems nearly infinite; no matter how ridiculous, ineffective, or potentially dangerous a given diet may be, desperate people will plunk down $24.99 for the latest fad in weight-loss advice. They'll eat tapeworms and drink concoctions made from cattle hooves,* have patches sewn onto their tongues so it hurts to eat, chew each bite thirty-two times (once for each tooth),** and blame themselves when they gain back any weight they've lost. Something is definitely wrong with this picture.

Traci Mann agrees. Mann, a psychology researcher and professor at UCLA, must be one of the few women in Western society who's never gone on a diet. Which is ironic, considering she's made dieting a major focus of her research. In 2006, she and a PhD student named Janet Tomiyama got to talking about Medicare's decision to start paying for "effective" obesity treatments. They wondered which treatments actually led to long-term weight loss, and decided to look at the evidence. The result of their investigation was a 2007 article confirming what many dieters already suspected: diets don't work.

The mind-boggling element here is that we've known diets don't work for a long time, and so has the medical establishment.

---

*The ProLinn Diet, popular in the 1970s, had dieters eat nothing and take only one daily four-hundred-calorie drink made from slaughterhouse by-products like hooves, horns, and tendons. Mmm, mmm, good.

**Fletcherism, also known as the chewing diet, was created in 1895 by one Horace Fletcher, an American dietitian who believed, as he often said, "Nature will castigate those who don't masticate."

Back in 1958, A. J. Stunkard, a well-known obesity researcher and professor at the University of Pennsylvania, wrote, "Of [obese] people who lose weight, most will regain it." In the 1970s and 1980s, scientists like Paul Ernsberger, now a nutrition professor and researcher at Case Western University, began to document the ways dieting did (and usually didn't) work. Nearly thirty years ago—thirty years ago!—Ernsberger and a colleague published an exhaustive review of the links between health and obesity.[7] They pointed out that sixteen long-term international studies had found that overweight and obesity were not major risk factors for death or heart disease; a US panel on obesity had relied heavily on data from the insurance industry, and since fewer heavy people bought life insurance (because they had to pay more for it), the mortality rates linked to obesity skewed higher.

Ernsberger also drew attention to the fact that mortality rates were lowest in the overweight category on the BMI chart—the very same *U*-shaped curve that would cause such a backlash when Katherine Flegal re-documented it in 2013. He and his colleague hypothesized that some of the conditions associated with obesity, like hypertension and elevated cardiovascular risk, actually came from failed treatments—that is, weight cycling, or losing and regaining weight over and over. And they suggested that many doctors' disapproval of obesity was based on "moral and aesthetic biases" rather than medical facts, a suggestion that has since been borne out by research into doctors' clear prejudices around obesity.

In the early 1990s, shortly after a slender, belted, and booted Oprah Winfrey rolled a red wagon carrying sixty-seven pounds of animal fat—the amount she'd just lost on Optifast—onto her television stage set, the Federal Trade Commission charged

Weight Watchers, Jenny Craig, and three other major diet companies with deceptive advertising.[8] In 1992, a researcher at the National Institutes of Health (NIH) concluded that "by five years, the majority of subjects beginning any weight-loss program have returned to their starting weight."[9] Around the same time, psychologist David Garner, who testified before Congress about the failures of the diet industry,[10] published an article that started with this sentence: "The purported benefits of weight loss are so well known that to question them is to defy almost unshakable beliefs."[11] That's still true today, twenty-four years later. Which I guess explains in part why Americans spend so much time and money chasing the elusive fantasy of thinness, and why most doctors continue to push diets on their overweight and obese patients. It's as if we don't *want* to know the truth, or believe it. Because despite what we know, anyone who questions the weight-loss paradigm even a little might as well be recommending crack for kids; people react with horror, judgment, and fear. And sometimes worse.

WHILE THE ULTIMATE effects of dieting aren't news, we do know more these days about the process, pros, and cons of dieting than we did forty years ago. We know, for instance, that dieting nearly always makes people heavier over time. In one study of Finnish twins, the more diets people went on, the higher their risk of becoming overweight and the faster they gained weight later in life.[12] The one exception to that rule involves set point, or settling points, theory, the idea that each of our bodies is geared to function best within a certain fairly limited weight range, usually ten or twenty pounds.[13] And our individual set points can vary wildly.

A friend who's the same height as me, and who probably weighs fifty pounds less, gained ten pounds recently from taking a short-term medication. She knew she'd finish the medication and her weight would return to its usual level. She's not particularly biased against fat or fat people, never diets, and is very physically active. But the extra ten pounds made her excruciatingly uncomfortable, physically and mentally. She couldn't wait to get off the meds so her body could revert to its set point. Which, in good time, it did.

By contrast, when I've weighed what she usually weighs—which falls well within the normal BMI range for our height—I've been utterly miserable: starving, fixated on food, and crabby as hell. All I could think about was what I was going to eat next and when. According to the doctor, that weight was ideal for my height, and I should have felt swell. But I just didn't. I feel stronger, fitter, and happier now, some fifty pounds heavier.

Set point theory suggests it's relatively easy to lose or gain weight within your range, but a lot harder to go outside it in either direction. And the stories I've heard from people who have lost weight and kept it off bear that out. Michelle, a magazine editor in her forties who lives in Madison, Wisconsin, lost about twenty pounds by walking seven miles a day. She says she's kept it off for nine years without having to diet, and with relative ease, and one explanation is that her lower weight still falls within her body's natural weight range. (Though some might argue that walking seven miles a day, every day, isn't so easy.)

Most people who want to lose weight want to lose more than a few pounds, though, and that's when they run into the unintended consequences of dieting and weight gain: the more you diet, the heavier you're likely to wind up. There are good reasons for those consequences, according to Janet Polivy, a researcher whose best-known paper is titled "Distress and Eating: Why Do Dieters Overeat?" Polivy grew up on Long Island, and her voice still carries the accent despite the thirty years she's spent as a psychology professor at the University of Toronto. She says watching her mother struggle with weight over the years inspired her own interest in exploring the psychological obstacles dieters face.

For instance, says Polivy, dieters tend to be more emotional and react more strongly than non-dieters to upsetting events, maybe because dieting itself creates so much stress. Dieters tend to have higher levels of cortisol, sometimes called "the stress hormone," and free fatty acids, both of which signal stress.[14] And dieters tend to exhibit diminished executive function, what economist Sendhil Mullainathan calls "strained bandwidth,"[15] maybe because using so much mental energy thinking, worrying, and negotiating about food choices leaves them too distracted to think about much else.[16]

Polivy believes a lot of the stress of dieting comes from the fact that we're surrounded by food cues, which may explain why people on diets react differently than lab rats whose food is cut back. "When rats are given food they eat it, and when they're not given food they're not necessarily stressing about it," explains Polivy. "They're just sitting there. So they live longer." She laughs. "Or maybe it just *seems* longer."

But when the rats' situation gets a little more real-world, their responses look more like ours. In one study, Polivy attached little baskets of Froot Loops above the cages of food-deprived rats, so the animals could see and smell the Froot Loops but couldn't get to them. *Those* rats showed much higher levels of stress hormones than the rats who weren't tormented by the Froot Loops.

And when they *were* allowed to eat as much as they wanted, the first group ate without restraint, gaining significant amounts of weight, while the second did not. The takeaway, says Polivy, is clear. "Unless you lock yourself in a room, have minimal food brought to you, don't watch TV, and don't have access to anything outside, you'll be surrounded by food cues," she explains. "Which ultimately take their toll. As soon as you *can* get food, you eat more and gain back everything and then some."

Physiology plays a role, too, of course. The drive to eat is so crucial to our survival that it's supported by a number of power-ful biological processes. For instance, a 2011 study showed that starvation (whether intentional or not) triggers neurons in the hypothalamus—a small almond-shaped organ deep in the brain— to literally consume themselves, which in turn amplifies hunger signals sent out by the brain.[17]

And the effects of dieting last long after the diet ends, at least in rodents. A history of dieting (or, actually, a history of being underfed) led to the rat equivalent of bingeing behavior—over-eating Oreos rather than their usual rat chow—in a study done by Mary Boggiano, a psychology professor at the University of Alabama–Birmingham. "Obviously there are lingering effects in the brain that were caused by dieting and produced binge eating," says Boggiano. "That was the novel finding—dieting can stay with you and put you at risk."

IN 2002, William Klish, a pediatric gastroenterologist featured in the movie *Super Size Me,* told a reporter from the *Houston Chronicle,* "If we don't get this [obesity] epidemic in check, for the first time in this century children will be looking forward to a shorter life expectancy than their parents."

As Klish later admitted,* he had absolutely no evidence for this frightening scenario; it was based on his "intuition." Which didn't stop it from being replayed in the media and cited by researchers. In fact, as I write, this claim is featured prominently on the websites of the American Heart Association, the Children's Defense Fund, the American Psychological Association, and other reputable organizations.

One reason no one questioned Klish's doomsday scenario is that it jibes with our deeply held assumptions around weight. In a culture so entrenched in the fat-is-bad/thin-is-good dichotomy, such a conclusion seems self-evident and, therefore, doesn't seem to need support. "People who talk about the 'obesity epidemic' often adopt a tone of absolute conviction," wrote Michael Gard in *The Obesity Epidemic*. "Both the extent of the problem and its causes are held to be self-evident."

There's another factor in play here, too, one that's related to that sense of conviction we have around weight issues. "The way we evaluate research related to weight is not neutral," explains Abigail Saguy, a professor of sociology at UCLA and author of *What's Wrong with Fat?*, "People, journalists, and researchers live in a world where it's taken for granted that fat is bad and thin is good. We know these influence the way we evaluate findings."

For instance, says Saguy, a 2004 study estimating that four hundred thousand people die each year from obesity got little or no public scrutiny because it reinforced what most people (including researchers) already believed—that fat will kill you. But the next

---

*According to "An Epidemic of Obesity Myths," published by the Center for Consumer Freedom. The CCF is a controversial source because it is, essentially, a front for food manufacturers, who have a vested interest in continuing to produce and market junk food to American consumers. Still, I haven't been able to find any evidence to support Klish's claim.

year, when the CDC somewhat sheepishly revised that estimate down to around twenty-six thousand excess deaths from obesity each year—a huge difference—reporters couldn't stop questioning the new estimate. "Almost a third of the journalists interviewed researchers who weren't the authors and who said the research wasn't good," says Saguy. "They didn't do that for the earlier study." The journalists were, of course, doing their jobs in taking a skeptical stance about the new number. The question is why they didn't feel the same skepticism about the original and much higher estimate.

So Klish's doomsday scenario lives on in part *because* it's frightening. And fear (whether justified or not) is a big part of the way we talk about weight—especially when it comes to children. The already heated debate about dieting gets even more volatile when it centers on kids.

According to the most recent numbers from the CDC, almost half of American kids and teens fall into either the overweight or obese category on the BMI chart. Like the categories for adults, those cutoff points were moved somewhat arbitrarily within the last fifteen years. Starting in 1994, the National Institutes of Health considered children whose BMI put them in the 95th percentile or above for their age overweight; those in the 85th to 95th percentiles were labeled "at risk of overweight." In 2005, the categories shifted; now kids above the 95th percentile are labeled "obese," while those in the 85th to 95th are "overweight."[18] And, according to University of Colorado law professor Paul Campos, author of *The Obesity Myth*, another little-known change happened at the same time: those percentiles were defined using data from the 1960s and 1970s rather than data on kids today, who are both taller and heavier than kids back then. In other words, writes Campos, "When Michelle Obama claims a third of our children are too fat, what she's really saying is that what was the 85th percentile on the height–weight charts forty years ago is about the 67th percentile today."[19]

The changing definitions make it hard to track how kids' weights (rather than their weight categories) have actually changed. Like adults, kids' average weights rose between 1980 and 2000, when they more or less stabilized. (What's rarely reported is that the percentage of young people who are underweight dropped from around 5 percent in the early 1970s to around 3.5 percent now— good news, because underweight is strongly associated with malnutrition and other health conditions.)[20]

Childhood obesity is commonly referred to as both an epidemic and a call to action: in 2010, when First Lady Michelle Obama launched her Let's Move! campaign, her goal was "to solve the challenge of childhood obesity within a generation." Some researchers have even called for obesity prevention starting in the womb.[21] Others, notably David Ludwig, a professor of pediatrics at Harvard Medical School, have argued that since "even relatively mild parenting deficiencies, such as having excessive junk food in the home or failing to model a physically active lifestyle, may contribute to a child's weight problem,"[22] obese children might need to be removed from their families, put into foster care, and, presumably, made to lose weight.*

---

*Ludwig made this argument in response to the growing popularity of bariatric surgery for kids and teens; he believes foster care would be a better solution than irreversible surgery. Putting kids into foster care is also a radical solution, though, and its effects might also be irreversible. And it has been happening. In October 2011, an eight-year-old Ohio boy was put into foster care because he weighed 218 pounds and was considered at risk for type 2 diabetes and high blood pressure. He didn't actually have either of those conditions, but the county still considered it a case of medical neglect. He went home five months later and more than fifty pounds lighter. I haven't been able to track what happened to him after that.

I wonder why we're not having the same conversation about, say, kids who live in homes where one or both parents smoke. We know the dangers of second- and thirdhand smoke very well: it causes and/or contributes to a range of diseases, including asthma, respiratory infections, lung cancer, and heart disease.[23] Yet no one is calling for children to be put into foster care if their parents can't or won't stop smoking. No one is calculating the health-care costs of secondhand smoke over a child's lifetime, or suggesting that cigarettes and cigars have any sort of environmental consequences.

Doctors and researchers know that dieting is no more successful in kids and teens than it is in adults—that in fact, it's probably even less successful and more damaging. Dianne Neumark-Sztainer, a professor of public health and epidemiology at the University of Minnesota, has studied weight, dieting, and health in children and adolescents since the 1990s, as the principal investigator for a series of ongoing studies known as Project EAT. Her research consistently links dieting in kids and teens with long-term weight gain and with patterns of dangerously disordered eating that can last a lifetime.[24]

Neumark-Sztainer has found that the younger kids are when they start to diet, the heavier they tend to become and the higher their chance of developing risky behaviors like purging, abusing laxatives, bingeing, and overexercising.[25] In fact, children and teens who diet are *significantly* heavier ten years later than those who don't—even if they weren't fat to begin with.[26] They feel worse about their bodies than non-dieters, which in turn makes them even more vulnerable to disordered eating, eating disorders, and weight gain.[27] And—here's the kicker—dieting kids and teens are also *less* likely to pursue healthy behaviors, like regular moderate exercise and eating balanced meals.[28] "People often feel like body dissatisfaction or being unhappy with how you look can be motivating," says Katie Loth, one of the researchers involved with Project EAT. "We've found that's not true."

So why, then, do we keep pushing kids to diet? It's one thing to make that kind of decision for yourself, as an adult; it's quite another to encourage or even force a child to diet, to start her on a set of behaviors that can last her whole life. A couple years ago, New York City mom Dara-Lynn Weiss had a moment of fame (or infamy, depending on your point of view) after writing an article for *Vogue* describing how she put her seven-year-old daughter on a diet. "There are lots of times I looked like a crazy, overbearing mom and I felt like a crazy, overbearing mom," she told a reporter for the *Huffington Post* after her book on the experience was published. "But it was the only way I found to help my daughter."[29]

In Recovery from Dieting

Mandy, thirty-six, works at an environmental nonprofit in Gainesville, Florida.

I developed early, around eleven, and was self-conscious about my body. My family made jokes about it a lot. There was a song that was popular, "Da Butt," and they would sing it to me: "Mandy has a big ol' butt." So I was hyperaware of my body even before I really understood that stuff.

The first time I changed the way I ate to lose weight, I was about twelve. My parents hid "their" food, the Oreos and ice cream, the things I wasn't allowed to have, so I would sneak food a lot. I became a secret eater and a binge eater for the next twenty years.

→

→

At fourteen I bought my first diet book and started doing exercises and eating fat-free foods, counting calories, chewing gum all the time, walking all the time. I became a compulsive fidgeter because being still meant I wasn't burning calories. I still do it and am completely unconscious about it.

By the time I was nineteen I was very skinny for me. There was some drug use going on in my life. I was restricting, and I was obsessive about eating. I was miserable, and so uncomfortable in my own skin. When I turned twenty-one, I stopped doing drugs and started putting on weight. For the next ten years I'd go on a diet, restrict pretty heavily, exercise a lot, lose weight, maintain it for a while, and then slowly gain. Every time I lost weight and regained it, I gained more and my weight stabilized at a higher level.

When I was thirty-one, my husband got into an accident and almost lost his leg. As soon as the accident happened, I gained thirty pounds. And something in my head just snapped at that point. I was just tired of it. I was exhausted with hating my body, being at odds with my body. It became so apparent how futile the effort was. And I thought, I can't do this for the rest of my life.

It's been a big realization for me that there's nothing wrong with me, that this is what your body does when you try to manipulate your weight.

That's the rub: we want our kids to be healthy and successful, so when the pediatrician warns us a child is in danger because of weight, we feel compelled to take action, which can mean anything from teaching a child to count calories to criticizing her body to locking the refrigerator. (Weiss, for instance, admits in her book to humiliating her daughter at parties and with friends about how much the girl had eaten.) As parents, especially as mothers, we not only bring our own baggage around food and body image to the table, but we're often directly blamed for our children's problems, especially with weight. And we blame ourselves.

I know I did just that when my daughter developed anorexia; in fact, on some level I wished her illness was my fault because then, I reasoned, I might be able to fix it. (No one thinks clearly after an anorexia diagnosis.) As I learned from talking to eating-disorders researchers and experts like Dr. Thomas Insel, director of the NIH, while many factors contribute to the development of an eating disorder, including genetics, neurobiology, and hormones, families do not. Specifically, the fact that I'd struggled with food and weight didn't cause my daughter's anorexia; if anything, it reflected our shared genetics and brain circuitry.

Given our love for and anxiety about our children, it's hard to go against the mainstream when it comes to kids and weight. When we hear that unless our child loses weight she'll be obese for the rest of her life, or she'll get diabetes or heart disease, or all of the above, of course we want to protect him or her, to *do* something, even if we suspect that that *something* is counterproductive or damaging. As renowned pediatrician William Sears told an April 2012 roundtable on childhood obesity campaigns, "For every eating disorder we might create, I think there are probably hundreds of health consequences of obesity that are much worse." It's tough to push back against a message like that, coming from an "expert." I can't help wondering if Sears has ever actually treated a child with an eating disorder, if he's seen the physical, psychological, and developmental havoc such disorders wreak on kids and adolescents. For a pediatrician, he seems curiously cavalier about these serious diseases.

And that tells me a lot. For one thing, it demonstrates that doctors like Sears either aren't looking at all the research or they're dismissing some of it. Their laser focus on the dangers of overweight and obesity—whether those dangers are real or exaggerated—prevents them from stepping back and seeing kids as whole people, more than a number on the BMI chart. Even if they truly believe, as Sears obviously does, that overweight and obesity are urgent health problems, they must also know that there are no effective long-term "solutions." We don't know how to make kids thin any more than we know how to make adults thin. But as the work of researchers like Dianne Neumark-Sztainer and Janet Polivy show, we do a hell of a lot of damage in trying.

Sears' comment also suggests that (a) eating disorders are incredibly rare, and (b) they're not all that bad, especially when compared with being fat. (It also ignores the reality that you can be fat and have an eating disorder.) That's precisely the kind of rhetoric that can and often does trigger kids into a spiral of unhealthy eating and exercise behaviors. And pediatricians really should know better,* as most eating disorders are diagnosed in childhood or adolescence—by pediatricians.

This end-justifies-the-means thinking is a big part of the national conversation about weight and dieting, especially when it comes to kids. Three years ago, when a pediatric hospital in Georgia created a series of controversial ads on childhood obesity, many people praised the campaign for telling the truth on a tough issue. The campaign featured stark black-and-white shots of fat children looking unhappy, with captions like "Warning: It's hard to be a little girl if you're not," "Being fat takes the fun out of

---

*Anorexia nervosa, for instance, has the highest mortality rate of any psychiatric illness.

being a kid," and "Big bones didn't make me this way. Big meals did." The children in the videos spoke about having hypertension and diabetes, though it later turned out they were actually healthy actors. A hospital administrator involved with the campaign told CNN, "Flowery ads don't get people's attention. We wanted to come up with something arresting and hard-hitting to grab people." They did grab people, but maybe not in the way the hospital intended. The backlash to the campaign went viral; critics said the ads stigmatized, shamed, and ultimately harmed the very children they were supposed to help. They were eventually taken down.[30]

The "means" here—shaming people into "doing something" about their child's weight, whatever that means—rarely if ever result in the hoped-for "end" of making kids thinner or healthier. Self-loathing in kids doesn't lead to positive change any more than it does in adults, despite arguments from experts like bioethicist Daniel Callahan, who has called for increasing stigma and shaming of fat people—which he described as an "edgier strategy"—to end obesity.[31]

Even when such efforts don't set out to shame kids, they can backfire in serious ways. For instance, many schools now require classes in "wellness" or "healthy eating," which may or may not be grounded in science. One student told me about a high school health teacher who instructed her class to go home, take off their clothes, stand in front of a mirror, and jump up and down. If anything wiggled that shouldn't wiggle, said the teacher, they'd know they were at an unhealthy weight.

Really?

Such classes often scare kids into destructive relationships with food and their own bodies. And that's the point, isn't it? To get kids to eat less and move more? But using fear as a motivator sets up all sorts of negative messages and behaviors. And while there's no evidence these classes help kids in any way, weight loss or not—in fact, decades of school-based initiatives to make kids thinner have repeatedly failed—many middle and high schools require them. And such classes can and often do trigger full-blown eating disorders in kids who are vulnerable.[32]

My daughter was one of them. A sixth-grade "wellness" class kicked off both her anxiety about eating and her interest in health. Though her weight was normal, she started to worry about being fat. She cut out desserts, telling us she'd learned that sugar was unhealthy. Over the next six months or so, her restricting took on a life of its own, and eventually turned into full-blown anorexia that nearly killed her.[33]

Researchers like Leora Pinhas, a child psychiatrist who directs the eating disorders program at Toronto's Hospital for Sick Children, have pointed out the risks of these targeted school-based health promotions. "These cases underscore the need to promote health, *regardless of size,* for all children and adults in the homes, schools, and neighborhoods they live in," wrote Pinhas in 2013. In other words, isn't it a good idea for *everyone* to be encouraged (not threatened) to engage in healthy behaviors like eating well (not minimally, but well) and exercising, whether they're fat, thin, or in between? Isn't the ultimate point health rather than weight?

I'm not so sure. We know putting kids on diets not only doesn't make them thinner in the long run, it often makes them fatter than they might otherwise have been later on. We know being thin doesn't necessarily equate with better health—on the contrary, for some children and adults, weight loss is a symptom of medical problems. We know the vast majority of people can't maintain

The End Justifies the Means

Joslyn, thirty-six, is an artist and legal assistant near Ithaca, New York. She grew up in Arkansas.

My history of dieting goes back to when I was eleven, when I started losing and regaining weight over and over. When I moved to California for college, I was at my heaviest. So I started eating less and walking a lot. I lost weight and immediately got all sorts of compliments from people. That progressed to me restricting calorically even more and exercising obsessively. I was walking about three miles in the mornings and evenings, and going to the gym for a couple hours, too.

I developed some health problems and eventually raised the issue with a nurse practitioner at school that I wanted to lose weight. At this point I'd lost sixty-five pounds, but my weight was still high based on the BMI chart. She didn't know how fast I'd lost the weight. She didn't ask what I was actually eating. She just gave me a goal weight and examples of what I should be eating, and had me come in weekly for weigh-ins to track my progress.

That was when I started purging. A couple months later I started abusing laxatives. But I lost weight every week. I was being monitored for weight loss, and being encouraged to keep losing. I lost about 115 pounds in eleven months, and then I started passing out randomly. Eventually I had an EKG and found I'd developed an arrhythmia. I needed to go into the hospital for inpatient treatment, but I was still overweight according to the BMI chart, and there was only one place that would take me.

I've now been in recovery from eating disorders for almost six years.

intentional weight loss, and so that first diet often triggers a life-time of weight cycling that may be far worse, healthwise, than staying at a stable but higher weight. But doctors keep prescribing diets for children of all ages. In fact, the latest twist in the race to "end childhood obesity" calls for putting infants on diets.[34]

Too many professionals still seem to feel that pushing weight loss on children and teens is not just a good idea but an imperative, that few of those young people will develop eating disorders or other problems in response, and that even if they do, the good of the many outweighs the potential harm to the few. One of those professionals is psychologist Thomas Wadden, a prominent obesity researcher at the University of Pennsylvania. "Although health professionals, teachers, and parents will continue to be concerned about misguided weight loss efforts in children and teenagers, all should be increasingly concerned by the growing epidemic of pediatric obesity," he has written.[35] But who really benefits from this kind of approach? Wadden's allegiance to the fat-is-always-bad perspective suggests it's OK to disorder kids' eating and self-image in the name of making the fat kids thin—which doesn't work anyway. (And what about the eating habits and physical and mental health of the thin kids? Is anyone paying attention to those?) Wadden also directs the Center for Weight and Eating Disorders at the University of Pennsylvania, a frightening thought given his clear priorities around children and weight. I'm glad my daughter wasn't treated there.

SO DIETING, it turns out, doesn't make people thinner in the long run. But it must make them healthier. At least that's the premise Janet Tomiyama, now a professor at UCLA, set out to explore a couple of years ago. Tomiyama, who describes herself as a "huge foodie," traces her interest in weight issues to the fact that she spent much of her childhood in Japan. "Everyone there is much thinner than in the U.S., and there's a more pervasive stigma against overweight," she says. "I went to an American school, so I heard two different messages around weight. The American message, was, *Your body is beautiful!*" She grins, making a dimple appear in one cheek. "And then I'd go home to people blatantly putting me down because of my body."

Tomiyama's most recent collaboration with psychologist Traci Mann investigated whether intentional weight loss—regardless of whether people kept the weight off or regained it—improves health. They reviewed studies of dieting interventions, looking for those with common health biomarkers, and chose five measures to compare: total cholesterol, triglycerides, blood pressure (systolic and diastolic), and fasting blood glucose. The results stunned them. "We found basically no relationship between any health outcome and the amount of weight lost or gained," says Tomiyama, adding dryly, "we had some trouble getting it published."

Their finding is deeply disturbing, given the fact that virtually everyone in this culture uses weight as a proxy for health. My neighbor who bemoaned the actress's body size, for example, was conflating weight and health. Ditto the doctor who told Dara-Lynn Weiss her daughter had to lose weight but who asked nothing about her eating or exercise habits.

Tomiyama's study doesn't mean that weight loss *never* benefits health, of course. Some people who intentionally lose weight see improvements in blood pressure or glucose levels or cholesterol or joint pain. It does underline the fact that health is essentially an individual measure. What's healthy for me might not be healthy for you, and vice versa. But that's not how the issue is typically framed. Instead, weight loss has become a reflexive prescription for improving nearly everyone's health, and we've all come to think of it that way, including doctors. When medical experts automatically recommend weight loss for any and every medical problem—and I've heard stories ranging from ear infections to brain malformations being blamed on being overweight—they're not only relying on an assumption that's untrue; they're also potentially missing other health issues.* Weight stigma is a real problem, especially among doctors (see Chapter 4).

One of the largest and most recent comprehensive studies on weight loss and health, the Look AHEAD trial, set out to see if weight loss via "intensive lifestyle intervention" could improve the prognoses for people with type 2 diabetes, who are more susceptible to heart problems, amputations, and other medical complications. The study followed five thousand or so overweight or obese patients with type 2 diabetes for close to ten years—far longer than the usual one or two years of follow-up most studies offer.

The results were somewhat mixed. People in the intervention group did lose more weight than those in the control group (though not much—6 percent versus 3.5 percent of body weight at the end of the study); they also showed significant improvements in fitness and biomarkers like waist circumference and glycated hemoglobin (a marker for blood glucose levels). But they had just as many heart attacks, strokes, other cardiovascular "events," and premature deaths as those who didn't get the

---

*To read some personal stories on the subject, visit the blog First, Do No Harm at http://fathealth.wordpress.com.

intensive interventions. In fact, the study was stopped ahead of schedule because it found no significant differences between the two groups.

That doesn't stop doctors from clinging to the weight-loss prescription for patients with type 2 diabetes. According to Rena Wing, the chair of Look AHEAD and a professor of psychiatry and human behavior at Brown University's Alpert Medical School, "There are many reasons you should be encouraging patients with diabetes to lose weight."[36] Twenty years ago Wing, who holds a PhD in social relations, developed the National Weight Control Registry to track people who lost "significant" amounts of weight and kept it off for "long periods of time," defined as anyone who's kept off at least thirty pounds for a year. She's also published more than two hundred research articles about obesity treatment and prevention.[37] Like many researchers in the field today, she has gotten financial support for some of her work from the weight-loss industries. And like them she's deeply invested on a number of levels in the idea that losing weight improves health, despite the lack of clear evidence supporting that hypothesis.

ONE OFTEN OVERLOOKED factor in the conversation around weight and health is the effect of yo-yo dieting, also known as weight cycling. An ever-growing body of research suggests that losing and regaining weight over and over correlates with higher levels of heart disease,[38] impaired immune function,[39] cardiometabolic risk,[40] insulin resistance,[41] triglycerides,[42] hypertension,[43] and abdominal fat accumulation.[44] In other words, weight cycling can be far worse, healthwise, than obesity. And these health risks apply whether you're thin or fat, judging by a fascinating 2001 study done in Japan.

Researchers at Nagoya University took five healthy, nonsmoking, "normal"-weight women in their twenties and thirties and put them through two major periods of weight loss and regain within 180 days. Studies of weight and health typically use self-reported measures of weight, height, food intake, and exercise routines, which are notoriously inaccurate; most of us under-report what we've eaten and our weights, and overestimate how much we exercise. These women were actually weighed, measured, and to a large extent supervised by researchers, meaning that the data was more accurate.

The subjects first dieted for thirty days, eating around 1,200 calories a day and losing six to ten pounds each. Then they were allowed to eat whatever they wanted for fourteen days; all of them gained back the weight they'd lost, plus a little more. Next came another thirty-day diet period, during which they didn't lose quite as much as they had the first time around. Finally, they ate freely for the last three and a half months.

At the end of the study, the women's weights were around the same as when they started. But their lean body mass had dropped, meaning they now had more body fat even though they weighed the same. Their resting metabolic rates had also dropped, meaning they now required fewer calories to sustain the same amount of energy. Finally, their blood pressure and triglycerides rose, too. They may have looked the same on the outside and on the scale, but weight cycling caused physiological changes that hurt their health and could likely lead to more weight gain and disease down the line.[45]

What's interesting about this study (besides the fact that researchers somehow persuaded five women to undergo such a grueling process) is that it tracked and monitored individuals, not groups. So while the sample size, five, is too small to generalize from, the study's design offers a window into some of the otherwise invisible changes that accompany weight cycling. While more research needs to be done (and no doubt will be), the bulk of the data suggests that yo-yo dieting is not benign. The kind of up-and-down weight cycling so many of us do, over and over, believing that we're trying to make ourselves healthier, is almost certainly hurting our physical health in ways we don't yet understand.

While many of the studies on weight cycling suggest it's dangerous, a handful have found no correlation with mortality[46] or disease.[47] (Nearly all of those, interestingly, were worked on by Harvard's Walter Willett, who refused to talk to me.) As with pretty much every aspect of the research on weight and health, there's no absolute consensus, and there's a lot we still don't know. Still, when a respected obesity researcher like Donna Ryan, a former director at the Pennington Biomedical Research Center in Baton Rouge who's worked on some of the biggest weight and health studies in the United States, claims not to be familiar with any negative effects of weight cycling, I have to wonder why. In an interview, Ryan told me, "I am not convinced there's any harm whatsoever in losing weight and regaining it. I think the risk reduction while you're at a lower weight is good for you."

That perspective, which appears to be shared by Willett, doesn't jibe with most of the research. It certainly doesn't match up with what we know about the psychological effects of weight cycling. Pretty much every study that's looked at the question has found strong connections between weight cycling and binge eating, which makes sense, since part of the body's physiological response to starvation is to up the drive to eat. Binge eating, in turn, is closely linked with mental distress. In a 2011 study of overweight and obese African American women, weight cycling correlated with a higher drive for thinness, lower body satisfaction, and lower self-esteem.[48] Earlier studies found correlations between weight cycling and disordered eating, higher stress, lower well-being, and less confidence about food and eating.[49] In other words, the more loops of the yo-yo you go around, the worse you feel about your weight, your eating, your very self.

AMONG THE HUNDREDS of women and men I interviewed for this book, I talked to maybe four or five who lost more than twenty pounds and kept the weight off for more than five years. In the world of obesity research they're known as "maintainers," the 5 percenters, and they're few and far between. Almost all of them say keeping the weight off is their top priority, and that when their focus slips even a little they start to regain weight. Almost all have done some weight cycling.

One of those "maintainers" is Patrick, a slender thirty-eight-year-old university librarian with deep dimples who grew up in Texas. He describes himself as a person with a big appetite. "I did a lot of eating and drinking in a celebratory way," he says. "I felt like it was part of my personality."

Patrick's first diet started nine years ago, after his doctor lectured him about his weight. "I knew I was overweight, but it had never officially been on the record before," he says. "It was like I was getting yelled at. And that was a very big incentive to me, to not upset the doctor." He started walking every day, eventually transitioning to running. He became more mindful about what and how much he ate. Over the next three years he lost eighty pounds.

Patrick's daily routine now starts with the same breakfast every day (shredded wheat with milk). He walks or bikes two and a half miles to work and goes to the gym at lunchtime. Lunch, too, is the same every day—currently several ounces of hummus, half a pita, cherry tomatoes, spinach and arugula with a little cheese and vinaigrette, and fruit. (He changes it up every few months.) He walks or bikes home, goes for a run, and then sits down to a small dinner with his wife.

He runs twenty to thirty miles a week and says it's become both his passion and his refuge. But he worries about what might happen if, say, he was injured, or found himself having to work three jobs. Or if, for whatever reason, he didn't have fifteen hours a week to devote to fitness. "The day-to-day practice of being a healthy person is ingrained in how I live now," says Patrick. "But what if the thing that I know works for weight loss, and that I enjoy, gets pulled out from under me?"

His concern illuminates one of the core confusions at the heart of the weight-health debate. When Patrick began walking, and then running, his health improved—not because he lost weight but because he started getting regular exercise, and the physical and psychological benefits of regular exercise are well known and well documented. But he attributes his improved health to the fact that he's eighty pounds lighter, not to the behavioral changes he made. It's as if a former smoker attributed his new improved health to the fact that his teeth were now whiter; yellow teeth are, after all, a risk factor for lung cancer, as I mentioned earlier. If we lived in a culture that fetishized white teeth the way it does thinness, we might agree. But of course the real reason for his better health is the fact that he changed his behavior; he stopped smoking.

Not long ago Patrick did indeed regain thirty pounds, mostly, he says, by just not paying attention to what he was eating and how much he was exercising. This time around it was much tougher to drop the weight.*

This is the reality for pretty much everyone who loses a significant amount of weight. As the researchers at Nagoya University learned, dieting changes metabolism. The body becomes more efficient after a period of restriction, spending its calories frugally. People who have intentionally lost weight generally use about 15 percent fewer calories than non-dieters to perform exactly the same activities,[50] which means they gain weight eating fewer calories than non-dieters. "We know scientifically even if someone loses weight, they will never be like a thin person," says Asheley Skinner, PhD, a research professor of pediatrics at the University of North Carolina at Chapel Hill. "They will always need fewer calories and will need to exercise to stay at that lower weight. We know there's some sort of derangement of the metabolic pathways, and that has a cascade effect on everything from the hormones involved with obesity to hunger."

A few years ago, Skinner used data from the NHANES study to test the concept. She analyzed two days' food intake for "normal"-weight and overweight children, and found that while heavier toddlers and preschoolers ate more than their thinner counterparts, older children and teens ate significantly less.[51] One possible explanation is that the older kids and adolescents might have lost and regained weight, even once or twice, making their metabolisms more efficient.

---

*A 2003 study of successful weight maintainers found that few if any were able to re-lose weight they'd regained, even small amounts. Patrick's success may have something to do with the fact that he doesn't have a history of weight cycling; this was his first yo-yo.

GIVEN WHAT WE know about how ineffective and often harmful dieting is, why is it still so widely prescribed, pushed, and promoted? I think one reason is that most of us feel trapped when it comes to weight. We're constantly hammered with the message that fat is bad, that we need to be thinner, that our kids and pets need to be thinner, that we're all going to die (or live alone with too many cats for the rest of our foreshortened lives) if we don't lose weight. We live in a time when we believe we can control our destinies, and that includes our bodies, despite mountains of evidence to the contrary. We believe we might even cheat death if we do everything exactly right—eat right, exercise enough, de-stress, make time for friends, fill in the blank. So when our bodies don't measure up, when our lives look less full or less desirable than other people's, we feel incredible shame. We live in a culture where failure in anything is a sign of unforgiveable weakness. So we keep pushing ourselves and our children; we keep running around and around the same closed loop trying to get it right. To get our bodies and our appetites right.

And one way we try to mold ourselves into the shape du jour is by controlling, obsessing, and angsting over food.

Chapter 3

Good Food, Bad Food

*"Although we learned long ago to abandon magical
thinking in connection with weather, crops, the care of
animals, and other natural phenomena, it still has us in
its grip when we think of diet."*

—Ruth Gay, "Fear of Food,"
from *The American Scholar,* 1976

*"The amount of misinformation about nutrition that is
circulated widely, especially by those who profit from
doing so, is overwhelming."*

—researcher A. E. Harper, University of Wisconsin

My most vivid childhood memory of eating took place at my grandparents' house. My family ate dinner there every Friday night, and
it was the highlight of my week. Not only did I get to spend time
with my grandparents, whom I adored, but my grandmother was
an excellent cook who catered to my sister's and my tastes. (For
years I thought chickens had four wings; my grandmother always
bought extra, knowing wings were my favorite part.)

This night I must have been around ten. I already felt too fat, though photos from that time show a short girl with curly dark hair and a perfectly ordinary body. We said the blessing over the challah and passed it around the table. My grandfather smeared margarine on his slice and urged me to do the same. "Come on, doll," he said. "Try it with some margarine." I shook my head—I liked my challah plain—and as I lifted the slice to my mouth, he said chidingly, "Looks like you're putting on some weight there." I remember sitting there, the bread halfway to my mouth, thinking even at ten years old *Now what do I do?*

I'd forgotten that experience until the day years later when the therapist asked *What if you were OK with your body the way it is right now?* And then it began to pop into my head at random moments, that vision of a young girl at the family dinner table, caught in the suddenly forbidden act of eating, frozen in shame and confusion. I still thought the therapist had misjudged me. I still thought she was insane. But for the first time in a long time, I found myself examining the roles food had played in my life. It took until I was thirty-eight years old to really bear down and think about the ways food—what I ate and how much—affected how I felt about my body. The subject had been so painful for so long that I'd literally taught myself to think around it. Now, though, I forced myself to sit down and consider how food made me feel. I had a ridiculously hard time getting myself to focus on it. My mind kept wanting to slide away, wander off into some immediate distraction, which told me how important the question was and how long I'd been burying it.

Eventually I was able to sit still long enough to come up with an answer: when I ate too much, I felt bloated and huge. When I ate too little, my body felt light and clean, but also, often, shaky and weak. The really puzzling thing, I realized, was that I'd had both sets of feelings at exactly the same weight. Today I might feel enormous; tomorrow I might feel svelte. But how could that be? It made no sense.

And, I realized, there were moments when I felt reasonably good about my body. That came as a bit of a shock, to be honest; I was so used to automatically ragging on myself I'd forgotten I ever had other feelings. But those good moments could turn in a second to rank, rancid shame. My flesh seemed just too much—too soft, too white, too hairy, too *corporeal*. It wasn't just my body that could provoke this shame, either; it was also my eating and not-eating and overeating, my anxiety about eating and the way food had come to dominate my entire life. I realized I was sick of it. I wished I didn't have to eat, which was a supremely odd thought for someone who loved food. But it was true. It would be much easier to just not eat at all than to keep going around and around this cycle of eating and dieting, bingeing and starving.

It occurred to me for maybe the first time ever that I had absolutely no idea what normal eating was or how to do it. I'd tried to suss it out by watching my husband, who's naturally wiry and athletic and who's never counted a calorie in his life. But as a role model, he was no help. Sometimes he ate a lot, and a lot of foods I never touched: fettuccine Alfredo, bread slathered with butter, macaroni and cheese, huge bowls of ice cream with whipped cream on top. Fatty foods. Scary foods. Bad foods.

Other times he didn't eat much at all—a peanut butter and jelly sandwich could keep him going for hours. I'd seen him forget to eat lunch, or postpone it when it wasn't convenient or easy to eat. I never did that, not just because I got too hungry but because the experience of not having food when I wanted or needed it made me feel both physically shaky and anxious. The few times I'd had outpatient surgeries or procedures, the not-eating before-hand was by far the worst part of the whole thing. Even if I wasn't physically hungry, that sense of deprivation sent panic screaming through my cells. And that shamed me, too, because I had plenty of meat on my bones. Missing a meal now and then should hardly matter. It would be good for me, wouldn't it?

I felt like a fly struggling in a spider's web, wrapping myself tighter the more I thrashed and flailed. So I went back to the therapist and put aside the question of weight, to focus instead on food. On, as she said, my *relationship* with food, a phrase that seemed oddly disturbing. I'd devoted so much energy to forget-ting I had a relationship with food; why would I want to undo that now?

But I turned up for our next session with a box of crackers, as she'd requested. At least, she told me to bring in a food I felt neutral about, and that was easy to eat. So I opened my box of Saltines, took out a cracker, and got ready to eat it. The therapist instructed me to "explore" the cracker in as many ways as possi-ble; so, even though I felt ridiculous, I sniffed it and struggled to come up with descriptive words for its smell (bready? bland? like cardboard?). I ran the tips of my fingers over it, felt its sharp corners, touched the salt crystals studding its surface. I looked at it just about every way you could look at a cracker, and just when I thought I couldn't stand another minute of it, the therapist told me to break the cracker and put half in my mouth. "Don't chew," she ordered. "Just let it sit on your tongue."

I would have rolled my eyes if she wasn't looking, but I did what she said, and immediately started to sweat. The cracker felt huge and heavy, swelling second by second on my tongue. I was going to choke on it. I needed to swallow it or spit it out. The therapist looked me in the eye, keeping me steady, and I managed to hold it in my mouth. Hours went by. Whole days and nights. Finally she nodded and I moved my jaw, intending to chew. But the cracker had melted to mush. The lump slid down my throat, and I startled both of us by bursting into tears.

"What happened?" she asked, and I tried to tell her about the feeling that I was about to choke, the sense of panic that rose in my throat, the grief and terror that came from sitting with half a Saltine in my mouth for what probably amounted to fifteen seconds but felt like an eternity. I couldn't make coherent words, but I didn't have to. She kept looking at me calmly, and slowly I felt calmer, too.

That was the beginning of our real work together. I spent the next ten years sitting across from her, taking my life apart and putting it back together, starting with that cracker. The act of eating, such a basic human experience, had become such a loaded, painful aspect of my life. And I knew even then I wasn't the only one who felt that way. As M. F. K. Fischer wrote, "First we eat, then we do everything else."

IMAGINE IF ONE of your great-great-great-great-great-great-great-great-great-grandmothers magically came to life in twenty-first-century America. Unless you're descended from royalty—and maybe even if you are—she'd likely be stunned by the abundance, accessibility, and array of food in this time and place. You could, of course, tell her that hunger is still a problem here, that fifteen percent of all American families go hungry at least some of the time.[1] And certainly malnutrition sickens and kills millions of people around the world. But here in the United States, where we spend about $4,300 per person each year on food,[2] most of us get enough calories to survive.

Then imagine you go on to describe how we feel about food. On the one hand we celebrate it: we pore over lavish four-color cookbooks studded with food-porn-style photos. We read magazines and blogs devoted to the sensual pleasures of preparing and eating food. Many of us spend a fair amount of our discretionary income in restaurants ranging from McDonald's to New York City's Masa, which serves an *omakase* (chef's choice) sushi menu that sets the average diner back about $1,200.

But then there's the other side of the story. Many of us fear and struggle with food. Three-quarters of American women eat in a disordered way a lot of the time; another third have purged (through vomiting or laxatives) to control their weight, and that's not counting anyone with an actual eating disorder diagnosis. My students aren't surprised by these statistics; they're living them. In one class where we talked about disordered eating, a young woman raised her hand and asked, "What is *not-disordered* eating?" That unleashed a torrent of confessions and questions from nearly everyone in the class. (For a good definition, see page 185.) A number of the young women (and a few of the guys) admitted eating only once a day, cutting out bread or other food groups altogether, avoiding anything with fat in it, spending two or more hours a day in the gym to "get rid" of the calories they did consume. These twenty-year-olds were just as tormented as I'd been at their ages. And like twenty-year-old me, they had no idea how to feed themselves well and feel good about it.

So yes, we're confused and screwed-up and anxious about food, which is unsurprising given the mixed messages that bombard us: enjoy your food but not too much. Eat what you like but don't get fat. Eat healthy but don't deprive yourself. Eat this but not that—never *ever* eat that. You'll die without food, but you're eating yourself to death.

The nutritional wisdom du jour is no better. One day meat will kill you and the next it'll add years to your life. Fat makes you sick and obese; no, it's carbs that give you diabetes. No, make that sugar. Eggs raise your cholesterol. Or do they? Too much salt leads to stroke, but wait—it turns out too little salt may be even worse.

Once-reputable doctors like Mehmet Oz take to TV to hawk "miracle foods" like green coffee extract, guaranteed to trim your tummy. No wonder we use so much of our bandwidth worrying about what to eat—or, more to the point, what not to eat. No wonder a friend who was torn between loving to eat and longing to be thin once told me she fantasized about having her taste buds surgically removed so she wouldn't have to choose.

At various times in my life I would have gladly joined her. If food was truly just fuel, nothing else, life would be so much simpler, especially in this era of thin-at-any-cost. But despite the views of food crusaders like Walter Willett, Brian Wansink, and even the popular Michael Pollan,* who encourage a fairly utilitarian perspective on eating, food is much, much more than the gas that fills our tanks. Food is nutrition, true, but it's also love and community and ritual. The need to eat is one of the few

---

*In her insightful book *Weighing In: Obesity, Food Justice, and the Limits of Capitalism*, University of California–Santa Cruz professor Julie Guthman points out that Pollan's book *In Defense of Food* advocates strategies like using smaller plates to trick yourself into eating less, and "reads like a diet book." Much of Pollan's work, she adds, seems "to suggest that if you act like him, by spending more money and time procuring, preparing, and eating food, you'll be thin." Which is, of course, completely untrue; I've never used a mix, eat few if any processed foods, cook everything from scratch, use local organic ingredients whenever possible, and have rarely in my life been thin.

experiences we all share. Coming together to prepare a meal, to serve it, to eat it, binds us to other people more often than sex and more closely than circumstance.

I didn't realize how much social connection revolves around food until my daughter's illness. For more than a year we didn't invite people over for dinner, didn't go out to eat, avoided brunches and lunches and backyard barbecues with friends and neighbors. Without a table full of other people to gather around, we didn't gather. We felt isolated. We *were* isolated.

The social aspects of eating made my daughter's recovery tougher at first. Early on she avoided any event where food would be served, afraid to eat and self-conscious about her fear. And since just about every gathering involved food, she wound up alone a lot. It was months before she could eat with friends, and even then it was a struggle. A few years later, when she was further along in recovery, eating with good friends actually helped her through some bumpy moments.

Which makes perfect sense to Montana-based psychologist and evolutionary biologist Shan Guisinger, who's come up with an intriguing theory about how early humans ate and why some people develop anorexia nervosa. Our ancestors were nomadic foragers, says Guisinger, following the food sources from place to place. She believes anorexia may have been an adaptation to periodic episodes of famine: most humans without enough food get hungry and weak. People with anorexia, on the other hand, become almost manically hyperactive, full of restless energy. They don't see themselves as too thin or think they have a problem. Their terror of food and eating seems to propel them despite the lack of enough calories—at least for a while.

Guisinger's theory is that people with the anorexic adaptation could lead a tribe to food when everyone else was too weak to think clearly or want to move. Once they found new food sources and regained strength, she says, the group would draw the person with anorexia back into health through the social routines of eating[3]—by including her, encouraging her, and supporting her eating until she'd regained weight and strength.

Our current anxieties around food and eating are, of course, nowhere near as severe as the ones that characterize anorexia nervosa. But our cultural attitudes around food are scarily reminiscent of those pathologies. "We've all been traumatized at least a little bit with regard to our eating," says Ellyn Satter, a registered dietitian and therapist who's written a number of books on children and eating.

A few years ago, Satter told me a story that made her point all too well. For many years her clinical practice in Madison, Wisconsin, focused on helping parents and kids deal with food, weight, and eating. One mom brought in a seven-month-old girl who was eating well and whose weight was steady. The problem, said the mom, was that the baby loved food too much. She would literally moan with pleasure and wiggle her legs as she ate. The mother was mortified by the moaning and, more important, scared of her daughter's appetite, afraid the girl would eat so much she'd become obese.

That story seems both relatable and terribly sad to me. Before my daughters were born, I used to worry about what traits they might inherit from me and their father, good and bad. I thought they might get my curly hair and passion for writing. I hoped they wouldn't inherit my anxiety disorder or tendency to gain weight because I didn't want them to suffer the way I had. I didn't want them to feel crippled or consumed by body anxieties, and I also didn't want them to be rejected or bullied because they weren't thin enough.

This is, of course, a common fear among parents. We want our children to be accepted and appreciated for who they are. We want to protect them from harm, including the kinds of harm people inflict on one another. A few years ago, when Rebecca Puhl, the deputy director of Yale's Rudd Center for Food Policy & Obesity, surveyed parents about the reasons kids and teens are bullied, weight concerns topped the list, far outweighing other potential sources of bullying like physical disability, race, class, or sexual orientation.[4] Tellingly, parents with thin kids worried about weight bullying, too, though not as much as parents of overweight or obese kids. No one really feels safe from such public criticism. We're all only five pounds away from being called out for being too fat.

So I understand that mother's fear of her baby's appetite. I even understand (sort of) why Dara-Lynn Weiss put her seven-year-old daughter on a diet (though I have more trouble understanding why she wrote about it in such painful detail for *Vogue* and later in a book). I understand the impulse behind Weiss's actions; I just wish she'd done a little more research first, investigated other possibilities beyond dieting..

If I hadn't been actively researching weight and health, I might have been one of those parents who preached the good food/bad food dichotomy and encouraged her daughters to "watch their weight." Maybe I, too, would have delivered the same mixed messages around food that my sister and I got at home. Growing up, we ate Tastykakes and drank diet soda with every meal. My mother kept the upright freezer full of desserts but locked it and hid the key. She commented freely and critically about what my sister and I ate and how much we weighed, and once went so far as to fill an empty ice cream container with garbage and put it back in the freezer, where she knew my sister would open it. (Inside, she placed a note reading "Gotcha!" I'm still trying to figure out what that meant. I caught you eating? I caught you enjoying your food? Sacrilege.) She herself dieted on and off until practically the day she died, recording her weight each morning on a chart in the bathroom, losing the same twenty-five pounds or so over and over.

I know what it's like to be afraid of food—of my own response to it, anyway. My personal experiences with dieting, restrained eating, and the bingeing that inevitably followed made me feel like I couldn't control my appetite, that once unleashed it might literally devour everything in sight. Now I know all too well that fear leads only to more fear, more disordered eating, more health problems. We bounce from one extreme to the other, eating nothing but salad and fruit one week (and feeling oh-so-virtuous for doing it), then inhaling nachos and cupcakes the next in a vicious and self-perpetuating cycle of defiance and despair.

Our personal fears about food have morphed into powerful cultural anxieties. Google the phrase "eating ourselves to death" and you'll see what I mean. Most of us believe the reason we're fatter than we used to be, as a culture, is that we eat too much and too many of the wrong things. That *sounds* reasonable, and it meshes with the "calories in, calories out" truism we're used to hearing. But despite the appealingly transparent logic of this proposition—eating too many calories is making us fat, so all we have to do is eat less—the reality is not so simple.

For one thing, nutritional science is more presumption than prescription. We know a lot about the general principles of nutrition, but we're more or less guessing about what particular individuals need to be healthy. "We make all these recommendations, with all this apparent scientific precision, but when it comes down to it, we don't know how much fat someone should have in their diet," says the University of North Carolina's Asheley Skinner. "We don't know how many months or years with high cholesterol will cause heart disease. We argue like we know

---

I Wore Shorts This Summer

Alyssa, thirty-one, works at a natural foods store on Long Island.

The first time I became really conscious of my weight was around eighth grade. Somebody made a comment about how my thinner sister would probably be a model but they never had to worry about me clearing a plate. I didn't go on a diet, but I exercised quietly in my room a lot. I didn't see it as an avenue to health. I saw it as something I had to do to get smaller.

The first time I went on a diet I was twenty-one. In three months I lost twenty-five pounds, and everyone was raving, "You look amazing!" That kind of fed me. But of course I gained it back. When I lived in New Paltz, I started running on beautiful mountain roads. Once this car full of college kids drove by, and a guy leaned out and said, "Keep running, flabby, you have a long way to go." I remember stopping and laughing because clearly I *was* exercising right then.

The second time I went on Weight Watchers the weight didn't come off as quick, and I wasn't as disciplined. I went back and forth between counting calories, trying to eat really healthy, and then the second a cheeseburger was put in front of me I would eat it. Things were either really good or really bad. I lost all balance.

I started working at a health food store and eating all this healthy whole food. I didn't count a single calorie and actually lost twenty pounds the first year. Then somebody made a comment about how much weight I'd lost, and I felt pressured to lose more. I started counting calories, and the weight just came back.

The worst part about Weight Watchers from a health standpoint is I ate more garbage on the plan than I did not counting calories at all. I ate so much crap, just to get the lower calorie counts. I've taken diet pills and done Engine 2. Eventually I started feeling like, *Why am I spending so much time on this?* I joined Tumblr and started following body positivity blogs, and it's funny—when you change your media environment and expose yourself to more than just the same three skinny white girls all the time, you put a lot less pressure on yourself.

It's still a daily struggle for me. Some days I feel amazing, and some days I don't want anyone to look at me. But I wore shorts this summer—I hadn't worn them in years—and I felt great.

what we're talking about, but we don't." As I'm writing this, for instance, a new international study of 100,000 people, published in the *New England Journal of Medicine,* suggests that eating too little salt may be just as dangerous as eating too much. The arguments over salt guidelines will likely go on for years. Meanwhile, what do we do?

Nutritional science is especially weak on issues of weight. Much of the research assumes, for example, that if a fat person drops enough weight, he or she will become "healthy" in the same way as a thin person, and will be able to eat and exercise like someone who's naturally thin. But that's not how it works. "We're putting people through something we know will probably not be successful," says Skinner. "And who knows what we're doing to their metabolisms in the process?"

We do have an idea about that, actually, thanks to an idealistic senator from South Dakota named George McGovern who was worried about hunger in America. In 1968, he created and chaired a special Senate committee—the US Senate Select Committee on Nutrition and Human Needs, informally known as the McGovern committee—to work on the problem. Over the next few years, the committee organized a conference on nutrition, food, and health, and gathered testimony on the subject from experts, teachers, doctors, academics, nongovernmental organizations, and citizens.

In 1974, McGovern broadened the committee's mandate to include setting national policy around nutrition—specifically, helping Americans eat less to avoid chronic diseases. His intentions were good; as he told attendees at the Church World Service conference nearly thirty years later, "I hope someday we will be able to proclaim that we have banished hunger in the United States, and that we've been able to bring nutrition and health to the whole world." But the committee's 1977 recommendations, while well-meaning and even logical, were not grounded in strong science.

For instance, the committee set detailed guidelines for how much fat, carbohydrates, cholesterol, sugar, and salt ordinary Americans should consume. Two of those dietary goals were to cut fat to 30 percent of a person's intake, and raise carbohydrates to about 60 percent, despite a complete lack of compelling evidence for those cutoffs.[5] The 1977 report set in motion a national experiment in eating that people like cardiologist Arthur Agatston, who created the South Beach Diet, believe contributed to or even triggered the so-called obesity epidemic.[6] It ushered in the era that brought us such cognitively dissonant "foods" as fat-free brownies and cheeses, and helped create a nation of lipophobes. And it set the stage for the government's Dietary Guidelines for America, first issued in 1980 and updated every five years, which have also come under fire for being driven more by politics than science. (The latest iteration led to the creation of the government's "My Plate" recommendations of five food groups that are part of a "healthy diet": fruits, vegetables, grains, protein foods, and dairy. Presumably everything else is not part of a healthy diet.)[7]

The McGovern committee's recommendations on fat were based loosely on research done by Ancel Keys, a physiologist and researcher at the University of Minnesota who spent a long and fascinating career exploring the relationship between nutrition and health. One of Keys's most important research projects, in fact, laid the groundwork for the modern understanding of anorexia nervosa as a physiological, not just psychological, disease.* In a study that would never be approved by institutional review boards today, Keys took thirty-six healthy young conscientious objectors and subjected them to an experiment in starvation. For three months he merely observed them, cataloguing their physical and psychological conditions, creating a kind of baseline for the experiment. For the next six months he starved them, feeding them so little that each man lost a quarter of his body weight.

---

*If you don't want to wade through the whole 1,585-page study (why ever not?), check out the much more readable *The Great Starvation Experiment: Ancel Keys and the Men Who Starved for Science*, by Todd Tucker.

(This may not sound like much, but consider that a 160-pound man would have dropped 40 pounds in six months.) For the final three months, Keys and his team re-fed the men, all the while observing and meticulously recording the minutiae of their physical and psychological health.

Keys's observations turned a lot of the conventional wisdom around food and eating upside down. His subjects' psychological well-being deteriorated along with their physical health. They became irritable, anxious, depressed, fatigued, socially withdrawn. They couldn't concentrate. They obsessed over food and over the act of eating, spending hours on a tiny meal, cutting their portions into minuscule pieces, rearranging them on the plate, dousing them with salt and other condiments. They daydreamed about cooking, concocting elaborate mental meals; in fact, several of them with no previous interest in cooking went on to restaurant careers. Maybe the most surprising aspect of the experiment, though, was that the men's symptoms hit their peak during the re-feeding phase, not the starvation phase. They showed nearly all the same behaviors as people with anorexia, including, for some, resisting food despite the fact that they were starving.

Keys's research was important in part because it showed that malnutrition affects the entire organism, brain and mind as well as body. And it suggested that the traditional perspective on eating disorders—that they're psychological diseases centered around issues of control and autonomy—was misleading, incomplete, or just plain wrong.*

---

*Unfortunately, it took the therapeutic professions many decades to incorporate Keys's findings into their understanding of eating disorders, and many therapists still resist the notion that the physiological process of starvation can affect thinking, feeling, and personality as well as physical well-being.

His interest in food and its effects on human physiology and psychology continued, leading him down a different path in the 1950s and 1960s. Keys had also observed that as food became scarce in Europe during World War II, fewer people there died from heart disease. He concluded that higher levels of dietary fat and cholesterol were linked to heart disease, strokes, and death.[8] Convinced that the correlation between levels of heart disease in developed countries, where diets tended to include more saturated fat, must be more than coincidental, Keys became a fervent anti-fat crusader, developing a formula (known as the "Keys equation") that he claimed predicted how cholesterol would rise or fall depending on how much fat and cholesterol a person ate.[9] His vilification of foods like eggs, butter, and meat triggered our current cultural fears around those foods, and still informs the way many of us eat, as the robust market for margarines and egg substitutes attests.

After the McGovern committee used Keys's conclusions about food to shape their nutrition recommendations (eat less fat! eat more carbs!), American food producers and consumers jumped on the bandwagon. Nutrition writer Gary Taubes, author of *Good Calories, Bad Calories: Fats, Carbs, and the Controversial Science of Diet and Health*, was later interviewed by *Frontline* about the recommendations. As he explained, "This belief set in that carbohydrates could be eaten to excess and wouldn't cause weight gain, that they were both heart healthy and the ideal diet."[10] Low-fat foods became de rigueur, an automatic menu must-do. Only now, nearly forty years later, are we beginning to look a little harder at whether low-fat is always such a health imperative. And we're realizing that the low-fat trend coincided nearly perfectly with the twenty years or so when

Americans gained weight. Maybe our horror of fat has had some entirely unintended consequences.

WE'VE LEARNED A lot about the complexities of food, nutrition, and metabolism since Keys came up with his equation. But the way we eat—and the way we *think* about eating—lags seriously behind and reflects few of those nuances. Take the notion that we're fatter now because we eat more. That idea is firmly established in the general population, and plenty of nutrition experts concur. Yet a number of studies have consistently found that we're not eating substantially more than we did thirty or fifty years ago.[11] In fact, children and teens in Western countries, especially girls, actually eat fewer calories now than in the past.[12]

Even if we were eating a little more than in the past, that still wouldn't account for the weight gain trend because the relationship between what we eat and what we weigh is far more complex than calories in, calories out. Back in 1989, two of the best-respected weight researchers in the world, sociologist Jeffery Sobal and psychiatrist A. J. Stunkard, concluded, "Even when food intake and energy expenditure are carefully monitored in field studies, the relationship between energy intake and body weight is weak."[13] In other words, what you eat doesn't necessarily correlate with what you weigh. Some people can take in 3,000 calories a day and never gain an ounce; others struggle to maintain their weight eating 1,200 calories a day. (And if you've gone around the dieting yo-yo a few times, that number may be even lower.) Other factors play more of a role than we think.

You and I might eat the exact same meal, but our bodies will handle the calories and nutrients very differently, thanks to a slew of elements including how well your thyroid works, the size and

Learning to Live with Food

Kelsey, twenty-five, is on staff at Johns Hopkins University.

I absolutely love food, all different kinds. I love fruit and chocolate and anything you can imagine. Unfortunately, I don't really love what it does to my body. I would say my body type is average, maybe a little heavier. According to my doctor, though, I'm obese and need to lose twenty pounds.

It's not like I haven't tried to lose weight. I was a skinny little child but I thought I was fat, so I started dieting. I looked at my mom, who I love, but she's an aerobics instructor, and she's weighed the same thing since she was fifteen. I saw how proud she was of one of my sisters who was really thin and fit.

In my sophomore year of high school I wanted to look good for my ring dance, so I stopped eating. I told my mom it was because eating made me feel sick, which was partially the truth. I felt sick about what it was doing to my body. The saddest part is even though I was pale and had huge purple bags under my eyes, people told me how great I looked, and it made me feel good about myself. I looked sick, but because it's what the models out there look like it's considered beautiful, which I find absolutely disgusting.

Anyway, after I decided I needed food, I ate and ate and ate and ended up being twenty pounds heavier than when I started. So that didn't turn out the way I wanted it to. Today I am a little heavier, but I am confident most of the time. I have a boyfriend who loves my body, and I love my body. It might not be exactly what a woman is supposed to look like by American standards, but it's mine, and I cherish it. I only wish more girls could feel the same.

type of bacterial colonies in your intestines, how often you've dieted, your parents' and grandparents' weight, your genetic makeup, how much you exercise, and other factors.

One of those factors, interestingly, is pleasure, which appears to be an integral part of the metabolic process. The more we enjoy our food, the more efficiently our bodies make use of its nutrients. In a now-classic experiment done in the 1970s, researchers in Thailand and Sweden fed volunteers from each country identical spicy Thai meals, then measured how much iron each volunteer had absorbed from the meal. The Thai volunteers absorbed 50 percent more iron from the meal than the Swedes; the researchers hypothesized that being familiar with the food served, and liking it, helped the Thai women digest it more effectively. In the next phase of the study, researchers took the same meal, mushed it into paste, and fed it to the volunteers again. This time the Thai women absorbed a lot less of the iron than they had before, presumably because mush is not quite as appetizing as real food.[14]

This may seem strange, but consider that the digestive process actually begins before you even open your mouth. When we see and smell a meal that appeals to us, our salivary glands start working, getting ready to begin breaking down the first bite. When a meal doesn't look or smell good (like the mush), it takes longer for those glands to kick into gear, and we don't metabolize the food as completely.

So even if we could have our taste buds surgically removed, we wouldn't really want to. Food looks, smells, and tastes good for the same reason the brain's hypothalamus (a small neuro organ resembling a kernel of corn) sends out hunger signals to the body: to make sure we eat regularly, and enough, to survive and reproduce. Our current anxieties about eating and appetite often keep us from enjoying food—*really* enjoying it, I mean, not just wolfing down something forbidden—and, ironically, likely contribute to overeating. You can't feel satisfied after a meal if you're barely aware you're eating it.

NOT LONG AGO, I sat next to a slender woman on a plane who spent most of the trip reading. Eventually we began to chat, and I asked about her book.

She looked up eagerly. "It's all about how sugar is killing us," she said. "Did you know it's in practically everything we eat? And that's what's making us so fat?" She talked on and on, with the zeal of a recent convert, about how high-fructose corn syrup (HFCS) was poisoning our children, skewing our taste buds, and making us all obese. Well, making other people obese, anyway.

Both her subject and her enthusiasm felt painfully familiar. We've been looking for a weight scapegoat for years; wheat, in the form of gluten, and sugar, especially in the form of HFCS, are the latest in a long line of foods to vilify and cut out of our diets. A quick cruise through Amazon turns up pages and pages of book titles like *Sugars and Flours: How They Make Us Crazy, Sick and Fat, and What to Do About It,* or *The Sugar Fix: The High-Fructose Fallout That Is Making You Fat,* or *Wheat Belly: Lose the Wheat, Lose the Weight, and Find Your Path Back to Health.* The notion that our modern taste for processed foods, fast foods, and junk food is to blame for our weight issues has been promoted by a number of experts, like Harvard professor David Ludwig, author of a diet book called *Ending the Food Fight: Guide Your Child to a Healthy Weight in a Fast Food/Fake Food World.* Ludwig believes that if we ate fewer refined grains (white flour, white pasta, cornmeal), sugars, and potato products, and made "a few other sensible lifestyle choices" (he doesn't say what exactly), we'd all be thin.[15] Or at least thinner. (Something that rarely comes up in this discussion is the fact that we eat way more fruits and vegetables than we did fifty years ago, now that we have access to them year-round.)[16]

Just to be clear: I'm not working for Big Food, and I'm not a fan of fast food or processed foods, maybe because I grew up eating great quantities of both (Hostess Sno Balls, Devil Dogs, Rice a Roni, Kentucky Fried Chicken—and these are just the first few that spring to mind). I don't like the way they taste, in general, and I find they often make me sleepy. I haven't drunk soda, sugared or diet, since I was sixteen, and I prefer water to juice and other caloric drinks. I eat a lot of fruits, vegetables, nuts, dairy, fish, chicken, and whole grains, not only because they're nutritious but because I like the way they taste and how I feel when I eat them.

The phrase "processed foods" is actually a little misleading, since a lot of what we eat is processed in some way (hello bread, wine, cheese, pickles, chocolate, and cooking in general).[17] Maybe it's more useful to think about packaged or heavily processed foods, which have been part of our diet for longer than most of us know. Trans fats, for instance, a signature ingredient in heavily processed foods until recently, first hit the grocery store shelves in 1911, with the introduction of Crisco.[18] Wonder bread, candy bars, commercial cereals, Velveeta, and other packaged foods have been around since the 1920s and 1930s. McDonald's, founded in 1940 in San Bernardino, California, sold its billionth burger way back in 1963, nearly twenty years before our collective weight began to rise.* HFCS entered the food main-stream in the mid-1970s, though it's certainly way more prevalent today than it was back then.

I'm not arguing that heavily processed foods are good for us, or that I personally want to eat more of them (or think other people should). On the contrary: I tend to avoid them because they have little nutritional value and, to my palate, don't taste good. Take HFCS, for example. Rats that are fed HFCS gain more weight and spike higher triglycerides than rats that are fed sucrose (table sugar), so HFCS may in fact be an endocrine disruptor that alters our metabolisms.[19] Of course, we're not rats, and animal studies can be misleading.[20] But without question, we eat a lot more sug-ars of all kinds than we used to, thanks to the "food engineers" who know exactly how to manufacture "foods" that appeal to our palates. (A good account can be found in Michael Moss's book *Salt Sugar Fat: How the Food Giants Hooked Us*.)**

We may wind up banning HFCS (and I rather hope we do). But it's worth remembering that despite our very human ten-dency to want a scapegoat, heavily processed foods are clearly not the sole drivers for diabetes, fatty liver disease, and other mod-ern health concerns. Poverty, stigma, other endocrine disruptors

---

*French women may not get fat, but 2 percent of the French population eats at McDonald's every day, and the fast-food chain is more profitable in France than anywhere else in Europe.

**The same manufacturers who design the foods we can't stop eating often also produce diet foods. *The Guardian*'s Jacques Peretti wrote a thoughtful exposé of this mind-boggling contradiction. "The food industry has one ostensible ob-jective—and that's to sell food," he wrote in 2013. "But by creating the ultimate oxymoron of diet food—something you eat to *lose* weight—it squared a seem-ingly impossible circle. And we bought it."

and pollutants all play a role, and likely there are other factors involved as well. And something we miss when we focus on HFCS and Big Food is the long-term damage, both physical and psychological, that comes from being rigid, chaotic, and fearful about eating. As my students have pointed out, we have no idea these days how to eat with pleasure and not fall into guilt or self-loathing or dangerous weight-control behaviors. The notion that we need to consciously restrain our eating (or try to, and feel shame when we fail), that we need to practice constant vigilance around food, that we need to follow someone else's food rules, whether they come from a diet manual, a nutritionist, or the *New York Times*, has become deeply embedded in our cultural psyche.

Those rules have made us worse off in every way imaginable. Dieting and the fear of food have made us fatter, sicker, more depressed and more obsessed.

NOT LONG AGO, a hypnotherapist named Iris Higgins published a letter in the *Huffington Post* that racked up more than twenty-three thousand shares on Facebook, which is where I came across it. The article was headlined "An Open Apology to All of My Weight Loss Clients," and in it, Higgins wrote about her former job at a well-known commercial weight-loss clinic, where she taught her clients all sorts of tricks for staying on a 1,200-calorie meal plan. "Volumize with vegetables," she wrote. "Start with a bowl of broth-based soup. Are you drinking enough water? Did you exercise enough?"

Higgins went on to apologize for things she did in the name of helping her clients lose weight. It's a brutally frank catalogue that will be familiar to anyone who's ever dieted, with or without a meal plan or company. She wrote that she regretted the "lies" she'd told her clients, like saying 1,200 calories a day was a healthy amount, and explained that she wasn't cynically trying to trick them or sell them something:

> I believed the lies we were fed as much as you did. And it wasn't just the company feeding them to me. It was the doctors and registered dietitians on the medical advisory board. It was the media and magazines confirming what I was telling my clients. A palm-sized portion of lean chicken with half a sweet potato and a salad was PLENTY. No matter that you had "cravings" afterward. Cravings are a sign of underlying emotional issues. Yeah, sure they are. Except when they're a sign that your body needs more food and you're ignoring it. Then they're a sign that your 1,200-calorie diet is horseshit. Then they're a sign that you've been played.

After three years of working in weight loss, wrote Higgins, "I am sorry because many of you walked in healthy and walked out with disordered eating, disordered body image, and the feeling that you were a 'failure.' None of you ever failed. Ever. I failed you. The weight loss company failed you. Our society is failing you."[21]

Higgins, who went on to publish several gluten-free cookbooks, had no formal nutrition training. That may have made it easier for her to critique what she saw as destructive food rules and eating patterns. Nutritionists and dietitians, on the other hand, are often more invested in the weight-loss paradigm and in a more black-and-white view of eating.* My interactions with

---

*One notable exception is Michelle Allison, who practices in Canada and writes at www.fatnutritionist.com.

nutritionists—usually with or on behalf of my daughter as she struggled with anorexia—have typically been unproductive or worse. Like the nutritionist I asked to explain to my daughter the science behind why the brain and body require fat. I hoped if my daughter understood cognitively why she needed to take in a certain amount of fat, she could use that knowledge to help fight the terror she felt as part of the eating disorder.

The nutritionist sat down with us, cleared her throat, and said, "Your brain and body need fat." She paused. We waited. My daughter looked twitchy. The silence stretched on. The nutritionist tried again.

"You need fat in your body," she started, and then said in a rush, "but not too much!"

Argh. I'm sure some professionals would have been able to give my daughter the scoop without panicking. But I also know many hold the same biases as this one, even if they don't blurt them out. The idea that food has an inherent moral component, and that we do, too, when we eat it (or don't), has become a meme, a contagious cultural idea that triggers an automatic response.

I saw an extreme example of this when my daughter was sick. Certain foods were "safe," and they were all low-fat or nonfat: pretzels, fat-free yogurt, grapes, carrot sticks, ramen noodles. Other foods terrified her, and they were usually the ones high in fats: avocados, cheese, any kind of dessert, pasta. Watching her made me realize I, too, thought of food in categories, though not nearly as rigidly or extremely as my daughter. For me, fruits and vegetables felt "safe," while doughnuts and fettuccine Alfredo might as well have come packaged with a skull and crossbones. My internal good food/bad food meter was for a long time organized around the same general principles as my daughter's, though calibrated differently. (For instance, I have no bad feelings about cake or pesto, both of which are higher in fat.)

Each of us probably has her own equivalent of doughnuts and fettuccine, foods we've come to think of as off-limits, untouchable, even dangerous. And there's no question that there's a lot of room for improvement in our national diet, especially among children. "If we look at behaviors, thin kids and overweight kids are not that different," says UNC's Asheley Skinner. "When it comes down to it, most kids in this country eat a crappy diet and don't exercise enough."

But much of what passes for nutrition education is essentially based around fear, on making us afraid of eating those less nutritious foods. And it's worked, up to a point; many of us *are* afraid of those foods. That doesn't mean we've become healthier eaters, though. On the contrary: As long as the discussion is framed as a dichotomy—food is good or bad, and *we're* good or bad for eating a specific food—many of us will keep bouncing from one end of the spectrum to the other, depriving ourselves or overeating, eating "healthy" or "unhealthy." Dichotomies by definition lack nuance; they're meant to be black and white. But black-and-white thinking doesn't work so well for humans. If it did, most of us would be following the USDA's latest food recommendations (for better or worse) without complaint or deviation.

The good food/bad food dichotomy leads to other problems, too. The conflicting messages we get around food and eating have already raised our cultural anxiety about what to eat and how much and how to prepare it. Adding in a new set of rigid food rules can tip some people into orthorexia, an obsession with eating "healthy" or "clean" that can contribute to people becoming terrified of eating anything they consider unhealthy, processed, or "contaminated" with artificial ingredients. But you don't have to officially be diagnosed with orthorexia to be vulnerable to some of those feelings.

Carolyn, a thirty-two-year-old in Sandpoint, Idaho, remembers the first time she decided to eat "clean" by cutting out an entire food group. She was five years old, and she gave up sugar after her first-grade gym teacher told her she was fat. A dozen diets and fifteen years later, a therapist threatened to stop working with her unless she changed her eating habits. "She told me, 'You can't possibly do psychological work unless you clean your body,'" recalls Carolyn. She starting eating only raw foods, becoming so restrictive she made rules for what her *husband* could and couldn't eat or bring into the house. She joined Overeaters Anonymous, which exacerbated her rigidity around eating, and eventually became a sponsor. "I was taking phone calls at all hours," she says now. "People would call and say, 'I had a piece of gum and I found out it had sugar in it. What do I do?'"

Eventually Carolyn found a nutritionist who helped her begin to unpack her feelings and routines around eating. "It's taken quite a few years to undo a lot of that mind-set of good and bad food, learning to eat again," she says.

It takes time, in this culture, because so many factors reinforce the disordered eating default. One of those factors is the medicalization of obesity. As doctors have gotten more deeply involved and invested in diagnosing and treating weight issues, they've (inadvertently or not) reified the healthy/unhealthy dichotomy around food and eating. And they've brought their own particular set of conflicts and concerns into the conversation. It's worth taking a look at how medicine and money have shaped our thoughts, feelings, and behaviors around food, eating, and weight.

Chapter 4

Money, Motivation, and the Medical Machine

"It is difficult to get a man to understand something when his salary depends upon his not understanding it."

—Upton Sinclair, from *I, Candidate for Governor: And How I Got Licked*

Not long ago, I rode up in a hospital elevator with a bariatric surgeon, a trim, smiling man in his forties holding a box of doughnuts. I didn't know he was a bariatric surgeon—he wore no white coat, no identifying badge—but we got off on the same floor, which housed both the bariatric wing and the ICU, and headed in the same direction, and I saw him approach a cluster of nurses (all women, as it happened) and present the doughnuts with a little bow. "This is for you lovely ladies," he announced. He turned, recognized me from the elevator, and explained, "Always looking for new customers." He patted his own flat stomach and rolled his eyes, as if to say he couldn't *imagine* eating a doughnut himself, and walked away.

That encounter disturbed me for days. For one thing, the surgeon was assuming (jokingly or not) that eating doughnuts makes people fat, that weight issues are all about personal responsibility, just saying no to sugar or carbs or fat. That bugged me; shouldn't a doctor who specializes in treating fat people know better? Then there was his self-righteous stomach-patting, the way he implied both his horror at the idea of eating doughnuts and his disdain for anyone who did. But what really bothered me, what has stayed with me since that day, was his self-serving cynicism. Can you imagine a lung surgeon handing out cigarettes as "gifts"? Or a hepatologist distributing bottles of vodka? And if they did, would they roll their eyes afterward, as if to say "People are idiots to smoke/drink/eat, but better for my business"?

I know the bariatric surgeon was only one doctor, and hey, maybe he just happened to be a jerk. I'm sure there are plenty of surgeons who genuinely care about their patients and who would never make that kind of tacky joke. At least I hope there are.

But I also know that bariatric surgery is very, very lucrative. And popular, especially since 2009, when Medicare started covering some weight-loss surgeries. In 2000, some 37,000 bariatric surgeries were performed in the United States; by 2013, the number had risen to 220,000. "Right now, every hospital wants to have a bariatric surgery program because so many obese people are looking for the surgical way out," says Bradley Fox, a family physician in Erie, Pennsylvania, who's written about money and medicine. "Bariatric surgery is a booming business. It's huge."

Other weight-loss treatments are cash cows, too, as evidenced by a series of advertising campaigns rolled out by the Center for Medical Weight Loss, a national for-profit program. With headlines like "Jenny Craig didn't go to medical school," "How weight loss improved my family practice," and "Increase your practice income by $20,000 per month," the ads try to recruit doctors to incorporate the center's programs into their practices. And it's no coincidence that they started running in late 2011, soon after Medicare announced it would cover treatments for obesity as long as they were supervised by doctors.[1]

Weight loss is a big business, and, since it's rarely successful in the long term, it comes with a built-in supply of repeat customers. And doctors have been involved in the business one way or another for a long time. Some two thousand years ago, the Greek physician and philosopher Galen diagnosed "bad humors" as the cause of obesity, and prescribed massage, baths, and "slimming" foods like greens, garlic, and wild game for his overweight patients. More recently, in the early twentieth century, as scales became more accurate and affordable, doctors began routinely recording patients' height and weight at every visit.[2] Weight-loss drugs hit the mainstream in the 1920s, when doctors started prescribing thyroid medications to healthy people to make them slimmer.[3] In the 1930s, 2,4-dinitrophenol (DNP) came along, followed by amphetamines, diuretics, laxatives, and diet pills like fen-phen, all of which worked only in the short term and caused side effects ranging from the annoying to the fatal.

The national obsession with weight got a big boost in 1942, when a life insurance company created a set of tables that became the most widely referenced standard for weight in North America. The Metropolitan Life Insurance Company crunched age, weight, and mortality numbers from nearly five million policies in the United States and Canada to create "desirable" height and weight charts. For the first time, people (and their doctors) could compare themselves to a standardized notion of what they "should" weigh.

And compare they did, using increasingly clinical-sounding descriptors like *adipose, overweight,* and *obese.*[4] The new terminology reinforced the idea that only doctors should and could treat weight issues. The word *overweight,* for example, implies excess; to be overweight suggests you're over the "right" weight. The word *obese,* from the Latin *obesus,* or "having eaten until fat," handily conveys both a clinical atmosphere and that oh-so-familiar sense of moral judgment.

By the 1950s, even as Hollywood glamorized voluptuous actresses like Marilyn Monroe and Elizabeth Taylor, medicine was taking a different stance. In 1952, Dr. Norman Jolliffe, director of New York City's Bureau of Nutrition, warned doctors at the annual meeting of the American Public Health Association that "a new plague, although an old disease, has arisen to smite us."[5] He estimated that 25 to 30 percent of the American population at the time was overweight or obese, a number he essentially made up. "No one loves a fat girl except possibly a fat boy, and together they waddle through life with a roly poly family," wrote Paul Craig, an MD from Tulsa, Oklahoma, in 1955.[6] Craig was enthusing over a 1907 study that claimed "gratifying results . . . on the problem of obesity" by putting people on eight-hundred-calorie-a-day diets and dosing them liberally with amphetamines, phenobarbital, and methylcellulose. (Craig concluded, in a comment that fails to inspire confidence in his methods of scientific inquiry, "Not all people who eat gluttonously grow fat, but no fat man or woman eats, as they claim, like a bird, unless they refer to a turkey buzzard.")

In 1949, a small group of "fat doctors" created the National Obesity Society, the first of many professional associations meant to take obesity treatment from the margins to the mainstream. Through annual conferences like the first International Congress on Obesity, held in Bethesda, Maryland, in 1973, doctors helped propagate the idea that dealing with weight was a job for highly trained experts. "Medical professionals intentionally made a case that fatness was a medical problem, and therefore the people best equipped to intervene and express opinions about it were people with MDs," says UCLA sociologist Abigail Saguy.

Those medical experts believed that "any level of thinness was healthier than being fat, and the thinner a person was, the healthier she or he was," writes Nita Mary McKinley, a professor of psychology at the University of Washington–Tacoma.[7] This attitude inspired a number of new treatments for obesity, including stereotactic surgery, also known as psychosurgery, which involved burning lesions into the hypothalami of people with "gross obesity."[8] Jaw wiring was another invasive procedure that gained traction in the 1970s and 1980s. It quickly fell out of favor, maybe because it stopped working the minute people starting eating again. (At least one dentist in Brooklyn still promotes it.)[9]

Bariatric surgery is the latest medical development in the world of obesity treatment. While such surgeries are safer now than they were ten years ago, they still lead to complications for many, including disordered eating, long-term malnutrition, intestinal blockages, and death. "Bariatric surgery is barbaric, but it's the best we have," says University of Alabama's David B. Allison, PhD. "And I hope we'll look back at some point in the future and say, 'We can't believe we did that.'"

Long-term success rates for these surgeries are hard to analyze because they take varying forms and they haven't been around that long. There's lapband surgery (laparoscopic adjustable gastric banding), where a band with an inflatable balloon is surgically fixed around the stomach; the balloon can be inflated or deflated to control how tightly the band restricts the size of the stomach. There's the sleeve gastrectomy, where part of the stomach is amputated and what's left is formed into a small tube that can't hold much food at one time. There's the duodenal switch, where most of the stomach is amputated and parts of the small intestine are altered so food is rerouted away from the intestine and calories and nutrients can't be absorbed. And finally there's Roux-en-Y gastric bypass, one of the most popular surgeries, which involves the same kind of intestinal rerouting as well as reshaping the stomach into a small pouch that holds very little food at one time.

The best estimates suggest that about half of those who have some kind of bariatric surgery regain some or all of the weight they lose.[10] Some doctors say the surgeries cure type 2 diabetes (though remission is likely the better word, since many cases recur) and therefore save health-care dollars. A 2013 review of thirty thousand cases found no such savings,[11] maybe because the surgeries are expensive—between $12,000 and $35,000, according to the National Institutes of Health—and require a lot of follow-up care.

The more weight loss is reframed as "obesity treatment" best left to medical professionals, the more doctors stand to gain from it. Medicalization tends to lead to more diagnoses, as the definition of a disease inevitably expands. And more diagnoses lead inevitably to higher revenues and profits. I don't have a problem with doctors making money; I want my physicians to be rewarded for their expertise and knowledge and dedication. I want them to stay in practice.

But I do have a problem with the fact that profits drive a lot of the research into and treatment of obesity. In these days of dwindling medical salaries, many doctors look for other revenue streams, and they find them. Bariatric surgeons and other physicians own weight-loss treatment centers and clinics. They hold stock in or take money from meal-replacement companies and pharmaceutical makers. They own surgical practices or are partners in hospitals that do bariatric surgeries. And these other ventures create conflicts of interest that directly affect patients.

Some doctors argue that being involved in these so-called subsidiary services—say, owning a bariatric surgery center—means better care for patients, since they're in a position to oversee and direct treatments, and can offer improved continuity of care. But the research does not bear this out. In fact, patients in doctor-owned clinics wind up going to (and paying for) 50 percent more office visits but getting no better care.[12] That's no surprise; in fact, professional medical organizations have been warning doctors of the dangers of double-dipping for years. "A perception that a physician is dispensing medical advice on the basis of commercial influence is likely to undermine a patient's trust not only in the physician's competence but also in the physician's pledge to put patients' welfare ahead of self-interest," says a 2002 position paper from the American College of Physicians–American Society of Medicine.[13] A list of best-practice recommendations from the Pew Charitable Trusts suggests setting clear, strong boundaries between academic doctors and industry.[14] A report from the National Academy of Sciences says bluntly, "Physicians' ownership interests in facilities to which they refer patients constitute a conflict of interest."[15]

Well, yes, though that doesn't stop them from doing it. Some people believe that telling patients about such potentially profitable ties makes them ethical. "No doctor is unconflicted, and there is no unconflicted research," says Justin Bekelman, a professor of radiation oncology at the Hospital of the University of Pennsylvania who has studied medical research. "But doctors should be disclosing their financial interests. If a doctor says, 'I recommend this but you should know I have a stock ownership in it because I believe in the company,' I don't think that discredits the doctor or interrupts the doctor–patient relationship."

Subsidiary services are only one of several kinds of conflicts of interest that plague the medical profession, especially when it comes to weight loss. One of the most fundamental of those conflicts came to a head on a cool June afternoon in 2013, when hundreds of doctors from around the country streamed into the Grand Ballroom of the Hyatt Regency Chicago. They were there, on Day 3 of the American Medical Association's annual meeting, to vote on a list of organizational policies—boring but necessary stuff, for the most part. But one item on the ballot that day would prove contentious, and not just within the paneled walls of the Grand Ballroom. Resolution 420 was short and to the point: "That our American Medical Association recognize obesity as a disease state with multiple pathophysiological aspects requiring a range of interventions to advance obesity treatment and prevention."

The question—whether to classify obesity as a disease in and of itself, or continue to consider it a risk factor for diseases like type 2 diabetes—had been under discussion for years, both within the organization and outside it. Months earlier, the American Medical Association (AMA) asked its own Committee on Science and Public Health to explore the issue; the committee came up with a five-page opinion suggesting that obesity should *not* be officially labeled as a disease, for several reasons.

For one thing, said the committee, obesity doesn't fit the definition of a medical disease. It has no symptoms, and it's not always harmful—in fact, for some people in some circumstances it's long been known to be protective rather than destructive.

For another, a disease, by definition, involves the body's normal functioning gone wrong. But many experts think obesity—the body efficiently storing calories as fat—is a normal adaptation to a set of circumstances (periods of famine) that's held true for much of human history. In which case bodies that tend toward obesity aren't diseased; they're actually more efficient than naturally lean bodies. True, we live in a time when food is abundant for most people and life is more sedentary than it used to be, when we don't have the same need to store fat. But that simply means the environment has changed faster than we can adapt. The body's still doing what it's supposed to, so how can you call that a disease?

The AMA committee also pointed out the correlation-but-no-causation links between obesity and illness, and obesity and mortality. Katherine Flegal and others had established over and over that carrying some extra weight often correlates with living longer, which again argued against the disease appellation. Finally, the committee worried that medicalizing obesity could potentially hurt patients, creating even more stigma around weight and pushing people into unnecessary—and ultimately useless—"treatments."*

---

*Rarely does the move toward medicalizing actually help people; for instance, the classification of homosexuality as a mental disorder in the *DSM-1* in 1952 led to President Eisenhower's ban on hiring gay employees in the federal government, Senator Joe McCarthy's claims that gays in the military posed security risks, and an uptick in anti-gay prejudice in American society that's only now, sixty-some years later, quietly evaporating.

The AMA membership didn't agree with the committee; they passed Resolution 420 in an overwhelming voice vote. I asked the organization's president, Ardis Hoven, MD, an internist who specializes in infectious diseases, to help me understand why the membership voted that way despite the committee's recommendation. She wouldn't talk to me directly, instead writing through a spokesperson, "The AMA has long recognized obesity as a major public health concern, but the recent policy adopted in June marks the first time we've recognized obesity as a disease due to the prevalence and seriousness of obesity."

In other words, obesity is a disease because there's a lot of it and because it's serious (though Hoven wouldn't define "serious.") And because there's a lot of it we should consider it a disease. This is just the kind of circular reasoning that's gotten us where we are on weight issues in the first place.

There are, of course, other possible explanations for the AMA's decision. As James Hill, director of the Anschutz Health and Wellness Center at the University of Colorado, told ABC News, "Now we start getting some standardization for reimbursements and treatments."

In other words, follow the money. Doctors want to be paid for delivering weight-loss treatments to patients (even if such treatments are ineffective and often futile). Coding office visits for Medicare, for instance, is a complex process that involves counting the number of bodily systems reviewed and the number of diseases counseled for. "Every time we see someone for a twenty-minute visit, we do a complete review of systems because we get paid more," explains Bradley Fox. "If someone comes in for a hangnail, you still ask if they're having chest pains. The more diagnoses that are covered, the more you can increase your coding." So, for instance, if Medicare goes along with the AMA and designates obesity as a disease, doctors who even mention weight to their patients could charge more for the same visit than those who don't.

But that level of cupidity is trivial compared with the sorts of financial conflicts of interest defended by some in the field. It's rare to find an obesity researcher who hasn't taken money from industry, whether it's pharmaceutical companies, medical device manufacturers, bariatric surgery practices, or weight-loss programs. The practice isn't limited to lesser-known luminaries, either. In 1997, a panel of nine medical experts tapped by the National Institutes of Health voted to lower the BMI cutoff for overweight from 27 (28 for men) to 25. Overnight, millions of Americans became overweight, at least according to the NIH. The panel argued that the change brought BMI cutoffs into line with World Health Organization criteria, and that a "round" number like 25 would be easier for people to remember.

What they didn't say, because they didn't have to, is that lowering BMI cutoffs put more people into the overweight and obese categories, which in turn made more people eligible for treatment. More patients to treat means new markets and more money to be made by everyone from doctors and hospitals to pharmaceutical companies and, yes, researchers.

The 1997 panel was led by Columbia University professor Xavier Pi-Sunyer, a researcher with a long history of taking money from the weight-loss industries. In fact, eight of the nine panelists had financial conflicts of interest.[16] Pi-Sunyer may have been the worst, with a list of ties that reads like a Who's Who of the weight-loss business, including pharmaceutical giants Eli Lilly, GlaxoSmithKline, Arena, Novartis, Novo Nordisk, AstraZeneca,

PRE-Diabetes	PRE-Hypertension	Childhood Overweight	Childhood Obesity
Blood sugar ≥ 100	≥ 120/80	BMI at or above 85th percentile*	BMI at or above 95th percentile*
(original definition of diabetes ≥ 140, current definition of diabetes≥ 126)	(original definition of hypertension ≥ 160/100, current definition of hypertension ≥ 140/90)	(original definition of 85th percentile was "at risk of overweight" and "overweight" was 95th percentile*)	(Did not exist as a term before)
CHANGED IN 2003	CHANGED IN 2003	CHANGED IN 2007	CHANGED IN 2007
QUADRUPLES the population deemed a market for intervention:	DOUBLES the population deemed a market for intervention:	TRIPLES the range of weights deemed a market for intervention and DOUBLES the population deemed a market for intervention:	CREATES a new disease category for children to be able to say, "1 in 3 children are overweight or obese."
8.3→40% US adults	30→60% US adults	16→33% US children	0→16% US children
			*percentiles defined using 1975 data

Amylin Pharmaceuticals, Orexigen Therapeutics, Sanofi-Aventis, and VIVUS.[17] When questioned about how these relationships might affect his objectivity, he defended his industry ties to a reporter from the Newark *Star-Ledger*, insisting that pharmaceutical companies "have no influence over what I say."

Pi-Sunyer's attitude is fairly typical, says Eric Campbell, a professor of medicine at Harvard Medical School and director of research at the Mongan Institute for Health Policy in Boston. "If you ask doctors whether an industry relationship affects what they do, they almost universally say it doesn't," explains Campbell. "But if you ask them how industry relationships affect their colleagues, they say it affects *them* in negative ways." In other words, *I'm* too smart to be swayed like this, but those other doctors aren't. (It's a lot like the phenomenon known as the third-person effect, where people believe *they* aren't personally influenced by media messaging but other less discerning people are.)

The perks that come with those industry relationships range from throwaways, like $5 refrigerator magnets, to big-ticket items, like research support worth hundreds of thousands of dollars. And it turns out the small stuff may actually shift doctors' thinking and behavior more than the bigger perks. "If I said I was going to give you $100,000, you'd wonder what I was about," says Eric Campbell. "If I gave you a ten-cent pencil that said 'Harvard' on it, you'd think, 'This won't influence me; it's so small.'" But you'd be wrong; smaller perks may carry more weight precisely because they seem innocuous.

In reality, the size of the perk is less important than the fact that such gifts reinforce the relationship between the company and the doctor. And those relationships are what it's all about, according to Michael Oldani, a former sales rep for Pfizer who's now an anthropology professor at Princeton University.[18] "As a rep you had to build trust and a rapport," he told the *Princeton Weekly Bulletin*. "You did those things in the industry because the bottom line was you wanted to generate prescriptions—that's the number-one goal."[19]

Those relationships build a sense of obligation between doctors and pharmaceutical companies, which can be subtle, even invisible, but still very effective at, say, getting doctors to change their prescribing habits.[20] In 2003, bioethicist Dana Katz and colleagues at the University of Pennsylvania found that even small, seemingly trivial gifts from pharmaceutical companies like notepads, lunches, and travel reimbursements set up a feeling of obligation that strengthened doctors' loyalties to the givers. There's a reason drug companies deduct the cost of such gifts as marketing expenses.[21] "Denying the influence of those relationships is akin to denying gravity exists," says Eric Campbell.

Yet doctors and researchers—like Pi-Sunyer—*do* deny such influences. So are they corrupt? Or impossibly naïve? Maybe the truth lies somewhere in between. Campbell observes that drug companies are really, *really* good at manipulating physicians. "They tell the doctors, hey, this doesn't affect you," he says. "But there's all kind of empirical data to show it does."

Other studies have proven, over and over, that when doctors attend drug company presentations, they go on to prescribe that company's drugs more often than docs who didn't attend—even when they were reminded beforehand of the potential for influence.[22] Apparently knowing that you *might* be swayed is no protection from actually *being* swayed. "One thing we can say with absolute certainty," says Campbell, "is these relationships benefit drug companies' bottom lines. Because if they didn't, they wouldn't cultivate them." No matter how ethical, educated, and professional doctors may be, they're still human beings whose inevitable and necessary self-interest blinds them (as it can all of us) to their own biases and conflicts of interest.[23]

How else to explain the blatant and plentiful industry ties of some of the top physicians and researchers in the weight-loss field? For instance, George Bray, chief of the division of clinical obesity and metabolism at Louisiana State University's Pennington Biomedical Research Center, recently coauthored an article arguing that drugs *must* be part of obesity treatment and that, in fact, we need to develop more obesity medications.[24] Given the utter lack of long-term success for diet drugs, you might wonder where Bray was coming from. A partial list of his financial disclosures sheds a little light: consulting fees from Orexigen Therapeutics, whose new diet drug, Crave, is under review by the FDA; Abbott Labs, makers of the diet drug Meridia, withdrawn

The Doctor Thought I Was Lying

Terri, thirty-eight, is a bank examiner in New York City.

I went on my first diet at age eleven with my aunt, which made it seem very grown-up. And then over the next twenty-five years I gained and lost a ton of weight. For a while I dated a health nut, and he was always on some crazy diet or another and usually dragged me along on it. I yo-yo'd between 122 to over 250, and I'm five two.

I started seeing a doctor who was adamant about my losing weight. We talked about options. I did what she told me and nothing worked. I tried for certain calories, and worked out more, and my body was just done. Just done with it. But the doctor thought I was lying about doing what she told me to do. The fact that I couldn't lose weight, in her mind, meant I needed therapy.

So I found a therapist who specialized in eating, who's a big proponent of intuitive eating, and with her I lost weight and started working out and got to really the healthiest I've felt. I got to 215, which is still fat but feels like a natural place for me. Maybe I would be smaller if I hadn't screwed up my metabolism.

I hope I don't diet again. Sometimes I find myself slipping into it again, thinking, "What if I'm wrong, what if the choices I've made are unhealthy?" It's hard to be on the minority side of an issue that's so prevalent. Sometimes I find myself saying things like, "Everybody dies." Because the message is if you don't diet, you're going to die.

from the market in 2010 because it increased the risk of heart attack and stroke; GlaxoSmithKline; Medifast; Amylin Pharmaceuticals; Theracos, which holds a number of patents for obesity treatments; and Herbalife, makers of Formula 1 Shakes meal replacements.[25] And that was just a partial list. Even the best-intentioned doctor might be influenced by the sheer number and breadth of those relationships.

Medical journals, too, can be subject to bias. In 2013, the prestigious *New England Journal of Medicine* published "Myths, Presumptions, and Facts About Obesity," an article (rather than a study or original research) that promised to set the record straight on obesity. Some of the article's "myths" seemed a little tongue in cheek, like challenging the number of calories burned having sex (closer to fifteen than three hundred, calculated the authors). Other claims were less entertaining. The authors dismissed the often-observed link between weight cycling and mortality, saying it was "probably due to confounding by health status," which is a more sophisticated way to say "We're sure this isn't right, but we don't know exactly why not." And the article's "facts" included plugs for meal replacements like Jenny Craig, medications, and bariatric surgery.

The *New England Journal of Medicine* is one of the few journals that publishes financial disclosures along with articles (many bury them online or don't run them at all), so it was easy to see that five of the twenty authors disclosed grants, consulting fees, or paid board memberships from Kraft Foods, makers of (among other products) South Beach Diet meal replacement bars. Three of the twenty took money from Jenny Craig, purveyors of packaged Jenny's Cuisine diet food and meal replacements. Two authors, Arne Astrup and UAB's David Allison, reported payments from multiple companies, including pharmaceuticals, surgical instrument manufacturers, the World Sugar Organisation, Red Bull, and the Coca-Cola Foundation. As one outside commentator wrote, "I don't think there is much doubt that these relationships influenced the content of the paper, and not for the better. How else to explain the choice of 'facts' the authors chose to highlight in the paper, and those they inexplicably left out?"[26]

I asked Allison how he would respond to the critique that financial conflicts of interest sway researchers and doctors. "My feeling is, that's essentially *not* a critique," he told me. "It would be no different than anybody saying about any other person who puts forth an idea, 'I want to comment that you have this background or personality, this sexual orientation, weight, gender, or race.' It's all irrelevant. These conflicts were disclosed, we didn't hide them, we weren't ashamed of them. And what's your point?"

It's not *my* point, actually. A large body of research confirms that conflicts of interest absolutely affect the way doctors practice, whether they're disclosed or not, whether doctors believe it or not, and whether they come from Big Pharma or other entities.

And if you still have any doubt at all about the intentions of Big Pharma, consider this story from a syndicated newspaper business column on how companies could improve their sales of diet drugs. After pointing out a number of medications that have been taken off the market because of "adverse cardiovascular events," the writer concluded that doctors see the risks of diet drugs as outweighing their potential benefits. "The path forward is becoming clear," he wrote. "Each of these drug makers must work on changing this common perception."[27] Note the wording here. He's not recommending that manufacturers actually make their drugs safer, but rather that they make doctors *believe* they're safer. I don't know about you, but that makes me want to question every word out of a drug marketer's mouth.

ONCOLOGIST BENJAMIN Djulbegovic knows all about medical conflicts of interest. The MD/PhD and professor of internal medicine at the University of South Florida–Tampa has studied and written about the issue for years.[28] "It's not a question of whether we're conflicted," he says. "We're all conflicted by definition. The question for me becomes 'What's the mechanism?'"

Some of those mechanisms take place behind the scenes, invisible unless you're looking for them (and sometimes even then). And some of the tactics pharmaceutical companies use to skew research results go way beyond the realm of reasonable. One of the most common is manipulating a study's methodology, or how it's set up and conducted, to change its results. A drug company testing its new medication against competitors' older ones can deliberately slant the outcome by, say, testing a higher dose of its new drug against lower, nontherapeutic doses of older ones. Believe it or not, this kind of deck-stacking happens in about half of all industry-sponsored medication trials.[29]

Companies often refuse to publish studies that don't make their products look good. Only half of all drug trials are ever published, says Djulbegovic; the rest are suppressed in a number of creative ways. Pharmaceutical companies fund about 70 percent of the research in the United States; the NIH funds the other 30 percent.[30] "If you want to do a bariatric surgery, and five negative trials of the surgery were never published, you'll have a really distorted view of whether that surgery works," explains Djulbegovic.

Funders usually control the raw data, which companies can and do withhold from researchers. (As one anonymous company executive explained, "We are reluctant to provide the data tape because some investigators want to take the data beyond where the data should go.") They hire "ghostwriters," usually professional medical writers whose names never appear in print, to write up studies from a packet of materials that make the company's product look good. They can and do threaten legal action if researchers try to publish results they don't like. They hold up the prepublication review process for months, hoping researchers will get frustrated and give up. They pull funding, or threaten to. And when researchers don't fall into line, they might deliberately set out to discredit those scientists.[31]

Another popular tactic is to influence definitions of diseases and guidelines for treating those diseases. Typically, panels of practicing doctors work together to develop guidelines for when, where, how, and how much to treat the ailments specific to their medical specialty. So, for instance, the American College of Endocrinology and the American Association of Clinical Endocrinologists, two professional organizations, put out guidelines detailing exactly how type 2 diabetes should be treated.[32] In theory, the doctors on those panels consider all the evidence and produce unbiased recommendations. In practice, it doesn't always work that way. A 2012 investigation by the *Milwaukee Journal-Sentinel* found that in nine of the twenty expert panels the newspaper examined, more than 80 percent of the doctors had financial ties to pharmaceutical companies.[33] That's a whole other level of industry influence.

Other kinds of conflicts can subtly (or not) shape how professionals look at and talk about weight and health. Plenty of top obesity doctors and researchers, for example, have written diet books. Amanda Sainsbury-Salis, an Australian researcher who last year called for an "urgent rethink" of body positivity for overweight and obese people,[34] wrote *The Don't Go Hungry Diet: The Scientifically Based Way to Lose Weight and Keep It Off Forever.* Harvard's

Walter Willett is the author of *Eat, Drink, and Be Healthy: The Harvard Medical School Guide to Healthy Eating*. David Ludwig, Robert Lustig, Yoni Freedhoff, David Katz, James Hill, Nicole Avena, David Heber—some of the most prominent names in obesity research—all have diet books or programs to sell.

Other "experts" build academic and clinical reputations around treating obesity. Internationally known doctors like Arya Sharma, a professor at the University of Alberta who's often quoted in the media, or Penn's Thomas Wadden, who's brought in millions of dollars in grant money, have staked their careers on the ongoing need for patients to lose weight. They stand to lose a lot more than money if the weight-loss paradigm ever shifts.

THE DOCTOR WITH the doughnuts is only one of many, many medical professionals with a financial stake in a particular view of weight and health. And, let's face it, money talks in just about every aspect of medicine, business, and life. But the doughnut doc and others who research and treat weight-related issues share another specific perspective that skews their views, and so our views, on weight and health: they don't like fat, and in many cases they don't like fat *people*. And they're not shy about showing it.

In fact, says the Rudd Center's Rebecca Puhl, medical professionals show sky-high levels of weight bias, which affect both their research and clinical judgments. "Weight bias remains very, very socially acceptable," says Puhl, a slender, dark-haired woman with an air of reserve. The doctors, nurses, and medical students she's studied don't even bother to disguise their attitudes around weight the way they might try to hide, say, racism or sexism. "Those aren't so politically correct anymore," says Puhl. "But with weight bias, I don't need to trick people. I can give them straightforward self-report surveys about their attitudes, and boom!" They're not embarrassed to say demeaning things about fat people.

In one of Puhl's surveys of primary-care doctors, for instance, more than half the physicians described their obese patients as "awkward, unattractive, ugly, and noncompliant." A third of the doctors went further, saying those patients were "weak-willed, sloppy, and lazy."[35] A slew of studies by Puhl and others have fleshed out those findings: doctors say fat patients are more annoying and less likely to benefit from treatment than thinner patients.[36] Nurses say they're "repulsed" by obese patients.[37] More than half the nurses in a recent survey agreed that overweight people were not as good, successful, or healthy as thinner people.[38] Psychologists, too, show a marked disdain for heavy patients, judging them as lower functioning, less sexually satisfied, more severely impaired, and less likely to improve than thinner patients.[39]

I'm not surprised by any of these findings, in part because I've heard so many stories of medical professionals disparaging fat patients. One woman I talked to saw an emergency room whiteboard with the word "whale" written in the slot for her room. Medical students say it's common to joke about finding Oreos or TV remotes in the folds of fat patients' bodies in the operating room. One medical student told researchers about a doctor who said to a woman on the operating table, "Jesus Christ, why can't you lose some goddamn weight and make my job a little easier?" Even the other members of the surgical team, not generally known for their sensitivity, were appalled. The woman, thankfully, was unconscious.[40]

On the flip side, many doctors overvalue thinness, to the detriment of their thin patients. When my father had a stroke and was hospitalized for several weeks, practically the first thing every doctor and nurse mentioned when they saw him was his weight. "He's a good patient," one nurse commented. "No fat on him. He must take excellent care of himself." Not a single one bothered to ask about my father's eating or exercise habits; if they had, they'd have known he never exercised and often skipped meals—not the healthiest regimen.

Even doctors who devote their careers to researching or treating obesity often dislike fat patients. In one 2003 study, bariatric doctors said they strongly believed their patients were lazy, stupid, and worthless.[41] (Stupid enough to eat the surgeon's doughnuts? I doubt it.) Imagine a neurologist saying that about her patients. Imagine going to a doctor who felt that way about you. You'd pick up on it, whether it was conveyed in words or not. As George Blackburn, an MD and professor of nutrition at Harvard, pointed out a few years ago,[42] plenty of medical conditions may involve some level of personal responsibility; he offered the examples of high cholesterol, lung cancer, and sports injuries. People who go to the doctor with those conditions, wrote Blackburn, "routinely receive medical treatment without being questioned about their lifestyles." Not so for anyone who's even a few pounds over the "normal" BMI category.[43] Which helps explain why overweight and obese women tend to delay or avoid going to the doctor[44] and get fewer Pap smears, mammograms, and other routine cancer screening tests,[45] which may in turn help explain the link between higher BMIs and cancer deaths.[46]

Why are medical professionals so biased against fat and fat people? Doctors live in the same world as the rest of us, and so are subject to the same cultural influences and attitudes and biases. Then, too, there may be a self-selection process involved.

"Obesity researchers and physicians, compared to the general population, are more likely to be thin," points out Asheley Skinner. "They're less likely to have experience with this. People who are thin, there's a tendency to think, 'I'm thin. Why can't you act just like me?'"

If you believe doctors are entitled to their perspectives on weight, think about this: as obesity treatment and prevention have gained legitimacy and entered the medical mainstream, more and more people are being pushed by doctors to lose weight and encouraged to see weight loss as a medical issue. For women, whose bodies already come under more scrutiny (and are more subject to judgment) than men's, this can have profound effects on the quality of their health care.[47] One of Rebecca Puhl's studies found that it takes only an average weight gain of twelve or thirteen pounds for women to start experiencing weight discrimination. (Men had to be a lot heavier before they became targets.)[48]

So gain a few pounds—whether from lack of exercise, eating junk food, taking psychotropic medications, or plain old menopause—and you may find any health problems that crop up, from tennis elbow to depression, are automatically attributed to your weight. Your doctor may not believe your description of your eating and exercise habits, and that in turn may change the way he or she prescribes treatment.[49] And it will certainly damage your relationship, which is a key part of any treatment.

Doctors' biases around weight can take other forms, too. In 2010, six-year-old Claudialee Gomez-Nicanor died in New York City after a pediatric endocrinologist—a specialist in childhood diabetes—misdiagnosed her with type 2 diabetes because the child was overweight. The doctor, Arlene Mercado, prescribed weight loss, and when the girl did lose weight the doctor stopped

My Doctor Wouldn't Touch Me

Kate, thirty-eight, studied anthropology at the graduate level at New York University.

My pediatrician and mother pretty much created a conspiracy of two to harass me as a child. I had asthma and was on prednisone for years, so there was a clear reason for weight gain, but everything was about focusing on how I was wrong and needed to do more exercise. It was all shame and guilt. I remember the doctor painfully pinching my stomach when I was seven or eight, when I was maybe a little overweight but not fat. My mother was very overweight so that was the fear, that I'd "turn out like my mother."

When I started seeing a primary care doctor in Sacramento, I'd already been diagnosed with ankylosing spondylitis, an autoimmune disease. He'd sit across the room and talk to me. When I was twenty-seven I got a sebaceous cyst under my armpit that got bigger, and I had some anxiety about it, so I went in to show him. And he wouldn't get near me. I said, "I need to make sure what this is, I'm having panic attacks about it." He got a glove and some tissue. And it was in that moment I realized he'd never listened to my breathing or actually touched me.

monitoring her blood. Mercado's only prescription, diet and exercise, was working; no need to keep checking.

If Mercado had continued to order blood work, she'd have seen Claudialee's blood sugar levels were continuing to rise even as she was losing weight. She'd have realized that Claudialee actually had type 1 diabetes, an autoimmune illness requiring immediate treatment with insulin. And the six-year-old would almost certainly not have collapsed into a diabetic coma and died.

The last time I needed a new doctor I went about it differently. I would go in and meet a doc and say, "I have a chronic disease that needs treatment. I have a lot of experience being judged for my weight. I'm doing the best I can to be healthy, so I need to know how you feel about fat people." I went through four doctors that way. They got defensive about the fact that I was asking them how they felt. They'd say, "I'm sure we'll be fine." And I would say, "The tone of your voice is telling me you do have a problem, and if I make you my doctor I'm just not going to come in, so I'm going to try somebody else."

I wound up with a really good doctor. The more I become an advocate for my own right to have a quality relationship with a health-care provider, the better health care I get. Sometimes it means kicking and screaming.

According to the Centers for Disease Control and Prevention, one in 5,000 children under age ten has type 1 diabetes, while only one in 250,000 has type 2.[50] Craig Alter, a pediatric endocrinologist in Philadelphia who reviewed Claudialee's records, later told a jury, "If you tell me there is a five-year-old with diabetes, the chance that they have type 1 is probably 99.99 percent. If you tell me they are obese, I would say, okay, the chance is 99.7. It's almost definitely type 1."[51] Type 2 diabetes, while certainly serious, is far less of an emergency than type 1 and requires completely different treatment. And while other issues likely contributed to the misdiagnosis, the doctor's weight bias here clearly played a major role.

Claudialee's death was preventable and horrific. (A jury found Mercado guilty of malpractice and awarded Claudialee's mother millions of dollars. As I write this, Mercado is still treating patients.) But while it may be an extreme example of how weight bias shapes medical care, it's not an isolated one.

A few years ago I gave a talk on eating disorders to a group of pediatricians. I meant to raise awareness of early symptoms and new treatments, since pediatricians are often the first professionals to see a child with an eating disorder. Some of the doctors were receptive, taking notes and asking questions, but a few sat with their arms folded, scowling or pointedly looking away. I had no idea why until one silver-haired pediatrician spoke up. "I have children in my practice who are obese and have type 2 diabetes," he said challengingly, as if that invalidated any potential concern about eating disorders. "My patients are too fat, not too thin."

Of course doctors are right to be concerned about diabetes; whether it's type 1, the autoimmune kind, or type 2, more often associated with age and obesity, diabetes is a devastating, potentially life-threatening illness. And while type 2 does correlate with obesity, we still don't know which comes first, the weight gain or the disease. Are more children developing type 2 diabetes these days? It's hard to tell. Few if any statistics were kept on type 2 in kids before the 1990s, so there's no true basis for comparison. The 2014 National Diabetes Statistics Report says the percentage of Americans under age twenty who are diagnosed with type 2 has gone up about 3 percent since 2002.[52] Are doctors now more aware that children and teens can develop type 2, and are they looking for it? Or does this represent a genuine leap in prevalence? We don't know yet.

Even if the pediatrician was right, though, and more kids and teens *are* developing type 2 diabetes, the question I keep coming back to is whether our efforts to reduce those rates through weight loss are causing more harm than good. The message that comes through loud and clear in the literature, in the media, and from doctors ("My patients are too fat!") isn't particularly helpful. And by now we have plenty of evidence that pushing kids to lose weight is not only ineffective but counterproductive, contributing to (if not out-and-out causing) the very conditions it's meant to prevent.

Now that obesity has been thoroughly medicalized, and treatments are backed by the full weight of the medical establishment (despite their less-than-stellar track record), it's more important than ever to understand that doctors are human, that money talks, and that you can't believe everything you're told. Or sold.

Chapter 5

The Truth About Beauty

*"I wondered if I could truly see myself at all. One day
I found myself all-right-looking and relatively slim . . .
and the next day I saw a sagging, bulbous grotesque.
How could one account for the change except with the
thought that self-image is unreliable at best?"*

— Siri Hustvedt, *The Blazing World*

*"If tomorrow, women woke up and decided they really
liked their bodies, just think how many industries
would go out of business."*

— Gail Dines, professor of sociology and
women's studies at Wheelock College in Boston

One of my favorite assignments in the class I teach on body diversity comes early in the semester. I ask students to bring in media images of bodies they think are thin, fat, and "normal." They usually press me to define those three categories, and I tell them to use their judgment.

For the thin category, they bring pictures of celebrities considered not just thin but beautiful. For "fat," they often wind up with the kinds of unflattering pictures used to illustrate news stories about obesity—Charlotte Cooper's "headless fatties."

It's the "normal" category that stumps them, and that is of course the point of the assignment. They bring images of bodies ranging from slender to solid. But the most revealing part of the class is what they say about those "normal" bodies. They nearly always feel obliged to explain, in great detail, why a particular body fits the "normal" paradigm. They get defensive, as if the rest of the class is waiting to pounce on their choice and rip it to metaphorical shreds. When I point out to them that that's exactly what happens—metaphorically and literally—to real bodies, that the threat of being critiqued, dissed, dismissed because your physical being doesn't meet the standards of the day is something we all fear and all experience, I can see the penny drop. And that's usually the beginning of a lively and enlightening discussion.

When we talk about the assignment, my students steadfastly deny that their ideas about body size are affected by what they see online and around them. They tell me they're smarter than that; they know all about advertising. They tell me they're digital natives who grew up in this media-drenched world, and they know how to navigate it. They insist their opinions are their own, that they're not influenced by the onslaughts of the beauty industry.

I tell them that, on average, women in North America say their ideal body weight is 13 to 19 percent *below* their medically ideal weight.[1] I tell them about the work of German neuroscientist Dennis Hummel, who came up with an illuminating experiment a few years ago. He showed young women photographs of themselves that had been digitally manipulated to make their bodies look subtly heavier or thinner. Then he put the women through a series of visual tasks that asked them how realistic they thought their bodies looked in a series of photographs that were also subtly altered.

Hummel found that after the women were exposed to a thinner image of their bodies, they judged everything else they saw during the test as fatter, and vice versa. When they looked at images of other women's bodies, they then judged their own differently. In other words, what they got used to seeing all around them influenced their sense of their own bodies and other people's.[2]

Which explains, in part, why, if I asked you which of the two bodies below was the most attractive, we all know which one you'd choose. Which one most of us would choose.

The image on the left, which you've probably seen before, is a four-inch-high statue known as the Venus of Willendorf, carved about twenty-seven thousand years ago. The image on the right shows American model Marisa Miller.

We'd choose Miller over the Venus for two reasons: because we're human and because we live in this time and place. What I mean is because of both our hardwiring and our environment. Nature *and* nurture. Our preferences grow out of both the need for the species to survive and the ideals and standards of our particular culture, which, whether we internalize or reject them, still affect us.

Let's start with nature. In her book *Survival of the Prettiest*, evolutionary psychologist Nancy Etcoff argues that beauty is a necessary element in human survival. "The obsession with human beauty is, at rock bottom, an evolutionary adaptation for evaluating others as potential producers of our child," she writes.[3] She believes specific perceptions of beauty—what we as individuals find attractive—are hardwired into the species as a kind of biological adaptation, driving both reproduction and pleasure.

The evidence supports this idea—up to a point. For instance, we tend to find symmetrical faces and bodies more attractive than asymmetrical ones, maybe because physical symmetry correlates with genetic resistance to disease and parasites.[4] This "good genes" theory suggests that our looks advertise our underlying biological health. A symmetrical face, then, advertises a strong potential mate. Other physical traits—firm breasts, strong cheekbones, and wide hips for women, and height and musculature for men—are consistently seen as attractive across cultures and over time for the same reasons.[5]

There's less evidence for Etcoff's insistence that beauty has little to do with culture, especially when we're talking about weight. Our judgments about beauty may *feel* like they're hardwired—doesn't everyone find Marisa Miller more attractive than the Venus of Willendorf?—but in fact if you'd lived twenty-five thousand years ago, you'd likely prefer the image on the left. Its pendulous breasts, fleshy stomach, detailed genitals, and covered face signal sexuality, fertility, and health. Food could be scarce back in the Paleolithic period, and nothing said "healthy and fertile" like a fleshy body with clearly delineated feminine attributes—breasts, hips, bottom.

But to us, Miller's flat stomach, round breasts, slender thighs, and protruding collarbones epitomize feminine beauty. We live in a culture where food is abundant, it's easy to gain weight, and fertility isn't a matter of immediate daily survival. Like most societies, we typically prize what's rare and dismiss what's commonplace. And what's rare in twenty-first-century America is a body like Miller's, which by some estimations is achievable by maybe 5 percent of the population. At most.

Which, of course, we know, just as we know the earth is round and revolves around the sun. We still *experience* the earth as flat (unless you live in the mountains), though, and it still *looks* like the sun rises in the morning and sets at night. And we still buy into the notion that we can, and should, sculpt our bodies to look like Miller's.

We also seem to believe that our current cultural body ideals represent the culmination of some forward-moving process of development—an evolution of sorts toward a higher plane. That we have these ideals in the first place because, damn it, that's how we're *supposed* to look. We think our preferences around beauty and bodies are innate and inevitable, that we're immune to outside influences. We just happen to like the way Miller's body looks, that's all.

But even a cursory look back suggests otherwise. Italian researcher Paolo Pozzilli studies paintings and sculptures for clues about diseases through history. For instance, he says, if you look closely at some of Michelangelo's figures, you'll notice that their eyes are bulging, a classic symptom of the thyroid disorder Graves' disease. Or look at Madonnas from the fifteenth and sixteenth centuries, who were often portrayed with goiters, a common sign of iodine deficiency.

Pozzilli has paid particular attention to the way weight is portrayed in art, looking for clues to the prevalence of type 2 diabetes over time. "The women in Renoir's paintings were seen as beautiful, and their BMIs were about 29," he explains. As recently as 125 years ago, what we would now call overweight and even verging on obese was considered desirable and attractive.

American beauty ideals have clearly been constricting over the last hundred years. In 1894, a medical professor named Woody Hutchinson wrote an article for *Cosmopolitan* magazine extolling the aesthetic virtues of plumpness, and advising readers that no matter how much they dieted or exercised they were unlikely to change their body size much.[6]

The winners of the earliest Miss America pageants in the 1920s, for instance, had BMIs around 22.[7] By contrast, a contestant in the 2014 Miss America pageant, Indiana's Mekayla Diehl, has been praised for having a "normal"-sized body, visibly fleshier than those of the other contestants; she wears a size 4 and her BMI is around 18, which makes her underweight on the BMI chart. But she's positively glowing with health compared with other contestants, whose average BMI these days is a dangerously low 16.9.[8]

As recently as the 1950s, one of America's most glamorous stars was Marilyn Monroe, who wore a size 10 and was at the time considered one of the sexiest women in the world. At five

My Husband Tells Me I'm Beautiful, But . . .

Shannon, thirty-three, is a social worker near Raleigh, North Carolina.

I've had body image problems for as long as I can remember. The classic moment was when I was eleven and my grandmother made a comment about how flat my stomach was. That became a trigger point for me. I started dieting around fifteen, and it was a kind of bonding thing with my mom. She's dieted her whole life; she thought she was fat but she was tiny. She'd be happy when I wanted to diet with her.

Now when I diet I have a fairly easy job losing weight. I did Weight Watchers two years ago and lost ten pounds, then got tired of it and gained it right back, plus a couple more. When I'm not dieting I go right back to where I started: five foot five and about 170 pounds.

My husband tells me I'm beautiful all the time. But when I'm not dieting, I have a huge sense of anxiety about the lack of control over what I'm eating. I get this "I'm fat" mind-set. I'm not happy when I am dieting, either, though I get this sense of self-righteousness, that I'm doing something good by losing weight.

The thing that terrifies me is that I don't want my daughter to turn out like this. She's not old enough to understand any of this yet, but I lived it, I watched my mother do this to herself, and I feel like I'm repeating that already. And I don't know how to get away from it.

foot five and 140 pounds, her BMI hovered around 23—a far cry from today's much skinnier standard.[9]

So yes, the cultural norms for women's bodies have shrunk over the last hundred years, especially in the West. That fact alone supports the idea that body image is culturally constructed, that we learn body-size preferences, and that those preferences can change. But where do they come from in the first place? It's not like there's a committee in a closed room deciding what the ideal women's dress size will be this year.*

That's where the "nurture" part comes in; the environment we are born into, raised in, observe, and learn from.

Our daily lives are filled with hundreds, thousands, millions of images depicting the unattainable thin ideal. We see women's bodies that look like Marisa Miller's, and those that are much, much thinner. We also, increasingly, see images of the unattainable buff ideal for men. Bodies like, say, Channing Tatum's are no more "normal" than Miller's. (In fact, Channing Tatum's body isn't even normal for him. In 2012 he told a reporter from *People* magazine, "When I'm not training, I get really round and soft.")

Frankly, it's a little scary to realize just how much what we see shapes what we think. And it doesn't take long: one minute of exposure to an image of a thinner-than-average woman is enough to shift our perceptions of attractiveness to a thinner ideal.[10]

It's also scary to understand how changeable those thoughts and perceptions are. When my daughter was at her sickest, her gaunt face and impossibly thin body came to look normal to me. Other people's bodies began to look too large, oddly distorted—especially my own, which came to feel grotesque. I avoided mirrors for years during and after her illness. I tried consciously reminding myself over and over that my body hadn't changed size, and that the emaciation of anorexia was abnormal, not my own body. But I couldn't talk myself out of my feelings any more than

---

*Well, not literally, though some people might argue that designer vanity sizing approaches that.

patients with the aptly named Alice in Wonderland syndrome*
can talk themselves out of the feeling that various body parts are
shrinking or growing. (Both Alice in Wonderland syndrome and
body dysmorphic disorder involve a part of the brain called the
parietal cortex, leading some researchers to believe the disorders
are related.) We are fundamentally visual creatures; there aren't
enough words in the world to cancel out the effects of so many
thousands of pictures.

Culture shapes our body image in other ways, too. Humans
are social creatures, biologically designed to rely on other people
to help us survive a hostile world. Early humans had to evolve
mechanisms for telling friend from foe, for quick categorizations
of the people around us—what Polish-born social psychologist
Henri Tajfel described as in-groups and out-groups. In-groups are
people we perceive as *like us* in fundamental ways; they share
basic characteristics and identities.[11] So some of my in-groups
are Jews, women, people with curly hair, New Jersey natives, college professors, and people classified as mildly obese on the BMI
chart. Out-groups have identities we don't share; some of mine
are heavy metal bands, California natives, and people who believe in alien abduction.

We develop our social identities—our sense of ourselves and
where we belong in our families, communities, and societies—by
comparing ourselves with others.[12] On a fundamental level we
need to fit in, to belong, to conform. Maybe that's why parents
google "Is my daughter overweight?" twice as often as "Is my son

---

*People with Alice in Wonderland syndrome see things, especially body parts, as
smaller or larger than they are, or as otherwise distorted. AIWS is associated with
migraines, brain tumors, and hallucinogenics; some experts think Charles Dodg-
son, aka Lewis Carroll, who suffered from migraines, had the condition himself.

overweight?" despite the fact that in reality, more boys are over-weight than girls. Maybe they know the world is harder on girls whose looks don't measure up than on boys. Parents are also three times likelier to ask Google if their daughter is ugly than their son. ("How Google is expected to know whether a child is beau-tiful or ugly is hard to say," wrote Seth Stephens-Davidowicz, an economist who covered these analytics, with great restraint, for the *New York Times*.)[13]

And research shows that the more we want to conform, the more likely we are to internalize cultural norms,[14] to not just buy in to them but to defend them with the passion of the true be-liever. We've invested in them; we may have spent months or years of our lives trying to achieve those norms. They damn well *have* to be true.

In twenty-first-century Western society, those norms are communicated in large part by heavily manipulated images in advertisements, magazines, websites, TV, and movies. We know intellectually that no living woman actually looks like Beyoncé or Katy Perry or Kate Moss. You've probably watched the Dove "Evolution" video, which shows a beauty ad being created from start to finish, including extensive photoshopping. Or maybe you saw the 2012 video showing how the image of actress Sally Gif-ford Piper, wearing nothing but red bikini bottoms, was tweaked and transformed until the final image looked much more like a typical model than like her.

We all *know* images are altered. We know they embody the ideal—at least someone's vision of the ideal—rather than the real. And like my students, we think knowing makes us immune to their effects. Which is why in recent years advocates have pro-posed a number of legislative fixes for the photoshopping problem.

Israel was the first and, as of this writing, has been the only country to pass a bill requiring advertisers to label images that had been retouched to make models look thinner. In 2011, British MP Jo Swinson made news by forcing beauty company Lancôme to take down billboards featuring heavily photoshopped images of celebrities, including Christy Turlington and Julia Roberts.

On this side of the pond, former marketing executive Seth Matlins helped put together a bill known as the Truth in Advertising Act of 2014, which charges the Federal Trade Commission with regulating the way images are digitally manipulated in ads (though not in editorial spreads). Matlins told Fashionista.com he didn't realize how harmful marketing could be until his three-year-old daughter asked him if he thought she was ugly. Better late than never, I guess, though I have to wonder why Matlins and so many others become alarmed about the effects of marketing only when it affects their own children. As I write, the bipartisan bill has been introduced in Congress.[15]

Unfortunately such efforts, while good at raising awareness, are unlikely to bring about real change. Knowing that images have been retouched doesn't diminish their power or change the way we react to those images, according to several recent studies,[16] including one by Marika Tiggemann, a psychology professor at Australia's Flinders University. Tiggemann and her colleagues found that young women who saw fashion-shoot images that were labeled as having been digitally altered reacted with the same levels of body dissatisfaction as those who saw unlabeled images.[17]

No wonder two out of three thirteen-year-old girls are afraid of gaining weight.[18] No wonder body dissatisfaction rises exponentially (especially for girls) from childhood right on through adulthood.[19] (Boys' body dissatisfaction rises, too, but seems to level out after high school.) No wonder 90 percent of adult British women feel body-image anxiety, and many continue to feel that anxiety into their eighties.[20] No wonder half of the women who took one *Esquire* magazine poll said they'd rather be dead than fat.[21]

Feminist scholar, filmmaker, and former model Jean Kilbourne has spent her career looking at the connections between images of women in advertising and issues like distorted body image, disordered eating, and violence against women. She's one of the most media-savvy people on the planet. But she admits that even she's vulnerable to the power of those doctored images. "I don't know any woman who isn't," says Kilbourne. "It's impossible to be in this culture and not be to some extent made to feel bad about yourself because you're not perfect looking, you're aging, whatever."

After forty years of teaching media literacy—helping people understand that what they're seeing on the screen and in magazines isn't real—Kilbourne says the climate has not improved. "The images of women in popular culture have gotten *monumentally* worse," she says with exasperation. "Marketers have even more power than they did before. They have a lot of control over what goes into media, more than they used to. Sometimes it's subtle but it's there."

There's more of it, too. A lot more. On grocery-store carts, on billboards, on websites and social media and in elevators. Sometimes it feels like everywhere you look, someone's trying to sell you something. (Because, well, they are.) In 1964, the average American saw around seventy-six ads a day;[22] today we're exposed to over a thousand, more if we spend lots of time online. And America has no corner on the marketing market. When researchers from the International Body Project surveyed more than seven thousand people from around the world, they found an interesting pattern: in countries and regions where people had more money and higher socioeconomic status, they also had a stronger desire to be thin and were less pleased with their appearance. Which jibes with the scarce-resources theory: in wealthier societies, where it's easier to put on weight, there's more prestige attached to being thin. In poorer regions, heavier people are seen as having more access to scarce resources, and therefore hold more status.

That makes sense. But the International Body Project researchers suggested another possibility: people living in wealthier cultures are exposed to more marketing and advertising as well as more media in general.[23] And their research also showed that the more exposure people had to Western media, the more dissatisfied they were with their bodies. So maybe the sheer volume of images that pass before our eyes—whether we think we take them in or not—affects us more deeply than we know.

A now famous study of teenage girls in Fiji examined their attitudes around eating and body image just after television was introduced to the country, and then again three years later. Psychiatrist and anthropologist Anne Becker, currently a professor at Harvard, chose Fiji for several reasons: large bodies were considered aesthetically pleasing there, dieting and disordered eating were relatively unknown (there'd been only one documented case of anorexia in Fiji, *ever*), and the advent of television in 1995 offered a unique chance to explore its effects.

Becker and her colleagues saw profound differences in teen girls after Western television was introduced. Before TV, no girls vomited to control their weight, and few reported dieting or body dissatisfaction. Only three years later, 11 percent of the girls said they vomited for weight loss; 69 percent acknowledged dieting at some point, and a full three-quarters of them said they felt too big or too fat at least some of the time.[24] As one 1998 study subject told researchers, "The actresses and all those girls, especially those European girls, I just admire them and I want to be like them. I want their size. Because Fijians are, many of us, I can say most, we are brought up with those heavy foods, and we are getting fat. And now, we feel that it is bad to have this huge body. We have to have those thin, slim bodies [on TV]."

Becker's study was the first, and pretty much the only one, to explore how media affects eating behaviors and body image in a population. And given the sheer ubiquity of the internet and other media, it's unlikely there will ever be another study like this. Her findings reinforce the idea that, as media scholars say, we're living in a media panopticon, named for the giant Panoptes from Greek mythology who had a hundred eyes, some of which were always open. A panopticon is literally a prison building where inmates can be observed any time; because they never know when someone's watching, they assume they're always under surveillance. The arrangement is an architectural solution to the problem of how a handful of people can control a much larger group.

The media panopticon isn't a literal construct, of course, but more of a context—the media context we all live in. The ideals and assumptions of the culture surround us, holding us constantly to those values and beliefs. We're more apt to conform, internally as well as externally, when the cultural norms are reinforced everywhere you turn.

And boy, are they ever. The panopticon now extends deep into our everyday lives, thanks to smartphones and social media.

Everything we say and do has the potential to wind up online, for-ever, without our consent, for all the world to see. Facebook is for the moment the most popular social network; the average Amer-ican now spends forty minutes a day on the site[25]—more time than we devote to checking personal e-mail.[26] Then there's Ins-tagram, Twitter, YouTube, LinkedIn, Snapchat, WhatsApp, Ello, and, no doubt, new platforms by the time you're reading this. The way we consume and interact with social media has the power to affect the way we think and feel about ourselves as well as others. How exactly it affects us depends on age, gender, where we live, and a host of other factors we don't understand yet. We know that for women, especially young women, time spent on social media is linked to lower self-esteem and body confidence, and higher levels of depression and loneliness.[27]

We also know that platforms like YouTube and especially Twit-ter perpetuate what Wen-ying Sylvia Chou, a researcher at the National Institutes of Health who has studied obesity and social media, has described as "acts of toxic disinhibition."[28] She and her colleagues are referring to comments, "jokes," rants about fat and fat people (especially women), and cyberbullying that tends to happen less often face to face or on more nuanced platforms like forums and blogs. "'Fat' has become this catchall word for all the various hot-button issues we as a culture are metabolizing and dealing with," Chou told the *New York Times*.[29]

New technologies bring the panopticon closer in other ways, too. At public bus shelters in Moscow, for instance, anyone who sits down to wait for a bus will get a rude surprise: his or her weight will be displayed in large numerals for the world to see, along with nutrition information and—wait for it—advertisements for the gym that's sponsoring these so-called weighing benches.[30]

Some government officials clearly thought this was a good idea, and probably a lucrative one. Let's hope it doesn't happen here.

Of course, media and social media aren't the only culprits. Plenty of real-life interactions reinforce the sense of being judged, watched, critiqued. Jason Seacat, a professor of psychology at Western New England University in Springfield, Massachusetts, set out to explore how often women in particular experience these kinds of judgments. He asked fifty women, all of whom fell into the overweight or obese BMI categories, to keep a journal for seven days, recording every instance when they felt insulted, bullied, or judged for their body size. The women reported an average of three incidents a day—every day. Some of those involved inanimate objects, like turnstiles and bus seats that were too small. But many involved interactions with other people. One woman said a group of teenagers made mooing noises at her in a store; another said her boyfriend's mother refused to feed her and commented that she was so fat because she was lazy.[31]

Seacat was inspired to do the study after watching a group of teens at his gym loudly harassing a fat woman, who eventually gave up and left the gym. His findings shouldn't come as a surprise to any woman, because body surveillance affects us all, whether it's "positive" (catcalls, innuendos, public comments from men) or more like the experiences of the women in Seacat's study. I've endured my share of humiliating experiences, including being barked at by a group of young men while riding my bike. Whether we're young, beautiful, and thin, or middle-aged and overweight, or—let's not mince words—old and fat, our bodies are fair game for anyone who cares to comment. And a lot of people apparently do.

Obviously we're not in prison; we're free to turn off the TV and step away from the smartphone. But to do that is to cut ourselves off. Our need to belong, to be part of our community, makes us vulnerable to the power of our culture's ideals. Our need to compare ourselves to others, which in turn helps us survive and thrive in a hostile world,[32] makes us susceptible to anxiety about every aspect of our selves, from how we look to how much money we make to how many friends we have.

My Mother's Worst Nightmare

**Ellen, fifty-eight, is a massage therapist
in western Massachusetts.**

I was my mother's worst nightmare. Her biggest fear was that she'd become fat or have a fat child. She's five eight and has weighed 125 pounds her whole life. She's ninety-four now and still anytime she sees anyone who's fat, she'll comment.

Looking back now, I don't think I *really* had a weight problem until my forties. But I always *felt* I had a weight problem, and one reason is I am a tall, big-boned woman. No one else was fat in my family. Weight Watchers at sixteen was my first diet experience. I lost twenty pounds, reached my goal weight, and became a life member. I dieted on and off after that, tons of different diets. I did Weight Watchers three or four times. Each time I reached goal weight and would slowly start back up again.

Around age forty I did a liquid diet through a hospital. I didn't eat food for a year, and I loved it. When I didn't have a relationship with food and had no choices, it was wonderful. I would have stayed on it forever if I could have. But you can't. It's not healthy.

→

→

I did get really skinny, down to a size 10, which is low for me because I'm five eleven and a half. But then I lost my gall bladder because it had gone to sleep and was making tons of stones. When I started eating again, there was nothing I could do to not gain weight. I ate five hundred calories a day for a year and a half and still gained weight. So when they say weight loss is about discipline and self-control, that's baloney.

Then I got cancer and had my thyroid removed and gained sixty pounds because I was on the wrong medication. I went to an alternative health practitioner who took me off gluten, and it did work for quite a while. I lost about fifty pounds. And then, slowly, I gained it back again.

I was told often as a child that nobody would ever want me: I would never get married because I was too big. And I've had tons of therapy around that, and it doesn't matter. Once you have that image of yourself it doesn't change. Now I cannot tolerate myself being overweight. I don't like the feeling in my body. I work with a lot of athletes, and I see these gorgeous bodies and I feel like an elephant. I don't think that when I look at other fat people, but I think it about myself. I would do anything, basically, besides taking cocaine, to lose weight.

My mother and I used to fight all the time about my weight. It really damages you. I have a sister who's gone into my cupboards, found a muffin, and told me I should never ever have a muffin in my house. I never asked for her help, but she felt she had the right to do that.

My latest foray is hypnosis. The hypnotist does three sessions and you're done. I feel great. All I'm eating is protein and vegetables. No carbs—no wheats, rice, grains, none of that. No scales; you can't weigh yourself. No reading of labels. The hypnotist wants you to stay in your subconscious mind. I hope to be able to eat this way for the rest of my life.

As Jean Kilbourne points out, advertising is based on making people feel they're inadequate, less than, imperfect, and then offering a product or service that will "fix" what's "wrong" with them. In the words of Don Draper, the fictional creative guru at the heart of the series *Mad Men*: "The advertising industry is inherently aspirational. Commercials create a fantasy that elicits both desire for a possibility and disappointment in the reality."[33] We aspire to things that are by definition out of our reach—money, fame, beauty, the perfect body.

And, more and more these days, perfect health. Or at least really, really good health. Like food and body weight, the pursuit of health has taken on a moral aspect: you're "good" if you're engaging in healthy behaviors (however you define them), and "bad"—weak, lazy, undisciplined, unworthy—if you're not. University of California sociologist Julie Guthman points out that since the concept of "health" is essentially a moving target, a condition that can never be achieved once and for all, "it requires constant vigilance in monitoring and constant effort in enhancing."[34] If you're not actively working all the time on getting healthy—which of course means different things to different people at different times—there's something really, really wrong with you.

The unattainable goal of perfect health gives marketers yet another way to exploit our deepest anxieties and aspirations. And here my advertising and public relations colleagues would object; they would argue, instead, that they help people, that they fill real needs for real individuals. Maybe so, sometimes. But if marketers were in it for the public good, they'd be called philanthropists. Most of the time, they're after something else.

For instance: In 2013, London-based media agency PHD questioned more than six hundred American women about when they tend to feel worst about their appearance. A write-up of the survey's findings suggested that since most women said they felt least attractive at the beginning of the week, Monday was a good day to target "beauty consumers," and added, "Concentrate media during prime vulnerability moments." The survey also found that women's confidence about their looks plummeted when they felt depressed, angry, worried, or lonely. Kim Bates, head of brand planning at the agency, commented, "The cultural and psychological implications of that response are significant, and from a marketing perspective, it could be a factor in everything from creative concept to media platforms to promotional offers."[35]

Smart marketing, sure, especially for the $250 billion global beauty business.[36] But not so good for the rest of us.

ONE OF THE most disturbing aspects of the thin-obsessed beauty culture is that it hits children and teens hard—maybe even harder than it hits adults.[37] As the parent of two daughters, I struggled with how to protect them from those effects. Should my husband and I ban TV, Barbies, makeup, the internet? No, unless we wanted to move to a mountaintop in Idaho and raise our children entirely off the grid. Which we did not. So we had to try to find a way to teach our daughters to live with the flood of messages that they weren't thin enough, beautiful enough, smart enough—an impossible task in a culture that routinely tells women that our main (or only) value lies in how we look.

Beauty culture takes root much earlier than you might think, as evidenced in three recent studies. The first, a 2011 Canadian investigation, found that children as young as three years old, *especially* those who were normal weight, were unhappy with their bodies.[38] I had to think about that when I first read it; the predictable result would be that heavier children felt worse about their bodies and thinner children felt better. The researchers wondered about that, too. Looking deeper into the data, they found that overweight preschoolers consistently *underestimated* their size. They hypothesized that maybe the fatter children had internalized the pressure to be thin (and had already gotten some grief over their weight, at age three), and were dealing with it by avoiding or not acknowledging the issue.

That could be true, especially when you add the moral dimension of body criticism. Maybe thinner children who got praise for their physiques worried about being considered "bad" if their bodies changed. And maybe the heavier children had already given up on being considered "good."

In the second study, researchers at Rutgers University in New Jersey gave preschool-age girls a list of six positive and six negative traits, and asked them to assign those traits to one of three dolls: a thin (Barbie-size) doll, an average-size doll, and a fat doll. The preschoolers chose the fat doll least often for traits like "smart," "happy," "has best friend," and, most tellingly, "pretty." And they consistently assigned qualities like "sad," "no friends," "gets teased," and "eats most" to the fat doll.[39]

Finally, a 2013 study done by researchers at the Leeds University School of Medicine in the United Kingdom asked four- to six-year-old girls to read a kids' picture book whose main character was either normal weight, in a wheelchair, or fat, and then answer questions about the character. The girls overwhelmingly said the fat character was less likely to do good schoolwork, like the way s/he looked, or get invited to parties. When asked who they'd like to be friends with from the book, only three out of seventy-three girls chose the fat character. The older the girls, the more negatively they viewed the fat character.[40]

None of these findings surprise Katie Loth of Project EAT. She and her colleagues at the University of Minnesota have collected more than ten years of longitudinal data illuminating how weight and body image concerns affect kids and teens. Their conclusions highlight the dangers of our cultural obsession with thinness at any cost. "When a young person doesn't feel comfortable with their body, they're more likely to turn to dangerous means to lose weight," says Loth.

Experts like Daniel Callahan and Walter Willett have suggested it's OK to make kids and teens feel badly about themselves because those feelings will motivate them to change—presumably to diet, lose weight, and live healthily and happily ever after, which we know to be about as likely as finding a magic needle in a haystack. (Remember the stigmatizing Georgia hospital ads?) Actually, the opposite is true. Kids who are unhappy with their bodies are *less* likely to exercise or be active than kids who feel good about themselves, whatever their size.

So not only does the pressure to be thin push kids into disordered eating and weight-loss behaviors; it also keeps them from doing things that are good for them (and for all kids). The same holds true for adults. "Weight dissatisfaction may actually *discourage* people from engaging in healthy behaviors," says Christine Blake, a professor of health promotion at the University of South Carolina who has studied the issue. People who are unhappy with their weight are more likely to give up on a health-positive activity before they even start, says Blake, while overweight and obese people who are reasonably satisfied with their bodies are more likely to be active in ways they enjoy.[41]

Internalizing the unattainable thin ideal, in other words, can only hurt young people. One of the most interesting findings from Project EAT was that teenage girls who liked their bodies, even if they were overweight or obese, gained less weight and engaged in more "healthy" behaviors after five years than the girls who didn't like their bodies and wanted to change them.[42] Which makes sense, given that body dissatisfaction leads to dieting, and dieting leads to long-term weight gain and weight cycling, which leads to serious physical and psychological effects.

So we should be worried, deeply worried, about the fact that nearly half the three- to six-year-olds in a recent study were anxious about being fat.[43] We should be worried that 99 percent—*99 percent*—of the girls in one 2011 study said their ideal figure was smaller than their current one. (And 66 percent of the girls in that study were African American; it was one of the few that incorporated nonwhite kids and teens. Which is especially worrisome given the research showing that African American girls and women tend to be happier with their bodies than white girls and women.)[44] We should be worried about the fact that body dissatisfaction increases exponentially for girls heading into adolescence (though, interestingly, it decreases for boys).[45] We should be worried about the fact that for many children, the pressure to be thin leads to patterns of disordered eating that can last the rest of their lives.

I worked briefly at *Redbook* magazine in the early 1990s, not long after I'd given birth to my older daughter. One of my enduring memories of my time there was sitting in an editorial meeting where I was by far the largest woman in the room in my size 12 just-past-maternity wear. One of the other editors mentioned that she never let her husband see her sitting up in bed without clothes on, because (here she visibly shuddered) he might see her bulging stomach. I'm guessing this woman, like pretty much everyone else in the room but me, wore a size 2; she had no obvious fat on her. But her comment started a cascade of similar body anxieties. I was the only one in the circle of high-powered women who actually *had* a stomach that bulged, and also the only one foolish or honest enough to say that of course I sat up in bed naked in front of my husband and what was the point of being married if you couldn't?

I didn't last long at the magazine. Big surprise.

LAST SPRING, Kelley Coffey, a personal trainer in Northampton, Massachusetts, blew up a tiny corner of the internet with a blog post called "5 Things I Miss About Weighing More Than 300 Pounds." Coffey, a petite blond with striking blue eyes and dimples, headed the post with a pair of photos: herself at three hundred pounds (longer hair, double chin, same gorgeous dimples) and a current shot. "The longer I'm thin, the more I miss the gifts of living in a body so big that people often turned away," she wrote, and went on to list what she missed: power (physical strength), comfort (cushioning), perspective (she wrote that being stigmatized gave her "more empathy, more character, more personality" than she would have had as a lifelong thin person), friendships (it was easier to be friends with other women when she was fat), and presence, the sense of taking up space in the room and in the world.

Coffey says she got a lot of hate mail after publishing that post. One commenter wrote, "For a personal trainer this list is the most rediculous [*sic*], idiotic, and dubious thing to write. You are mentally NOT fit to train anyone obviously. PLEASE! Stop."

She says she wrote the post in the first place to illuminate one of the rules of her practice: no self-criticism. "My clients are not allowed to judge themselves aesthetically or get down about their strength or stamina," she explains. "You say good things or you say nothing." By writing a love letter to her former self, she figured she'd show them she meant it when she told them they were beautiful. "I'm daring to suggest there are beautiful things about the one thing we in this modern era and first-world country have collectively agreed is evil—fat," she says. "That there are beautiful things about these other bodies we're telling people we should hate."

So far, so good. Then Coffey followed up her original post a few weeks later with another called "Loving My 300-Pound Body Keeps Me Thin." This time she framed her appreciation for her former body a little differently. "If I've learned anything in the last 11 years about weight and wellness, it's this," she wrote. "The secret to happy, healthy weight loss and, in my case, to maintaining a lower weight, is to LOVE YOUR FAT." Self-love and self-acceptance, in other words, is a means to an end, and that end feels awfully familiar.

I asked Coffey, who describes herself as a "food addict," to clarify the seemingly mixed messages. "I don't believe they're mutually exclusive," she said.

I asked if she'd be OK with regaining the weight, which she lost after having gastric bypass surgery. "It's very important to me to maintain this body I have now," she said. "I'm comfortable in it. I'm invested in maintaining it because it's a symptom of me maintaining a healthy mind and soul. That's the highbrow answer. The lowbrow answer is I love to look at myself in the mirror. I think I am beautiful, and I enjoy that very much."

The longing to be thought attractive, even beautiful, is a powerful driver. And that's OK, really. It's OK to appreciate beauty, to strive to achieve it; it's human nature. And as with so many other things, knowing that beauty culture exists pretty much for the sole purpose of triggering our insecurities and anxieties doesn't change that longing. What helps, I think, is shifting our focus just a little, asking a different question, in a way. So long as we consistently look to other people and to the culture to tell us we're OK, we're attractive, we belong, even those of us who are the most beautiful and self-confident will struggle. I think we have to learn not to look outward for that stamp of beauty approval. It's not quite self-acceptance, a concept I find confusingly vague and impossible to put into practice. I can tell myself I'm beautiful all I want, but (a) that doesn't make it true, and (b) it doesn't make me believe it. When I look in the mirror and repeat "I'm beautiful," I feel silly, not inspired. I definitely don't notice any rise in confidence about my looks.

I think of it more like looking inward for that sense that we're OK, we're attractive enough, we fit in. Letting go of the imperative to be seen by others as beautiful lets me *feel* more attractive, maybe because I'm not measuring my looks by society's standards. I'm freer to appreciate what I find pleasing about myself, whether it's socially valued or not. My Jewish nose, for instance, is a perfect replica of my adored grandfather's nose, and therefore looks good to me if not to the world at large.

Kelley Coffey did get one thing right, though: self-loathing leads only to more self-loathing. Some of the most interesting research I've seen on body image comes from two psychology researchers at the University of Gothenburg in Sweden. The researchers interviewed a small group of young Swedish teens who scored high on a test of body satisfaction,[46] trying to understand what made them different. How did these adolescents manage to feel good about their bodies at such a vulnerable point in their lives and in a culture that seems bent on tearing down physical self-esteem?

"Positive body image isn't simply the opposite of negative body image," explains Kristina Holmqvist, one of the Swedish researchers. "And promoting positive body image is not done simply by reducing negative body image." She's right, of course, and once she said it, it seemed perfectly clear. Yet I'd never before thought of body image in that way.

Holmqvist and her colleague, Ann Frisén, found that this admittedly small, homogenous group of teens shared certain physical and emotional characteristics. First, their appearances more or less fit within current body ideals. On the surface this seems disheartening, suggesting that you have to be tall, slender, and big-breasted (girls) or muscular (boys) to feel good about yourself. But, as the researchers pointed out, plenty of teens who fit those norms still feel unhappy with their bodies. So there's got to be more to the story.

The teens also saw their bodies as functional, as giving them the ability to do what they wanted rather than simply look good. For instance, one girl who said she liked her legs explained she liked having muscles so she could run fast. Nearly all of them were physically active in ways they enjoyed, like dancing, sports, and jogging, and they saw exercise as something that made them feel good, not a chore to be ticked off a list. Though they reported hearing some negative comments about their bodies from friends and family members, they tended to brush off the comments rather than internalize them deeply.

Finally, and maybe most important, the Swedish teens shared the ability to think critically, especially when it came to body ideals. The reason they didn't tend to internalize the comments from others is that they were more likely than usual to question and challenge those cultural beauty ideals. They didn't accept them as gospel; they were able to step back and consider them more objectively.

That last quality may be the easiest to convey to kids and adolescents. I teach my students to understand beauty in the context of social trends, and to remember that both beauty and body image are culturally mediated. For example, we talk about the fact that the ideal woman's body here in America would be seen as sickly-looking in the desert society of the Niger, where girls' bodies are praised for their lush, voluptuous rolls of fat. And the most beautiful woman there would be considered unattractively obese by most Americans today.*

My twenty-year-old students are surprised to learn that beauty ideals in America have changed radically over time; they think things have always been the way they are. And when they start to understand the connections between women's body ideals and women's social status, a lightbulb goes off. "You find curvaceous women's bodies that accentuate reproductive potential as an ideal at times like the 1950s," says anthropologist Anne Bolin of Elon University in North Carolina. "That was an ideal that emphasized femininity." No coincidence, then, that the Marilyn Monroe ideal dominated at a time when Americans were under pressure to breed like bunnies and grow the post–World War II economy.

---

*For a fascinating first-person account of this phenomenon, read "Ideal," by Rebecca Popenoe, in *Fat: The Anthropology of an Obsession,* ed. Don Kulick and Anne Meneley (Tarcher, 2005).

Those of us who grew up with second- and third-wave feminism know this, or at least we did know this once upon a time. Writer Naomi Wolf, for one, drew attention to this link in her bestselling 1990 book *The Beauty Myth*. Wolf pointed out that in the 1910s, the lean, androgynous flapper look became the ideal just as women were fighting to get the vote. In the 1960s, when the birth control pill gave women the freedom to be sexual without the fear of unwanted pregnancy, the model du jour was Twiggy, who looked—well, twiglike, certainly childlike. You'd never mistake her for the Venus of Willendorf. And now that women sit on the Supreme Court, make up more than half the professional workforce,[47] attend college in higher numbers than men,[48] and fill medical and law schools, the body ideals have become punishingly narrow. Boobs on a stick, as one of my daughters once described them.

But we seem to have forgotten this hard-won insight, at least judging by our current levels of body angst and self-loathing. Older women feel as much body dissatisfaction as younger ones, though there are some important differences in what they experience. A 2001 study by Australian psychologist Marika Tiggemann found that while older women's rising BMIs lead predictably to rising levels of body dissatisfaction, those feelings were mitigated at least a little by a decrease in self-objectification.[49] It seems the older we get, the less likely we are to see our bodies as objects to be looked at by others, and therefore the less likely we are to feel shame and anxiety about our bodies. The two conditions balance each other out.

Here's where feminism could really help. By acknowledging that there's a historical context for beauty standards, and that the context is inextricably tied to social trends, feminism can remind us that we've taken this ride before and wound up in exactly the same place. That how attractive we judge ourselves, and are judged by others, depends in part on the changing social dynamics between women and men.

Personally, I've found that getting older has helped, and I don't think I'm alone in that. A 2014 Gallup survey found that more Americans over age sixty-five reported feeling good about their appearance than those who were middle-aged. Even more interesting, the midlife dip in physical self-confidence hit whites much harder than African Americans or Latinos, maybe because advertising and media in general are aimed at and feature more white people than other races and ethnicities.[50]

Now that I'm not (usually) angsting over every lump, bump, and stray hair, I have a lot more mental bandwidth for what I really care about and, frankly, what really matters. And when I wake up and just know in every pore it's going to be one of those days when I feel about as attractive as the inside of a burlap bag, I stay away from mirrors and go about my life.

Maybe comedian and actress Melissa McCarthy said it best when she told *People* magazine, "A recent article referred to me as 'America's plus-size sweetheart.' It's like I'm managing to achieve all this success in spite of my *affliction*. My weight? It is what it is. Like most people I know, it's like, you gain a little, you lose a little. You have a good hair year, a bad hair year, you manage money well, you don't manage it that well . . . your entire life is ebbs and flows and ups and downs. And you could be hit by a bus tomorrow. It's about being content. And sometimes other priorities win."[51]

Amen, sister.

Chapter 6

It's All in How You Look at It

"You know what the meanest thing you can say to a fat girl is? 'You're not fat.'"

—"Fat waitress" Vanessa, played by actress Sarah Baker,
in a scene from Louis C.K.'s comedy series *Louie*

A few years back, I got the chance to interview the executive chef at a hospice. I was fascinated by her descriptions of how she worked with patients to offer both nutrition and emotional comfort through food. She visited each resident every morning to ask what, if anything, he or she could eat and *wanted* to eat; many of them could no longer eat, or had problems tasting or digesting certain foods. And then she came up with creative ways to work with the patients.

For instance, for someone who loved chocolate cake but couldn't eat it anymore, the chef would bake one every day and put it in the room, so the patient could breathe in the aroma and, also, offer it to visitors. Patients loved being able to give pleasure to visitors, and took vicarious pleasure themselves in watching others eat what they could not.

Working at a hospice might seem like a depressing job, but the chef told me how much she loved it. In fact pretty much the only thing that distressed her—aside from the inevitable—was the fact that many of the women who *could* still eat refused bread, salad dressing, butter, chocolate, desserts, and other "fattening" foods. Being thin and being "good" about their eating had become such integral parts of their identities, they couldn't bear to leave them behind.

If ever there was a WTF moment, this was it. These women couldn't let go of their dieting *even though they were dying.* Who in the world were they still dieting for? What a perfect metaphor for the Mobius strip of crazy we're caught in.

The more I thought about it, the more I wondered if the thin-is-always-better mentality might have what psychologists call corollary benefits. That is, does it fulfill some emotional or psychological needs beyond weight loss or body size? Maybe one reason these dying women could not, would not eat the butter or the pasta or the cake was that it would violate some fundamental sense of themselves. It would alter some core aspect of their identities at a time when they were already losing so much.

Certainly the way we think and talk about weight and health and beauty can serve other purposes. Take the phenomenon known as "fat talk." We've all done it, ruefully or cheerfully or with real despair, telling a friend, a colleague, a stranger in a clothing store, "I've just got to do something about these thighs!" Or arms, or stomach, or neck or hips or waist. We do it to ourselves, a kind of self-bullying we wouldn't stand for from a friend, in part because we think it makes us feel better about our bodies.[1] We disparage our own physical selves, whatever size they are, in a kind of call-and-response that's come to be a ritual among American women. The conversations typically go something like this:

"I feel so fat!"

"You're not fat! I'm the one who needs to do something about these thighs."

"Get out—your thighs look great. You're a stick. I'm the one with the problem!"

"Stop it! You look fantastic. Me, on the other hand, I really shouldn't have eaten that half of a mini-cupcake. Now I have to work out an extra hour to burn it off."

"No, I'm the one who pigged out on breadsticks!"

And so on, and on, and on. We do it without planning it or thinking about it, for the most part. We do it because it's become a social norm, something we expect others to do and do ourselves because *they* expect it from us.[2] A lot of the time we don't even know we're doing it, that's how automatic it's become—like saying "God bless you!" to someone who sneezes.

Most of us think this kind of self-disparagement makes us feel better about our bodies; we think (if we think about it at all) we're looking for validation from other women that no, we're not fat, and yes, we look good. And we get it, or think we do.

In reality, though, what fat talk actually accomplishes is to reinforce the idea, to ourselves and others, that we *should* be thin and that our bodies need policing. On the surface it may sound reassuring ("You're not fat at all!"), but dig a little deeper and you'll understand how such talk *enforces* those rigid ideas around weight. Think about it: to knock your own body for being too fat is to show your support for the notion that fat is bad, unattractive, unhealthy, unacceptable. Even if the reassurances you get from others are well intentioned, they're still coming from the perspective that fat is not OK.

Which is why, for instance, on the show *Louie,* when comedian Louis C.K. tells Vanessa, a waitress who has just asked him out and been rejected, "You're not fat," she responds, "That's the meanest thing you can say to a fat girl." He's perplexed; he was trying to compliment her. But, as actress Sarah Baker, who played Vanessa, explained to Vulture.com, his reassurances ring false because they're still predicated on the idea that to be fat is "awful, like that it's the worst thing a woman can be, overweight." He's denying a basic truth about her, an aspect of her identity, one that she sees as no big deal, just part of who she is, like the color of her hair and her height. He's the one perpetuating the stereotypes; she's just a woman asking out a man.

Even as we use fat talk to get others to reassure us, we know it's hollow and meaningless. The more we fat talk, the worse we feel about ourselves,[3] which in turn makes us more likely to gain weight, exercise less,[4] develop type 2 diabetes,[5] and eat in a disordered way.[6] And we're not dumb; we know we don't feel better about ourselves after a back-and-forth bout of fat talk. But we keep doing it, in part because it's a way to reach for a sense of belonging—even though that belonging often leads to misery, obsession, and despair. We need to be part of the zeitgeist, even if it makes us feel crappy about ourselves.

I've done my share of fat talking, especially earlier in my life. But I didn't think about it much until I watched, with sadness and horror, my daughters and their friends going through the same rituals. It reminded me of the way dogs behave in a group, especially dogs that don't know one another and need to establish a hierarchy. The more submissive dogs bare their throats, demonstrating that they aren't going to challenge the leader. That's what fat talking sometimes feels like to me, a way to signal to other women that we're not challenging their place in the pack.

And it brings up another vexing question: Who are we doing all this for? Who benefits from the fat talking, the dieting, the endless closed loops of body angst? When we stand in front of the mirror in despair, when we starve ourselves or overexercise, when we cry in the store because the clothes don't fit, when we walk down the street judging other women's bodies, who are we trying to impress?

One answer is that we want to be considered sexually attractive. We want partners and lovers and mates, and we are taught over and over that we won't find love or success or happiness or sexual satisfaction if we're overweight or obese. None of that is true, of course, and we pretty much know it. We certainly know that men find a range of women's body sizes attractive. One example: a 2012 poll conducted by the British *Grazia* magazine found that men are most attracted to women with curvy rather than ultrathin bodies. And we also know that lesbians and bisexual women are most attracted to curvy women who are heavier than social norms dictate.[7]

So I don't think that fully explains our obsession with thinness, or why we pursue it so single-mindedly. It doesn't illuminate, for instance, the real distress of a student who sits in my office crying because she wears a size 8 and not a size 0. The range of body types our culture deems attractive is much broader (in both meanings of the word) than the range, or lack of range, we see every day in ads and media.

Another answer is that loathing our bodies has become part of our identity as modern women. We've grown up and continue to live in a culture that tells us our worth comes in large part from our bodies and our appearance. And even the most revolutionary among us can find it tough to push back against that equation. UCLA sociologist Abigail Saguy coined the term "moral panic" to describe the blame, fear, and disgust we're now conditioned to associate with overweight and obesity. As we've discussed, being thin has come to represent not just a physical condition but a spiritual and moral one. The divide between thin and fat marks a line between good and bad, virtue and sin, success and failure, beauty and ugliness, health and sickness. And who among us wants to construct an identity around being sinful, ugly, sick, and a failure?

So while the women in the hospice who couldn't or wouldn't let go of their lifelong dieting rules seem extreme, to say the least, many of us can relate to the fear of losing some fundamental element that makes us who we are. And yes, many of us feel that body anxiety defines us and our social roles. Dieting stories are, like childbirth stories, our ticket into a club, a shared experience that bonds us in suffering and hope. If you're a woman who doesn't diet, you inevitably wind up feeling like an outcast because you don't know or care how many points are in a slice of bread or a serving of cake, because you won't engage in the white noise of fat talk and self-disparagement that sometimes passes for small talk among women.

That feels both terribly sad and infuriating to me. We've gotten to a place where one of our core human needs, the need to belong, now requires us to hate our bodies (or say we do, which amounts to the same thing). Where we believe, deeply, that we need to police ourselves and one another when we break the unwritten rules, when we don't look or behave the way we're "supposed" to.

I've certainly learned to put on my inner hazmat suit whenever I publish anything about weight and health. A few years ago, I wrote a story on weight bias among health professionals for the *New York Times*. The piece was reporting, not opinion, and cited a number of specific research studies documenting attitudes among doctors and other medical professionals. It racked up more than seven hundred comments on nytimes.com, many of which were angry, nasty, and cruel (even more than usual for online comments). "Being fat and disgusting is a personal choice," wrote one. "Fat people take up handicapped parking spaces when they should be parking further away than anyone! The only handicap they have is laziness and self-control."

Many of the *New York Times* commenters defended doctors' bias against fat patients and became furious when others suggested such attitudes might not be constructive—including doctors themselves. A self-identified cardiac surgeon wrote, "I am generally repulsed by [obese people] and am acutely aware of their eating habits in public. It is really quite simple: calories in and calories burned; just change the ratio and you can lose weight. It's not the fault of others that you make the wrong choices, and quit blaming them."

A number of comments went something like this one from "Gary": "When I gained thirty pounds my freshman year of college, I sold my car and bought a bicycle. I've never worried about exercise since. When I suggest this to people struggling with their weight, I consistently get some form of 'It's too hard for me.' Well, suck it up. I did the work. You do not get to complain just because you find it challenging."

If you've ever seen *The Devil Wears Prada*, this attitude will feel familiar. Psychologists call this attitude "queen bee syndrome," and use it to describe women who have worked their way up the corporate ladder, usually in a male-dominated career, and think other women should have to do the same. They refuse to mentor younger women, and are often much tougher on women in the workplace than they are on men.[8] I call it misery-loves-company syndrome. *I sucked it up; you should, too. Why should I give you a hand when no one helped me?* Or, in the realm of weight, *I suffered to achieve this body, and if you want to look like me you can damn well suffer, too.* "People may feel losing weight is their proudest accomplishment," notes Abigail Saguy, "and they don't want it to be devalued."

Another piece I wrote for the *New York Times,* on the obesity paradox, attracted even harsher comments. You'd think we'd be relieved to learn we're not doomed to an early death if we gain five pounds. But the suggestion that in some cases there might be some health advantage to being heavier really makes people mad.

And I get it. Sort of. We've bought into the notion that being thinner is always better—some of us more than others. People who have struggled or are still struggling to lose weight are deeply invested in the process and in the idea that it's necessary. Many of us literally organize our lives around the imperative of getting or staying thin: what we eat and how much, whether and how much we exercise, how we shop, how we dress, how we raise our children, how we think and talk about ourselves—some of the most fundamental elements of our lives can be driven by an emphasis on thinness at any cost. Especially for people who are not naturally thin, who are what psychologist Deb Burgard refers to as "weight suppressed," meaning they're fighting their biology to stay at a lower weight. Because that's the kind of tunnel vision it takes to maintain a significant weight loss. As Debra observed in Chapter 2, keeping weight off is not a lifestyle, as weight-loss advocates often say; it's a job, the hardest job you'll ever have. And a more-than-full-time job at that.

Prejudice of any kind comes from a place of fear. In a culture where many fear fat more than they fear death or disease or bereavement, people feel free to voice the most vitriolic opinions on the issue of weight. They get angry enough to end friendships, send hate mail to strangers, publish mean-spirited tweets like this one, written by University of New Mexico evolutionary psychologist Geoffrey Miller: "Dear obese PhD applicants: if you didn't have the willpower to stop eating carbs, you won't have the willpower to do a dissertation #truth". They're afraid that they, too, could someday be fat, or fat again if they've lost weight. (By "fat" here I mean anything from five pounds "overweight" on up.) And that, apparently, is a terrifying prospect.

Other factors come into play beyond fear. Part of our concept of identity, how we see ourselves in the world, can derive from a sense of privilege, a special advantage granted to members of a particular group. Being thin in this culture certainly confers privilege, and lots of it. Thin people don't have to worry that someone will make fun of them for eating in public, will give them dirty looks on an airplane, will repurpose their photos to ridicule people with larger bodies. They enjoy the privilege of not having to deal with the shame and stigma heavier people encounter every day. And, let's face it, no one wants to let go of privilege. Once we have it, we feel entitled to it. "People don't want to be told privilege is undeserved," says Saguy thoughtfully. "They want to think they've earned it by working hard and counting calories, and they cling to it."

Several years ago, when Saguy published a book called *What's Wrong With Fat?*, she got plenty of nasty letters and hostile comments. A few of them surprised her. "People have said to me that I don't know what I'm talking about because I'm a fat woman," says Saguy, and laughs. She happens to be both slender and conventionally pretty. Before she started writing about weight, she studied sexual harassment, another topic that inspires passionate debates. The responses she got to that work, says Saguy, were nothing compared with how people have reacted to her work on weight. "I had an awkward moment at a dinner party when a friend actually screamed at me over weight," she says.

The good news—if there's ever anything good to be said about prejudice—is that people on the receiving end of weight stigma are beginning to speak up about it. Last year a young woman named Rachel Fox, who'd just graduated Wesleyan with a degree in biology, wrote an essay for the *Chronicle of Higher Education* titled "Too Fat to Be a Scientist?" where she described some of her experiences with weight shaming in the STEM fields. One research professor who was interviewing her for a lab job commented that her employees worked collaboratively, adding that she didn't need someone who was "going to eat more than their fair share of the pizza, if you know what I mean." When Fox, stunned, stammered no, she really didn't know, the professor abruptly ended the interview and didn't return any of Fox's follow-up e-mails.

During a summer fellowship, Fox was accosted by a senior colleague who told her she shouldn't be eating "more than 1,200, maybe 1,400 calories a day." When Fox responded, "How do you know I'm not?" the colleague clearly didn't believe her. She suggested maybe Fox wasn't measuring her portions accurately.

"Here was a woman with whom I worked side by side, a colleague who counted on me to keep her cell cultures alive while she went on vacation, insinuating that I didn't know how to use a measuring cup!" Fox fumed. "How could she trust me with the future of her research one minute and then imply that I'm too dumb to read a nutritional label or a food pyramid the next?"[9]

The prejudice hurts even more, she added, when it comes from scientists who are supposed to understand complexity and nuance, especially when it comes to the workings of the human body, but who revert to the same stereotypes and assumptions as the rest of us when it comes to weight. Fox is now working toward a master's in narrative medicine, which she hopes to use to do advocacy work. It's sad that a clearly talented scientist—and a woman scientist at that—was driven away from the field she loved. But the fact that she was willing to take a stand and make a very public statement about it gives me hope. Because that's the only way things will ever even begin to change.

Former pharmaceutical rep Chevese Turner used her experiences with weight stigma to launch the Binge Eating Disorder Association, a nonprofit that advocates and lobbies for awareness and treatment of binge eating disorder, which affects up to 5 percent of the population. (Not all overweight and obese people have BED, and not all people with BED are overweight or obese.) Turner herself has struggled with BED and knows weight stigma from the inside out. "People look at it as if it's the person's choice to be fat and so they're to blame," she says. "I can tell you firsthand that boy, we didn't choose this. It's a set of circumstances. You get there, and then you have to deal with it." Turner's "dealing with it" has included creating a national organization that brings information, awareness, and resources to thousands of people.

One TV anchorwoman who found herself on the receiving end of weight prejudice fought back in an inspiring way. When Jennifer Livingston, a broadcast journalist in La Crosse, Wisconsin, got a nasty e-mail criticizing her weight, she read it on the air and then took the opportunity to call out the e-mail for what it was: bullying. "What really angers me about this is that there are children who get e-mails as critical as the one I received each and every day," she said, with enviable poise. "To all of the children out there who feel lost, who are struggling with your weight, with the color of your skin, your sexual preference, your disability, even the acne on your face, listen to me right now. Do not let your self-worth be defined by bullies. Learn from my experience that the cruel words of one are nothing compared to the shouts of many." Her passionate, articulate response racked up millions of online views.

At least Livingston's critic stopped with an e-mail. Filmmaker Lindsey Averill from Boca Raton, Florida, wasn't so lucky. Along with her business partner Viridiana Lieberman, Averill put up a Kickstarter last spring to fund a documentary called *Fattitude,* about the ways culture encourages fat prejudice. Along with the early pledges, they got a few negative e-mails, messages that read "Shut up and eat your doughnuts" and "Get off your couch and exercise, you fat slob." This didn't surprise them; anyone who blogs or writes or speaks about weight issues learns to expect messages like these, whatever their body size.

It's a little harder to laugh off the hate when it hits closer to home. After Averill and her business partner initiated their Kickstarter, they found two videos on YouTube that used clips from their trailer inappropriately (one video spliced them with snippets of racist and anti-Semitic footage). Averill asked YouTube to take them down for copyright infringement, and that's when the campaign against her started in earnest. On top of the usual vicious messages, she started getting deliveries of pizzas and other things she hadn't ordered—evidence that the haters knew where she lived. Her husband began getting calls at his real estate office, recordings from the movie *Casino* of someone saying "When I get out of jail, I'm going to come kill you."

"At that point we started to feel freaked out," says Averill. She called the police, who were sympathetic but couldn't do much, even when an anonymous online poster claimed he lived in her town and wrote, "I can find this bitch and kill her." A local news station covered the story, and soon media outlets around the country picked it up. Which, ironically drew attention to the project. The Kickstarter funding came through, and the documentary is in process.

I asked Averill why she thinks her project attracted such violent hatred, and her answer jibed with Saguy's perspective. "Fat or thin, the entire American population has internalized this idea about fat being terrible," Averill told me. "They're overexercising and undereating and living in a constant state of fear and panic about this horrible, hateful thing we must avoid at all costs. So if they allow someone else to say 'It's OK to be fat and you should stop being mean to fat people,' their entire life of self-torture is a waste."

Back to misery loves company, in other words, mixed with a fair amount of judginess. And everyone feels entitled to dish it out. Not long ago a student at my university published an opinion piece in the daily student newspaper arguing, basically, that while it's OK to eat an entire pint of ice cream once in a while, it's just not OK to be fat, and that if you do wake up one day and find yourself fat, you have an obligation to do something about it. "Everyone should be inspired to live a wholly healthy life," she wrote. "It is not OK to accept yourself as something that is blatantly unhealthy and, in most cases, changeable."[10]

I invited the student to come talk to me, and to her credit, she showed up. But she couldn't, or wouldn't, even begin to question her assumptions around weight and health. I understand that's a scary process, whether you're questioning assumptions about weight, race, climate change, or fill in the blank. I understand that a twenty-year-old runner who's healthy and conventionally attractive might find it hard to put herself in other people's shoes.

What I don't understand is the veneer of concern that overlays so much of this judgment. Nobody says you have to like fat people or marry one; weight-based prejudice isn't illegal, and it's certainly commonplace. But if we were really worried about people's health, we wouldn't be OK with the nasty tweets and e-mails and public comments. We wouldn't be OK with the fat-shaming and the death threats and the anonymous letters. We'd be talking about how best to support people to be as healthy as they possibly can be—and not just fat people, or white people, or affluent people, but everyone. Judginess and disapproval don't come from a place of promoting health. They're part of the cultural tsunami of shame we're *all* swimming in.

That shame and stigma have physical repercussions as well as emotional ones. Stigma of any kind, whether it's around weight or race or class or gender or mental health, can increase levels of cortisol, the so-called stress hormone, which in turn raises blood sugar and blood pressure and—ding ding ding—can lead to weight gain.[11] Peter Muennig, a professor of health policy at Columbia University, has investigated the connections among

The Worst Kind of Judgment

Pat, who's in her sixties, teaches communications law at a university in the Northeast.

I first found out I was a fat person in kindergarten, when people I didn't know before told me I was a fat person. I have over the course of my life been of normal weight three times by doing extraordinary dieting. Each time I do that I ratchet my metabolism down one more notch, which has been counterproductive in the long run.

The tragedy for me is that I judge other large people the way people have judged me. I find myself looking at a large person and assuming they don't care enough to look right. And that they probably are lazy. And that they're probably stupid. And I know that's how people have judged me in the past. It's incredible to me that I do that. And I wish I didn't.

So I've tried to consciously make myself see people as individuals, as people who have a being underneath whatever their body type is. I hope more people can learn how to do that, and I hope we can share how to do that in the years to come. It's very, very difficult. The idea that there's a "right" way to look is so deeply ingrained, even in those of us who don't look "right."

stigma, weight, and health, and concluded that the stress of being fat in a culture that demonizes it is not good for your health.[12] "If we believe being overweight is stigmatizing, and we believe stigma is psychologically stressful, why wouldn't we believe that at least some of what we're observing with obesity is coming from psychological stress?" asks Muennig. His findings suggest that people belonging to all sorts of stigmatized groups are more likely to develop diabetes and other weight-associated diseases.[13]

He also points out that until recently, there's been little sense of identity or community among people society considers fat. "Even obese people believe their weight is their fault," says Muennig. "Therefore, anybody else you see who's obese, it's also their fault." We truly can be our own worst critics. It's so much harder to face off against the nasty voice in your head than against any amount of prejudice from the outside.

Rebecca Puhl and others see weight-based discrimination as a social justice issue. "Millions of people are potentially affected by this kind of discrimination," she says. "It's just as damaging as other forms of prejudice but it's not much on the radar of the public health community." Tell that to people like Daniel Callahan, who continues to insist that prejudice makes a good health-care strategy for fat people.

EVEN IF YOU never suffer from weight bias yourself, it's likely to affect you if you have children, or nieces and nephews, or friends with children. While heavy children are bullied more than thin ones,[14] even thin kids are sometimes harassed about their weight. A 2011 study by Rebecca Puhl found, surprisingly, that plenty of teenagers with average and just-above-average BMIs reported being teased and humiliated about their weight. Puhl can think of two explanations: maybe current beauty ideals are so narrow, so restrictive, that even the tiniest deviation can trigger shaming. Or maybe teens tease one another about weight because they know it will hurt; they know it's a vulnerable spot, even if their victims aren't overweight.[15] Because the anxiety about getting or being considered fat has become so pervasive, even naturally thin children internalize it.

Which contributes to the fact that it's damn near impossible to know how to handle (or not) the issue of weight with your children, especially daughters. It's impossible to say the right thing or do the right thing when you're struggling with all the same issues as your child. In my interviews, I've talked with many mothers grappling with their own body issues and trying to figure out how to help their children. The story that's haunted me the most came from a mother who was obese, and had suffered enormous shame because of her weight as a child; her own mother had set up booby traps with food around the house, to catch her in the act of eating something she wasn't supposed to. She didn't want her daughter to go through what she had. "So I'd interrogate her, around and around, about what she'd eaten," she told me. "I'd grab her by the double chins." The interrogating led to screaming, tears, and a ruptured relationship, one the mother is hoping to mend now that her daughter is grown up.

The pain of having a parent, someone you love and trust, criticize your body, which feels indistinguishable from your essential self, stays with a person. When Rebecca Puhl surveyed kids and teens who'd been at weight-loss camps, she found that more than a third of them said they'd been teased or bullied about their weight by their parents. Another half said they'd been bullied about weight by teachers or coaches, and virtually all said they'd been bullied by peers.[16] Maybe some of those parents were just plain mean or even abusive, like the father of a twenty-five-year-old woman named Crystal from Elizabethtown, Kentucky, who pointed to her thigh, when she was about eight years old, and said, "Your thigh is bigger than mine." When he picked her up from his ex-wife's house, he'd tell her, "You're bigger than last time I saw you." When she dressed up to try to please him, he'd curl his lip and tell her that her feet were fat.

But I'm guessing some of the parents in Puhl's study were trying (however misguidedly) to spare their children the kind of stigmatization that comes with being obese in this culture. Once you're labeled a fat kid, once you take that on as part of your identity, you never let it go.

In one disturbing study headed by Janet Latner, a psychology professor at the University of Hawaii, subjects read descriptions of two categories of people: those who had been obese and were now thin, and those who had been fat, lost weight, but were still considered obese. Then they filled out questionnaires on their feelings about those imaginary people. Unsurprisingly, the people who were described as having lost weight but were still considered obese came in for the highest levels of stigma. The unexpected finding was that people described as thin now but formerly obese also came in for a heavy dose of blame and shame.[17] Once a fat person, always a fat person, at least in the eyes of the world.

On the other end of the spectrum, I've heard stories of pediatricians leaving the hospital room of a teen with anorexia and commenting, "I'd have anorexia, too, if I had a mother like that."* Never mind the fact that parents don't cause anorexia and that any parent whose child is hospitalized for an eating disorder is probably half out of her mind with anxiety and guilt, and has been for a while. Some days when my daughter was in the hospital I

---

*In her book *Fasting Girls: The History of Anorexia Nervosa,* Joan Jacobs Brumberg describes how the language around anorexia has shifted over time. When young women in medieval Europe starved themselves, they described it as a way of showing devotion to God; young women today talk about the fear of fat. The disease is the same, but the context shifts with each culture's obsessions.

felt like I was walking around with a huge sign on my face that read "Yes, I damaged my daughter."

It's really, really hard for parents to help their children navigate the waters of weight, body confidence, and health. Most of us can barely do that for ourselves. I'm sure I never criticized either of my daughter's bodies, partly because I never *felt* critical of them. But I do remember standing in front of the mirror and criticizing *my* body when they were young, even as I reassured them they were beautiful just the way they were. At the time I had no idea that in trash-talking my own body I was giving them a far more potent message than all the compliments in the world. That's still one of my biggest parenting regrets.

ANYONE WHO'S EVER lost weight, even for a little while, knows it can dramatically change the way other people see and react to you. I remember one of the benefits of losing weight at age fifteen was that boys suddenly took an interest. I went from romantic untouchable to object of at least some desire. And that was just twenty pounds.

Which is, of course, a big part of why we go on diets in the first place: to change the way others react to us. In our weight-loss fantasies, our friendships and romances will bloom, our problems will vanish, and a magical unicorn will deliver a giant pot of gold to our doorstep. And then we're surprised when things don't turn out that way.

Terri, the New York City bank examiner whose doctor thought she was lying about what she ate, remembers the feeling of losing eighty-six pounds on Weight Watchers about fourteen years ago. It wasn't what she expected at all. "I felt really vulnerable," she says. "I didn't like the way people treated me. My identity is I'm smart and capable, and I suddenly felt like people treated me like I was weak and helpless and stupid." She also got a lot of unwanted romantic attention from people she'd considered friends.

Patrick, the librarian who became a runner and lost eighty pounds, never thought of himself as unhappy with his looks or his lifestyle before he went on his first diet. He was motivated by his doctor's concern rather than by distress over his appearance. Maybe that's why he was shocked to find that his relationships with other people changed dramatically as he became thinner. "It's horribly depressing to realize that nothing has changed, really, you're the same person, and people treat you differently," he says. "It reveals these things about the world that are just gross, that have nothing to do with who you are. I'm sure for women it's a hundred times worse." It was a relief, he admits, when he and his wife moved to a different part of the country a few years later. "Here, not everybody knows I had this big weight loss," he says. "I only share it with certain people now."

It took losing eighty pounds for Patrick to realize that people had been judging him for his appearance all along, even people who knew him. Even his friends. Which wouldn't surprise most women; we're trained from birth, pretty much, to know others are constantly judging our bodies, and to inflict such scrutiny on ourselves.

Carole, a fifty-six-year-old arts consultant in upstate New York, had gastric bypass surgery four years ago and lost 175 pounds over the next two years. After the surgery, as the weight was coming off, many friends and acquaintances made a point of telling her she'd been beautiful before the surgery. Their comments confused and then angered her. "Nobody looked me in the eyes for those twenty-five years and said, 'You're really beautiful,'" she says now. "No one *ever* said that to me."

She's all too familiar with the experience of being stigmatized from her "fat years." Before she started consulting, she was a dean at a prestigious university, where she was successful and, she thought, well liked. But she'll never forget the day four of her faculty members showed up in her office to let her know she was an embarrassment to the school, especially in her role as a fund-raiser—a role she was extremely good at. "They told me a new faculty member had described me by blowing out his cheeks. That was supposed to give me something to think about," she remembers. She kicked them out of her office and held it together until they were gone. Then she cried.

Plenty of other work-related fat-shaming incidents came her way over her nine years as dean. Colleagues told her, for example, that she was perceived (always by *other* people, of course) as not very smart. Coworkers and supervisors felt free to ask, "So what is it with the weight, anyway?" Eventually the gossip and ridicule and sheer unadulterated scorn, even from people she considered friends, drove her to quit the job she loved and opt for bariatric surgery.

Since losing weight, Carole has seen her relationships with many former colleagues and friends change. A lot. "I'm convinced people believe I'm more energetic and smarter than I was four years ago," she says. "And that is so untrue. If you think about all the workarounds I had to do to manage the world when I was almost two hundred pounds heavier. Just walking into a space and having to figure out where I was going to sit, and do that in a way that's opaque to everyone but me. To navigate place and space all the time on top of the highly analytical job I was doing."

I Do Not Have a Disease

Lizabeth is a business consultant in Washington, DC.

My mom has muscular dystrophy. It's a disease that wastes the muscles and grows increasingly more serious. My mom will die with a brain as sharp as a blade but a body that disintegrates on her, her diaphragm losing its strength and her heart slowly losing its ability to pump. She has lost use of the muscles in her legs, and her chest and arm areas have withered to the extent that her heart sits at a funky angle.

My mom has a disease.

I am fat. I have a big, beautiful body that does all the things I ask it to, and for that I am very blessed. I would be clueless if I was not aware of all the things my body can do in comparison to my mom's, and thoughtless not to acknowledge the privilege of that.

I do not have a disease.

There are many things that get casually conflated when people speak about size and shape related to health. To call my shape a disease when I know what a disease truly does to the body, to the mind, and to a family perks me right up and challenges my ability to remain gracious in conversation—not because I'm ashamed of my mom or of the idea of "disease" or even disability, but because comparing my shape to something that will kill my mother hits a very raw nerve.

But what about the fact that my *mom* conflates them? Ugh.

Mom, when she was healthy—or should I say physically able—was the same height I am and the standard bearer of what women in my family "should" look like. To this day, mostly housebound, unable to walk unassisted and with all the other issues impacting her health, she still diets. She believes that a "pouch" on the belly is something to fight against, even in a social circle of one.

My mom was, like many moms, the model of body acceptance (or lack thereof) as I was growing, and did the best with what tools she had. She wanted to keep me out of harm's way, out of the line of fire, and so she taught me to diet and strive for the thin ideal and criticize and hate anything short of that. Today she smokes like a chimney, drinks, isolates, and as you would imagine, has serious bouts of depression and anxiety. Her disease, I believe, contributes significantly to that.

For me, on the other hand, proper rest, nourishing myself, loving self-talk, and mindfully enjoying movement are essential to keeping myself confident, mentally balanced, and happy. I gained so much in my life when I learned about size diversity, engaging in thankfulness rather than self-critical monologues. You see, I have been in the shame spiral and depression my mom is in now, only I felt it due to my size and the "understanding" that being fat meant I was sick.

It's funny to view this from the external perspective and see the hypocrisy of unsolicited opinions in action. The behaviors that some people wouldn't *really* mind *too* much if I engaged in; a little shame here, a little self-loathing there, a lot of diet talk and attempts at body change are the exact behaviors my mom engages in, but since she's disabled with muscular dystrophy, they fall all over themselves to assure her that's misplaced angst. They are the same people that would call my body shape a disease and want me to make those changes, but since her disease is different, by all means she should show herself compassion. Wasting disease = compassion; fat disease = hate the weight off.

The fact that I don't try to change my body but my mother does, that I'm healthy and my mom is not—that's a whole big bag of unfair. The further fact that she can't see how self-compassion, self-care, and self-love have changed my life for the better and won't engage in it herself, that's simply a cruel truth.

I'm going to continue to talk to my mom, the person who thinks I'm wrong, that my body is wrong, and the fact that I can and do love it is wrong. I'm going to try to get her to learn to love the body that's been on her journey with her, no matter what state it's in now, because if I don't, nobody else will.

And then there are the not-so-subtle shifts in her relationships with male friends and coworkers. One former colleague, a married man about ten years older, has completely changed the way he approaches her. Before, their relationship was collegial but not close. "Now he shimmies up to me, wanting to gossip and have lunch," she says. "This is now how he wants to be my friend because he thinks I'm more attractive. Honestly, I prefer the way he treated me when I was fat, because it was more authentic about who I am."

IN A CULTURE where body-snarking is practically an Olympic sport, I'd be shocked to find anyone who hasn't fielded some of it from time to time. You don't have to be obese or even significantly overweight, either, at least if you're a woman, as Rebecca Puhl's 2008 research on weight discrimination showed.[18]

Even if you haven't directly been called names, denied airplane seats, or humiliated because of your weight, you've likely worried about other people's perceptions of your body. The fear of getting fat starts early and lasts a lifetime; nearly half of those who took one now famous online survey said they'd give up a year of their lives rather than be obese. A third said they'd rather be divorced than fat, and a quarter chose infertility over overweight.[19]

That fear and prejudice play a huge role in driving our obsession with getting and staying thin. Joseph Majdan, sixty-five, is a cardiologist in Philadelphia who has gone around the weight-loss yo-yo too many times to count. He's lost the same hundred pounds on Optifast, Medifast, Weight Watchers, Jenny Craig—you name it, he's tried it. But each time he's regained the weight. "Really, the obese patient knows how to lose weight," he says. "But how to keep it off? There is no pathway to that."

Fat-shaming has driven Majdan to lose weight (and, ultimately, to regain it) again and again. Most of that shaming has come from medical colleagues. In medical school, a doctor approached him in the cafeteria line one afternoon and said loudly, "You know you should watch what you eat. Don't you see yourself?" During Majdan's third-year medicine clerkship, the attending physician who was teaching the group regularly marched the whole team up nine flights of steps on humid summer days in Philadelphia, announcing, "One of you has to lose weight." At an interview, a cardiologist directed him to choose a different seat because he didn't want to have to buy a new chair. Other doctors told his friends and colleagues they would never refer patients to Majdan because of his size. Another cardiologist stopped him on the street one day to tell Majdan he looked disgusting, and asked, "Don't you feel any shame?"

"When a person has recurrent cancer, the physician is so empathetic," says Majdan. "But when a person regains weight, there's disgust. And that is morally, professionally abhorrent and wrong."[20]

I've talked with Majdan several times over the course of a few years. When I first interviewed him, he'd lost about a hundred pounds and was maintaining his lower weight with a program of strenuous daily exercise (biking twenty miles and rowing on the Schuylkill River) and eating more or less the same restrictive menu every day: egg whites, fish, Greek yogurt, vegetables, salad (no dressing), sugar-free Jell-O, and one piece of fruit. When I commented that his routine sounded an awful lot like what I'd observed in people with eating disorders, he quickly agreed. "But this is what I have to do to keep the weight off," he said. For him, the trade-off was worth it.

Two years later, he'd regained half the weight and was caught up again in the cycle of shame and self-loathing. This time, though, he was outspoken about the bigger picture. "Where in the Constitution or Declaration of Independence does it say all men are created equal except obese people?" he asks. "Society makes you think of yourself as a second-class, third-class, twentieth-class citizen when you're overweight or obese."

And that's one of the issues that causes so many of us so much pain and anguish over our bodies: what we know about our own lives, our own struggles with weight, and our own behaviors inevitably bumps up against what society "knows," or at least insists is true. To be "overweight" or obese here and now is to feel shame and despair and all the frustration of being trapped in a situation you probably can't change. It's to feel stuck where being heavier-than—whether it's by 5 pounds or 105—makes you feel less than, and your identity depends on whether your collarbones protrude or your butt fits in an airplane seat.

So I'm delighted that people are starting to talk about weight in a different way. That they're outing weight-based prejudice and pushing back on the narrow cultural body norms of the day. A change is beginning, I think, and the next big question we face is what that change will look like and how we can help it along.

Chapter 7

Now What?

"Tell me, what is it you plan to do with your one wild and precious life?"

—Mary Oliver, "The Summer Day"

Last June, a Senate subcommittee led by Missouri Senator Claire McCaskill held a hearing on the often deceptive advertising of weight-loss products and gimmicks. Its star witness was the not so great but still powerful Dr. Mehmet Oz, a Harvard-trained cardiothoracic surgeon with a huge TV following who got his start on *The Oprah Winfrey Show*. McCaskill took Oz to task for his claims about a number of diet supplements, which he touted on air and in print as "miracle cures" that would "bust your body fat for good"—unproven and untested supplements like green coffee bean extract, raspberry ketone, and garcinia cambogia.

"I get that you do a lot of good on your show," said McCaskill. "I understand that you give a lot of great information about health in a way that's easily understandable. You're very talented, you're obviously very bright, and you've been trained in science-based medicine. I don't get why you need to say this stuff when you know it's not true. The scientific community is almost monolithic against you in terms of the efficacy of the three products you called 'miracles.'"

Oz's response was telling. "My job, I feel, on the show is to be a cheerleader for the audience," he said to the committee. "And when they don't think they have hope, when they don't think they can make it happen, I want to look, and I do look everywhere, including in alternative healing traditions, for any evidence that might be supportive to them."[1]

What Oz was really saying was that people's longing for weight loss is so desperately important to them, so relatable, so *understandable,* that it's OK to sell them questionable supplements because it gives them hope. He was saying that being overweight or obese is such a terrible fate that it's OK to put lives at risk just so people don't fall into a sinkhole of despair and give up on ever being thin. It's OK to encourage people in the folly of thin-at-any-cost because, hey, there's a one-in-a-million chance they might pop some green coffee bean extract and "burn fat fast," as Oz said.

It's a perfectly absurd conclusion that grows directly from the perfectly absurd situation we find ourselves in when it comes to weight. As a doctor (and reputedly a good one, at least at some point), Oz has to be aware of the long list of weight-loss drugs and supplements known to cause serious side effects or death: fen-phen, sibutramine, rimonabant, ephedra, kava kava, and a slew of others. He's got to know that there is no magic pill, no fat-burning compound that (a) works and (b) does more good than harm. His real crime, then, is ignoring reality and continuing to act as though being thin is so crucial that it's worth trying anything to achieve it.

In researching and writing this book, I've had many, many moments of extreme cognitive dissonance, jolts of realizing what a ridiculous and pointless and dangerous cycle we're caught up in. I had one of them not long ago, reading an editorial in a medical journal that bemoaned the rise of severe obesity among young people and called for new and "serious treatments," including more diet drugs and more bariatric surgeries for children and teenagers.[2] Nothing new there; I've read such opinions before. The sentence that made me want to bang my head on the desk was this one: "The good news is that healthy lifestyle changes, when implemented during childhood, appear to be relatively effective in reducing adiposity."[3]

I had to read this several times before its absolute ludicrousness sank in. These physicians are advocating for "healthy lifestyle changes" (which isn't defined, so could mean almost anything) just to make kids lose weight. But isn't the whole *point* here making kids *healthier*? We've become uber focused on weight as a proxy for health, what doctors call an endpoint or surrogate, a kind of marker for other conditions. Wouldn't it be more useful to focus instead on the actual goal of better health for kids, teens, and adults? Why are we still talking about weight as if it was the only thing that mattered? (And how do we keep ignoring the fact that only 5 percent of people at most maintain weight loss over time, that we *actually don't know how* to make people lose weight over the long term?)

We'd do better for ourselves and our children if, instead of pushing diets and surgeries and medications, we looked at real-world strategies for eating more fruits and vegetables, getting enough sleep, dancing and playing sports, and other joyful physical activities. And especially if we supported those things for everyone, no matter what they weighed.

This is the big disconnect at the heart of our conversations about weight and health. Michelle Obama's Let's Move! campaign, for instance, includes some smart, constructive recommendations: starting school and community gardens, calling out food marketing to kids, getting rid of food deserts, bringing back recess. These excellent and much needed ideas could go a long way toward making all Americans healthier.

The trouble is, the campaign has been framed exclusively around weight loss. Obama famously promised to "solve the challenge of childhood obesity within a generation," and that's the fundamental goal of her campaign. The Let's Move! website is full of statistics about childhood obesity, and its components are all offered in the context of making kids thinner. The implication is that if they're thinner, they'll be healthier, which we know isn't necessarily true. Kids and families who do make changes but don't lose weight will likely feel like they've failed, because the only yardstick available is weight loss. Obama's campaign uses weight as a proxy for health, and so falls into the same diet-and-exercise traps as every other weight-loss program, no matter how well disguised or well intentioned. And that's a missed opportunity, not just for the First Lady but for all of us.[4]

So the question is, given everything we've come to know about how and why we struggle and obsess and despair over weight, how do we move forward? How do we begin to broaden the conversation, bring in other kinds of information, and inspire the kind of social change around weight that will promote health and well-being rather than destroy it?

The good news is that people have been moving in this direction for the last fifty years or so, singly, in small groups, around the country and overseas. And it's taken a while, but there's beginning to be some momentum around the idea of taking the emphasis off weight.

One early pioneer in this effort is a former engineer named Bill Fabrey, who was furious at the kinds of prejudice his wife, a fat woman, confronted every day. In 1969, Fabrey helped found the National Association to Aid Fat Americans (NAAFA), now known as the National Association to Advance Fat Acceptance, with a focus on ending size discrimination.

Another pioneer is dietitian and social worker Ellyn Satter, who for years gave her clients the standard nutritional advice of the day: watch what you eat, control your portions, count calories. At some point it began to dawn on her that her advice and guidance wasn't making the people she treated thinner, healthier, or happier. On the contrary: demonizing whole categories of food, trying to undereat, and relentlessly worrying and feeling guilty about what and how much to eat pushed people into a pattern of restricting/overeating, and taught them not to trust their own appetites.

Satter began developing a different approach. She'd observed, for example, that babies instinctively knew how to eat. A baby who's had enough will turn his head and press his lips together. He *knows* when he's done, and he'll stop eating, unless parents or caregivers consistently overrule him, forcing him to eat more than he wants or withholding food when he's hungry. Then he learns not to trust his own feelings around food, and begins to look outside himself to know when to eat, what to eat, and how much.

That's exactly what had happened to many of her clients, Satter realized. Those dysfunctional patterns had been set up early and were still shaping the ways her clients handled the primal act of feeding themselves. The best way to help them, she decided, was to support them as they repaired their relationships with food, eating, and their own bodies.

She called this new model competent eating, and outlined its four basic components: having a positive attitude around eating and food; being tuned in to internal cues of hunger and fullness; being able to eat a variety of foods; and trusting yourself to manage food well. Every one of these elements stood in sharp contrast to the advice she'd been doling out for years.

Satter's competent eating is all about *providing* yourself with food rather than *depriving* yourself. It doesn't classify foods as "good" or "bad" but focuses instead on the idea of feeding yourself a range of delicious foods—some of which will be more nutritious than others—in a structured, organized series of meals and snacks throughout the day. It gives people permission to honor their appetites, being aware of when they're hungry, what they're hungry for, and when they're satisfied.

More than that, it supports the idea that there's joy in eating. Remember the mother who brought her baby to Satter, embarrassed and worried because the girl loved eating so much she would moan with pleasure? While most of us would probably avoid moaning audibly at the table (at least when we're eating with other people), Satter believes we not only can give ourselves permission to enjoy food but that we should. That it's a necessary part of learning to take care of yourself with food. Because if you're not enjoying what you eat, you're consuming it out of duty or responsibility or to deprive yourself of pleasure. And that's a very different process than eating to sustain and nourish yourself.

Competent eating makes sense on a lot of levels. Research has shown that competent eaters have lower blood pressure, blood sugar, triglycerides, and overall cholesterol, (and, yes, BMI) than those who are constantly dieting and weight cycling.[5] And there are psychological benefits, too. People who become competent eaters can let go of a lot of food-related angst. I know this from personal experience, because Satter was the therapist who asked me the fateful question years ago and who taught me the principles of competent eating.

Like many women who've dieted on and off for years, I was scared to stop counting Weight Watchers points or calories or fat grams or whatever I was counting at any given moment, afraid that if I stopped restraining myself, my hunger would be insatiable. I had to learn to trust my own appetite, and man, was that scary. I mean, if there were no rules, what would stop me from just eating and eating and eating until I weighed five hundred pounds? How would I know when to stop eating the foods I loved if there was no one to tell me to stop?

I was not so different from my students now, who are so invested in disordered eating that they have no idea what "normal eating" means. Many of us don't. Here's Satter's definition, which I find immensely helpful:

> Normal eating is going to the table hungry and eating until you are satisfied. It is being able to choose food you like and eat it and truly get enough of it—not just stop eating because you think you should. Normal eating is being able

to give some thought to your food selection so you get nutritious food, but not being so wary and restrictive that you miss out on enjoyable food. Normal eating is giving yourself permission to eat sometimes because you are happy, sad, or bored, or just because it feels good. Normal eating is mostly three meals a day, or four or five, or it can be choosing to munch along the way. It is leaving some cookies on the plate because you know you can have some again tomorrow, or it is eating more now because they taste so wonderful. Normal eating is overeating at times, feeling stuffed and uncomfortable. And it can be undereating at times and wishing you had more. Normal eating is trusting your body to make up for your mistakes in eating. Normal eating takes up some of your time and attention, but keeps its place as only one important area of your life. In short, normal eating is flexible. It varies in response to your hunger, your schedule, your proximity to food and your feelings.[6]

I had to essentially learn how to feed myself again. For one thing, I had to figure what I actually liked and didn't like. I was so used to automatically avoiding or bingeing on "bad" foods like cheese and chocolate and pasta, I had no idea whether I actually *wanted* to eat them. For another, I didn't know how to tell when I was hungry and when I was full. That sounds ridiculous, I know, and before I began the process I would have said of course I know what I like to eat and what I don't, and of course I know when I'm full. But I didn't. The truth was, I was more ignorant than even the newest newborn. I had to completely reboot my relationship with food and figure out how to eat all over again.

Intuitive Eating

Stacey, fifty-three, is a therapist who treats eating disorders and body image problems in Wisconsin.

My mom was always dieting, and my maternal grandmother was a die-hard dieter as well. All the women on that side of the family were dieters. My sister and I took after our mom, who was short and pear-shaped. I have never been severely obese, but I had a belly as a little kid and have always had bigger thighs and hips.

I started dieting in early adolescence, and I also struggled with some binge eating, because of the long dieting. Even when I would lose weight, I would still be preoccupied with my thighs. I was convinced they were the cause of every bad thing that ever happened to me.

After college I worked for an eating-disorder therapist doing research and working on the unit at the hospital. All of us who worked for him used to go to these breakfasts, and one day my colleagues looked at me and said, "What are you using margarine for?" They introduced me to the works of Geneen Roth, who wrote *Breaking Free from Emotional Eating*. I started working on intuitive eating, literally doing what she wrote in the book, eating foods I used to overeat because they weren't allowed in the house or we weren't supposed to be eating them. One day it was cookies, one day it was peanut butter. It didn't take long, about a week maybe, before I was like, Oh, OK, I get it now.

When you really listen, your body tells you what it needs. So it's all about paying attention, and it's amazing. For instance, I was eating some potato chips yesterday and suddenly I was like, I'm done with these. It's still a wonder to me that I can stop eating potato chips. It was the most mind-blowing thing! But I'm still not perfect at intuitive eating. Old habits die hard.

→

→

When you're a dieter and you lose weight, you feel confident but fragile. At any minute you could gain that weight back. For years I had four or five different size clothes in my closet. Now I've been a size 16 for the past ten years. To wear the same clothes, season after season, is wonderful. Never in my life would I think I'd be happy at this size, but I feel so free and confident.

The last time my mother commented on my weight was about seven years ago. She said, "You know, honey, it wouldn't hurt to lose a few pounds." And I ripped her a new one. I was like, "I couldn't ever do that again, and I wouldn't even know how to do that again." No one walks away from conversations like that feeling good, even women who are on the "good" end, who have dieted and lost weight. They still have that fragile feeling. It's such a negative way women relate to each other. Trying to fit in to this culture on that level is really very painful.

The process of reconnecting with an internal sense of appetite is a huge part of moving the needle on weight and health. "Many people have been taught the diet behaviors and thought distortions, and are unaware now of the hard-wired appetite and satiety cues they were almost certainly born with," says Deb Burgard, a psychologist in Los Altos, California, who treats people across the weight and eating spectrum.[7] "They are innocently and with increasing desperation trying to use cognitive means to regulate their eating 24/7, and cognitive means are lousy tools for this project." In other words, we turn to diet books and programs and manuals, looking for structures and plans to tell us what to eat, how much to eat, and when to eat it. But like Dorothy in the land of Oz, the answers we long for don't exist in the outside world but are already within us; we just don't know it yet.

Burgard is one of a growing number of activists and advocates who are challenging the weight-loss paradigm in all sorts of ways, including blogging, writing, speaking, belly-dancing (yes, belly-dancing), and "fatshion." Marilyn Wann, whose 1998 book *Fat!So?* is the so-called fat acceptance movement's de facto manifesto, is another, along with Ragen Chastain, Kate Harding, Marianne Kirby, Linda Bacon, and many more. Social media can often function like a petri dish bubbling over with toxic bacteria, spreading its poison far and wide. But in this case it's actually been a force for good. Platforms like Tumblr have become known as supportive fat-positive spaces where people can connect with and encourage one another.

Satter's concept of competent eating is similar to intuitive eating, a term coined in the mid-1990s[8] by Evelyn Tribole, a dietitian in Newport Beach, California, and Elyse Resch, a dietitian and therapist in Beverly Hills. As the name suggests, intuitive eating encourages people to honor their appetites, reject dieting, respect their bodies, and pursue healthy behaviors regardless of weight. To eat intuitively, in tune with their own senses and feelings, rather than according to an external plan.

Intuitive eating is, in turn, linked to a larger movement called Health at Every Size, or HAES (pronounced hays), which grew organically from many of the ideas forged in the 1980s and 1990s. Nutrition professor and researcher Linda Bacon literally wrote the book on HAES, publishing *Health at Every Size: The Surprising Truth About Your Weight* in 2008.

In many ways, HAES is the social justice movement Philadelphia cardiologist Joseph Majdan wished for. It emphasizes process—the experience of living a joyful and healthy life at any weight—rather than outcome, that is, a particular number on the scale. One of its tenets is that people naturally come in many shapes and sizes rather than in one narrowly defined, culturally approved package. Another is that no matter what people's body type or size, they can incorporate behaviors into their lives that foster health, eating well, and exercising with pleasure rather than focusing on weight or weight loss.

Critics like Tam Fry, who made the famous "black forest gateaux" crack about Katherine Flegal's 2013 study, deride HAES as a license to sit on the couch and eat bon-bons all day. They say it promotes obesity and unhealthy "lifestyles." Advocates say nothing could be further from the truth. HAES, they explain, is actually *more* focused on health because it's not chasing the red herring of weight loss. "The traditional dieting, weight-loss paradigm blinds us from being able to look at health directly, because we're so stuck on the fact that the only way to mediate it is through weight," explains Bacon. In fact, the US Department of Agriculture, one of the most conservative government agencies in existence, endorsed HAES after a two-year study found it superior to more traditional approaches on pretty much every score.[9]

Bacon and others describe HAES as "weight-neutral." If people pursue health without focusing on weight, they may (a) gain weight, (b) lose weight, or (c) stay the same as their bodies find a set point that's comfortable and sustainable. "For some people, weight is a symbol of something going wrong in their bodies. For some, it's just about natural diversity," explains Bacon. "So it's important that we separate behaviors from weight, because we also know fat is not always a sign of disease or bad behavior. Studies show there are many metabolically healthy fat people living long, healthy lives. There may be a smaller percentage of them than in the normal-weight category, but it shows you *can* be fat and healthy and fit."

Robin Flamm, forty-nine, from Portland, Oregon, found her way to HAES two years ago after a lifetime of dieting. "If anybody asked me 'What do you want most in your life?' I'd say 'To be thin.' Besides having a family," she says. She'd done practically every diet plan in existence—Weight Watchers over and over, the Paleo Diet, Overeaters Anonymous, even Medifast. Every weight-loss plan she tried worked—for a while. She'd lose thirty pounds and gain back thirty-five, lose thirty-five and regain forty. Mentally she was just as single-minded, just as committed, the tenth time as she was the first. But physically the pounds came off more slowly each time. It was as if her body was fighting to hang on to every ounce.

Flamm convinced herself she'd been lazy; she just had to work harder, walk faster, eat less, keep at it. And she tried, she really did, in between full-time parenting and doing advocacy work for a national nonprofit. When stomach pains and rising liver enzymes sent her to a gastrointestinal specialist, he told her to lose twenty pounds and come back in a month. On her way out of the office he called, condescendingly, "Just keep your mouth shut!"

At first she took his comment as a wake-up call, an inspiration to try harder, find a new program or approach. But the more she thought about it, the more she realized she didn't *need* a wake-up call; she'd been "awake" since middle school, and what had it gotten her? More doctors who attributed every health problem that popped up to her weight, who didn't believe her when she described what she was eating and how much she was exercising. More pressure to eat less and work out more. "I thought, wait, how many times did I set my mind to losing weight?" she says now. "I've always wanted to be thin. I've been obsessed with it my whole life."

Instead of going back to the doctor she wrote him a letter, explaining how she felt about the way he'd spoken to her. That was satisfying, but it left her in a familiar dilemma. She still blamed herself, really, for the fact that after all this longing and effort and anguish she wasn't thin. She knew she'd internalized the message she got from doctors, nurses, magazines, movies, friends: being fat is a question of personal responsibility. But she couldn't seem to shake it off.

By the time she worked up the courage to see a therapist at Being Nourished, a center in Portland run by two therapists who practice HAES, she was desperate for a change. Even so, the thought of putting away her scale and getting rid of her calorie-counting app terrified her. She stuck with it, though, using the same determination that had seen her through so many diets and exercise regimens. And slowly, she started to relax. She saw her therapist weekly and started taking yoga classes because she liked the way they made her feel.

But when her clothes started to feel a little tighter, she panicked. Her first impulse was to bolt back to the familiarity of Weight Watchers. Instead, she asked herself if she was eating mindfully, if she was exercising in a way that gave her pleasure, if she, maybe, needed to buy new clothes. "It's really hard to let go of results," she says. "It's like free falling. And even though there's no safety net ever, really, this time it's *knowing* there's no safety net."

When Robin Flamm talked about giving up the safety net, what she really meant was giving up the fantasy of being thin.

How I Started to Learn to Love My Body

Dawn, forty-five, is a therapist in Columbus, Ohio.

My mom, who's five eight, weighed 148 pounds the day she gave birth to my brother. My dad, on the other hand, is built like Lou Grant. Guess who I take after? I quickly internalized the message that something was wrong with my body—wrong with me—although I thought I'd hit the teen years and get long and leggy like my mother.

My mom was strict about what food we could eat and what we couldn't. Part of this was about money and part of it was about staying thin. When my sister would reach for seconds my mom would say, "Why don't you just slap that directly on your ass?" But it was my dad who was constantly on a diet (the Mayo Clinic Diet was xeroxed and posted on our fridge).

As a young adult, I remember sitting behind a woman at a conference. I liked her style—kind of funky, messy, short hair and no makeup—and I liked the smart questions she asked during the presentation. We got to talking and she seemed very attractive to me, very charismatic. After we became friends I realized that she felt she was too fat. The only thing I'd noticed when we met was that she was attractive, not that she didn't fit a particular mold of attractive.

That's when I realized that perhaps people saw *me* and not what I perceived as lacking about my appearance. Or if they did notice how I was fat and stocky and built like a linebacker (so said one of my high school boyfriends), maybe it didn't matter because they also saw *me*, and I felt I was pretty likeable or at least interesting. I thought, "What if I just lived as if I knew this was true?" and I started working toward that. That was nineteen years ago, and I haven't totally nailed it, but today I am more like my attractive, charismatic friend (with far less negative body talk) than the insecure bundle of nerves I was when I met her.

This growth and love and acceptance thing—it's an ongoing negotiation, and I imagine that's true for all of us.

Letting go of the idea that someday, something would happen, and she would lose the weight forever, that she'd suddenly become a 5 percenter, one of the rare few who could lose weight and keep it off. But it's intensely, incredibly hard to buck the mainstream on an issue that holds so much power over our lives. At the end of the day, we all have to come to terms with these issues in our own way and for ourselves.

The last time Flamm and I talked, she told me a story that illustrates how far she's come: one day she felt a craving for a hamburger, a food she wouldn't usually have eaten. But she ordered a hamburger and fries for lunch that day, and ate it. She expected her inner critic to let loose, pile on the recriminations, blitz her with guilt, send her into a spiral of anxiety and self-loathing. Instead, nothing happened. No more cravings, no obsessing over calories, no guilt or anxiety. No cycle of restricting and bingeing, depriving herself and overcompensating for feeling deprived. No "feeling fat" and staying away from exercise. She ate a hamburger and fries and that was that. And that, she says, was an incredible gift, one that made her wish more people would take the time to understand what HAES is and isn't.

One person who clearly doesn't understand is Amanda Sainsbury-Salis, a researcher at the Boden Institute of Obesity, Nutrition, Exercise & Eating Disorders in Sydney, Australia. Last year, Sainsbury-Salis published a commentary calling for an "urgent rethink" of HAES, arguing that it's impossible to be both fat and healthy and that for anyone who's overweight or obese, things will inevitably go badly wrong, healthwise. She characterized HAES as the idea that "people can have health at every size," which is inaccurate, since HAES is about the pursuit of health and the idea that people can incorporate healthy behaviors into their lives no matter how much they weigh.

Sainsbury-Salis opened her commentary with a reference to how her grandmother used to warn her not to make an ugly face because it might freeze that way, adding, "I say 'Don't eat an ugly diet or let yourself stay fat, because if the wind changes you may become stuck with permanent obesity.'" The dubious literary quality of this analogy makes it hard to take it seriously (if the wind changes?), and so do its underlying assumptions. She conflates eating "an ugly diet"—presumably Cheetos, McDonald's, and ice cream at every meal—with permanent obesity, though thin people are just as likely to eat junk food and processed food as fat people. She also suggests that "staying fat" is a mistake and implies that HAES encourages such risky behavior. How exactly does Sainsbury-Salis propose that people avoid "staying fat"? Diets, exercise, and medications don't work for most people; surgery is dangerous, expensive, irreversible, and doesn't work for at least half the people who undergo it. As we've already seen, people who keep doggedly chasing weight loss usually wind up weight cycling, which may be even worse for health than "staying fat." Oh, and they usually wind up fatter than when they started.

Reading commentaries like this makes me feel like I'm right back inside that M. C. Escher drawing. Sainsbury-Salis describes herself as a neuroscientist who studies diet, appetite, and body weight; surely she's seen all the research. Yet she and other scientists talk about these issues as if they live on another planet where different rules apply. For instance, she acknowledges the well-supported fact that overweight and obese people can make "substantial health gains" without changing their weight at all, which is one of the foundations of HAES. But in the very next paragraph, she insists it's still not healthy to have a BMI outside certain parameters, and concludes "even for obese people who are metabolically healthy, it is only a question of time before a variety of issues raise their heads." As an example, she offers the correlation between higher BMI and greater risk of developing knee arthritis, which she attributes to "the mechanical effects of excess weight and the resultant gait abnormalities, combined with systemic inflammation."[10]

I laughed out loud when I read this, mostly because Sainsbury-Salis' "urgent rethink" turns out to consist of the same arguments that have been made for the last fifty years. They're no more accurate or relevant now than they were before. And she offers no new evidence or strategies for making people thinner in the long term and in the real world. As psychologist Deb Burgard puts it, "People who have maintained a weight loss, who eat flexibly, who are truly at peace with food—they're like unicorns."

Which is why Linda Bacon and others see HAES as not just a health movement but a social justice movement, one that speaks to psychological well-being as much as physical health. "We can't tell people you're wrong, you're bad, we want to make you different," says Bacon. "That's what the whole model of obesity treatment is based on—something being wrong."

Bacon told me about a sixteen-year-old girl who interviewed her for a school project and broke down crying on the phone. The girl's school was holding an anti-obesity campaign, and she was being bullied at lunch for her food choices, even when she ate exactly what the thinner kids were eating. That kind of tunnel vision about food and weight, said Bacon, not only gives the thin kids permission to think there's something wrong with the fat kids, maybe even to bully them; it also absolves them from worrying about their own health. As long as they're thin, they think, they're healthy. Only now we know that's not true.

YEARS AFTER THAT day in the therapist's office, I still *think* I should weigh less than I do, though I no longer care about being thin enough to fit into the appropriate BMI category (especially since I've gotten shorter in the last few years, which means I'd have to hit an even lower weight to have a "normal" BMI). I've been there and done that and it's not a happy or sustainable place for me. I still think I might *look* better if I weighed, say, fifteen pounds less than I do; though I no longer see being thin as the only way to be beautiful, it's hard for me to see my own fleshy body as attractive. I'm working on it. I choose instead to focus on what I do rather than what I weigh.

I rarely waste time and energy and creativity flailing and angsting over my body the way I did in my teens and twenties and thirties. I don't wallow in shame or despair. I don't obsess about food or my body. I don't want to spend my life caught in that cycle of self-loathing. I *can't,* I won't live that way anymore. How many mornings was I late for work because I couldn't find an outfit that magically changed the way I felt about my body? How many evenings did I stand in the middle of a grocery-store aisle, paralyzed with fear and indecision? It's not just the time I regret; it's the loss of who I might have been if I wasn't so consumed. It's who I might have loved, how I might have lived, what I might have accomplished. I might have been a force to be reckoned with. Instead, I spent way too much time weeping on my bedroom floor, surrounded by crumpled shirts and pants turned inside out.

Back then, self-care for me meant "making an effort," as my grandmother might have said, starving myself, jogging despite my bad knees, trying my best to fit my body, literally and metaphorically, into the image it was "supposed" to resemble. Now taking care of myself means what I *do* rather than what I look like. And over time I've figured out what I need to do to feel healthy and creative and, yes, joyful physically and emotionally. What I need to do will no doubt look different than what you need to do, but I'll tell you anyway in case it's useful:

- Some kind of physical exercise every day; a brisk stroll around the neighborhood works, but I also love cycling and hiking
- Making and eating foods I like, and letting myself enjoy them
- Being able to stop eating when I'm full
- Getting enough sleep
- Spending time with friends and family
- Taking medication for my depression and anxiety disorder; I resisted this for years, in part because the meds make me gain weight, but finally decided I wanted to live a wholly functional life, and this is what I need to do that

And, finally (and this has been the hardest of all)
- Letting go of self-loathing

Notice I'm not saying "love myself." While that concept and that phrasing might work for others, it's always seemed irrelevant to me personally. I find it more helpful to think "inhabit myself," meaning stay in my body, know that it's my body, and appreciate what it does. And, yes, actively deflect those self-loathing thoughts when they intrude, as they do.

It's a tough process for anyone who's spent a long time constructing an identity around a particular vision of herself, even if it's a negative view. Or maybe *because* it's so negative. I think of that quote by spiritual writer Marianne Williamson: "Our deepest fear is not that we are inadequate. Our deepest fear is that we are powerful beyond measure. It is our light, not our darkness, that most frightens us." Given the culture we live in, the pressures that come at us from so many directions to feel anxious, insecure, less than, especially when it comes to our bodies, no wonder we sometimes cling to our own feelings of inadequacy.

It gets easier, though. It really does. One of the most useful teaching tools I've found on this issue is Harvard's Project Implicit test on weight bias (implicit.harvard.edu), which measures how closely a person's underlying feelings about weight align with the culture's norms. I'm sure if I'd taken the test fifteen years ago, I would have gotten the same results my students do when I have them take it: a strong preference for thinness. (They're always upset by their results, which leads to some fruitful classroom conversations.) When I take the test now, it shows a moderate preference for fatness. Given how overwhelmingly our culture prefers thinness, I consider that major progress.

I regret feeling the way I did about myself for so many years, though regret isn't exactly the right word. Regret implies sorrow, and sure, I feel sorry about it. But mostly I feel mad—at the culture I grew up in, at myself for being susceptible to it, at the fact that it's 2014 and we're *still dealing with this* and it's so much worse than it was when I was a girl. I'm furious that so many children and women and men are suffering for no good reason.

Learning to trust myself, my body, my appetite, and my feelings has been one of the most empowering experiences of my life. Yet even as I write this, I can imagine what the Walter Willetts and Daniel Callahans and Tam Frys of the world would say—something along the lines of "Most Americans already feel *too* empowered around food/appetite/body image." As one writer suggested in an online opinion piece for *Philadelphia* magazine, "The stigma once rightly associated with obesity is disappearing as quickly as fat is accumulating. How do we get to the bottom of this problem? For starters, shame. Because no matter what else is attempted, if shame is not the cornerstone of the solution, the situation will never improve."[11] Anyone who thinks we don't do enough shaming of fat people should dip into the comments section for that story.

This attitude comes from and perpetuates the kind of assumptions we know aren't true. And it's precisely the type of rhetoric that got us into this dysfunctional relationship with food in the first place, that's left us eating chaotically, not competently. Articles and attitudes like this have helped make us fatter and less healthy in every way.

SO IT SEEMS to me we're at a crossroads. This is a moment, as people say, meaning an opportunity to stop and take stock and make choices. The conversation that's been taking place in the background and on the fringes and out of the mainstream—about competent eating and intuitive eating and HAES and health rather than weight—is slowly, tentatively becoming a little more

Eating Well for Health

Marsha, sixty-five, is a dietitian who runs a "non-diet" center in Vermont.

I developed body image issues very young. I'm tall, five eight, and the rest of my family was very thin, so I was always singled out for my weight. In my teens I started dieting and developed an eating disorder. It took me about ten years to overcome that.

In my midfifties I started getting really ill, with ailments ranging from severe fatigue to joint and muscle problems. Eventually I was diagnosed with fibromyalgia. I discovered I was gluten sensitive and had a lot of chronic inflammation going on in my body. I was hungry a lot, having cravings, and that was affecting my weight, too. I was probably twenty-five pounds heavier than my normal weight.

By really focusing on dealing with the chronic inflammation and gluten sensitivity, my weight normalized for my body, and there haven't been any ups or downs since then. My focus was to feel better, to get rid of the aches and pains. It wasn't intentional weight loss.

When I work with women now, we start out with gentle guidelines. So many of them are lost when it comes to being able to know how their body feels in response to eating different types of foods in different ways. We move people away from the "burn those calories because you ate that piece of cake" mind-set around physical activity. The other big thing is stress management, helping women and men recognize that body dissatisfaction is a huge source of stress in our lives. We help them figure out what they can do on a regular basis that's going to really help them feel well and stay feeling well.

Weight loss rarely takes people where they want to go. If they focus on health and how they feel, they find themselves in a much better place in the long run.

visible, thanks mostly to social media. Much of what I've covered in this book is still considered by many to be crackpot or self-serving or just plain wrong—fat people rationalizing why they can sit on that couch and eat those bon-bons all day. And the messages we get from the mainstream—the beauty industry, medical professionals, advertising, and media of all types—are so dominant, so loud, and so scary that it's hard to even consider questioning them. Clearly we are, as individuals and as a society, still under their spell. We've been drinking that Kool-Aid for a long time, and we're understandably nervous about putting down the glass.

No one's going to force us to, either. We can keep drinking from the same glass, keep running around that hamster wheel of self-loathing, keep teaching our children that while they'll never be good enough, thin enough, buff enough, healthy enough, pretty enough, they have a moral obligation to keep trying to live up to those unattainable ideals. We can keep right on teaching them what we've learned and internalized, and we can expect them to have all the same feelings we do about their bodies, their appetites, and their lives.

But we need to realize that staying with the status quo is no longer just a default position but a choice, and it's not the only one on the menu. We can also, for example, take a step away from the kind of either–or thinking that permeates our belief system around weight and health. We can make a mental paradigm shift away from the black-and-white perspective we've grown up with and take, instead, a broader view. A this-*and*-that perspective.

If each of us is willing to just consider the possibility that what we think we know about weight and health isn't as simplistic and clear-cut as we believe, we'd have the beginning of a truly constructive conversation. If we could become aware of how the rhetoric around weight and obesity has shaped the way we think, and challenge ourselves to imagine other truths and perspectives, we can potentially help create real and lasting change for ourselves and our children.

So what does that mean exactly? In the ideal world (you know, the one we don't live in), we wouldn't starve ourselves or spend four hours a day at the gym or crouch over a toilet or refuse to swim because we didn't want to wear a bathing suit. We wouldn't avoid mirrors. We wouldn't torture ourselves. Instead, we would each explore our own definition of health, based on our individual physical, psychological, and emotional needs. We'd acknowledge that health and weight are complicated issues, that they're not the same for everyone, and we'd be free to make our own choices about how to live and take care of ourselves. We'd be kind to ourselves and to one another.

On a more practical level, we would at least be open to hearing points of view beyond the mainstream. We'd be willing to think critically about weight and health; right now, our culture makes it nearly impossible to do that. We have to make the effort. It might not change what we do or how we behave, but I think regardless of outcome it's an important and even crucial step.

There are also some specific strategies that can help us grapple with the issues day to day. As I researched this book, especially the section on beauty standards, I kept thinking about the phenomenon of social comparison, our innate tendency to compare ourselves against others, first described by social psychologist Leon Festinger in the 1950s. According to Festinger, the more similar we are to others (or the more similar we *think* we are, which isn't always the same thing), the more likely we are to judge ourselves against them.[12]

We can compare ourselves to others in two basic ways. *Upward comparison,* where we judge ourselves against those we see as better than us, tends to make us feel more depressed, enraged, and worthless. *Downward comparison,* where we judge ourselves against those we see as worse off, makes us feel better about ourselves.[13] (This notion is closely related to, but not exactly the same as, the delightful concept of schadenfreude, or taking pleasure in others' misfortunes.)

When we look at pictures of impossibly thin models in magazines or online or in advertisements, we're basically engaging in upward comparison, judging ourselves against those we see as superior. Researchers at the University of South Florida-Tampa, who published a 2000 study on body image and social comparison, think it's important to broaden the field, so to speak.[14] For instance, they suggest, spend time in a public place people-watching. Unless you're standing on a Hollywood movie lot, you're bound to see a range of people who run the gamut of attractiveness and body type. Look at all kinds of shapes and sizes, not just the one kind we see most often in media and marketing. Think of it as resetting your inner beauty detector.

Interestingly, exercise can also help, though not in the way you might expect. In one 2012 study, women and men who were randomized to a group that exercised six times over two weeks felt better about their bodies afterward, even though their weight and fitness levels stayed the same. (A control group who read rather than exercised felt worse about their bodies at the end of the two weeks, though this may have had something to do with the fact that they read at the gym, where everyone else was exercising.)[15]

One survey of college freshwomen turned up a range of coping mechanisms for what researchers called "bad body image days." These included exercise, talking to friends and family, spending time alone, getting out and doing something, and self-acceptance.[16] Different strategies seem to help different people, so a little experimenting might be in order.

That's the challenge I want to leave you with: to think beyond the messages we're getting a thousand times a day. To question the conventional wisdom. You may wind up making the same exact choices in your life as you do now, but at the very least you'll be making those choices more consciously. Or you may wind up with an entirely different point of view, one that could help set you free from the painful and punishing rules we've been living by for so long.

NOTES

Introduction: How My Life Changed
with One Sentence

1. Body image issues are clearly on the rise for boys and men, but there are few statistics on the subject yet, maybe because men are far less open about such concerns than women.

2. Charlotte Cooper, "Headless Fatties," 2007, accessed on October 23, 2014, www.charlottecooper.net.

3. C. Y. Chang, D. S. Key, and J. Y. Chen, "Essential Fatty Acids and Human Brain," *Acta Neurologica Taiwanica* 18, no. 4 (2009): 231–241.

4. According to a 2008 survey done by *Self* magazine and the University of North Carolina at Chapel Hill. See www.med.unc.edu/www/newsarchive/2008/april/survey-finds-disordered-eating-behaviors-among-three-out-of-four-american-women.

5. According to an NPR story, "Skinny Isn't All That: Survey Finds Fewer American Women Are Dieting," aired January 7, 2013.

Chapter 1: Four Big Fat Lies
About Weight and Health

1. B. Chaix et al., "Food Environment and Socioeconomic Status Influence Obesity Rates in Seattle and Paris," *International Journal of Obesity* 38 (2014): 306–314; Susan Everson et al., "Epidemiological

Evidence for the Relation Between Socioeconomic Status and Depression, Obesity, and Diabetes," *Journal of Psychosomatic Research* 53 (2002): 891–895; Supriya Krishnan et al., "Socioeconomic Status and Incidence of Type 2 Diabetes: Results from the Black Women's Health Study," *American Journal of Epidemiology* 171 (2010): 564–570; Jessica Robbins et al., "Socioeconomic Status and Diagnosed Diabetes Incidence," *Diabetes Research and Clinical Practice* 68 (2005): 230–236; Mei Tang et al., "Gender-Related Differences in the Association Between Socioeconomic Status and Self-Reported Diabetes," *International Journal of Epidemiology* 32 (2003): 381–385; and Timothy Lee et al., "Socioeconomic Status and Incident Type 2 Diabetes Mellitus: Data from the Women's Health Study," *PLOS One*, 2011.

2. Duk-Hee Lee et al., "A Strong Dose-Response Relation Between Serum Concentrations of Persistent Organic Pollutants and Diabetes," *Cardiovascular and Metabolic Risk* 29 (2006): 1638–1644; and J. S. Lim et al., "Inverse Associations Between Long-Term Weight Change and Serum Concentrations of Persistent Organic Pollutants," *International Journal of Obesity* 35 (2011): 744–747. Also, environmentalist Sarah Howard, the national coordinator of The Collaborative on Health and the Environment's Diabetes-Obesity Spectrum Working Group, has created a website exploring links between diabetes and POPs at www.diabetesandenvironment.org.

3. Bruce Blumberg and Amanda Janesick, "Endocrine-Disrupting Chemicals and the Developmental Programming of Adipogenesis and Obesity," *Birth Defects Research* (Part C) 93 (2011): 34–50.

4. E. L. Dirinck et al., "Exposure to Persistent Organic Pollutants: Relationship with Abnormal Glucose Metabolism and Visceral Adiposity," *Diabetes Care* 37 (2014): 1951–1958.

5. *America's State of Mind Report*, 2011, http://apps.who.int/medicinedocs/documents/s19032en/s19032en.pdf.

6. Amresh Shrivastava and Megan Johnston, "Weight Gain in Psychiatric Treatment: Risks, Implications, and Strategies for Prevention and Management," *Mens Sana Monographs* 8 (2010): 53–68.

7. Marion Nestle, "Diet Wars," *Frontline,* first aired April 8, 2004.

8. Jotham Suez et al., "Artificial Sweeteners Induce Glucose Intolerance by Altering the Gut Microbiota," *Nature* 514 (September 2014): 181–186.

9. National Obesity Forum, "State of the Nation's Waistline Obesity in the UK: Analysis and Expectations," 2014.

10. Michael Stones, "'We Exaggerated Obesity Crisis': Pressure Group," Foodmanufacture.co.uk, January 20, 2014.

11. William Ernest Henley, "Invictus," from *Book of Verses* (1888), http://www.poetryfoundation.org/poem/182194.

12. J. A. Bell, M. Kivimaki, and M. Hammer, "Metabolically Healthy Obesity and Risk of Incident Type 2 Diabetes: A Meta-Analysis of Prospective Cohort Studies," *Obesity Reviews* 15, no. 6 (2014): 504–515.

13. Per the Mayo Clinic website, accessed October 23, 2014, www.mayoclinic.org/diseases-conditions/prediabetes/basics/treatment/con-20024420.

14. Attia's TEDMED talk on the subject is provocative and fascinating. See it at www.ted.com/talks/peter_attia_what_if_we_re_wrong_about_diabetes.

15. Eugenia Calle et al., "Body-Mass Index and Mortality in a Prospective Cohort of U.S. Adults," *New England Journal of Medicine* 341 (1999): 1097–1105.

16. Robbins et al., "Socioeconomic Status," 2004; Tang et al., "Gender-Related Differences," 2003; Lee et al., "Socioeconomic Status," 2011; Everson et al., "Epidemiological Evidence," 2002; and Krishnan et al., "Socioeconomic Status," 2010.

17. Michael D. Wirth et al., "Chronic Weight Dissatisfaction Predicts Type 2 Diabetes Risk: Aerobic Center Longitudinal Study," *American Psychological Association* 33 (2014): 912–919.

2: The Amazing! Seventeen-Day! Flat-Belly! Grain-Brain! Biggest Loser! Raw Food! Diet

1. Sadie Whitelocks, "Trendy Crash Diets This New Year Are Likely to Last Just 15 Days and Could End Up with Women Weighing

MORE," Mail Online, January 2, 2002, accessed October 24, 2014, www.dailymail.co.uk/femail/article-2081315/Trendy-crash-diets-New -Year-likely-just-15-days-end-women-weighing-MORE.html.

2. "100 Million Dieters, $20 Billion: The Weight-Loss Industry by the Numbers," ABC News, May 8, 2012.

3. According to statistics from the Eating Disorder Foundation of Denver, Colorado, www.eatingdisorderfoundation.org/EatingDisorders.htm.

4. "The U.S. Weight Loss Market: 2014 Status Report & Forecast," accessed October 24, 2014, www.marketresearch.com/Marketdata -Enterprises-Inc-v416/Weight-Loss-Status-Forecast-8016030/.

5. R. L. Corwin, N. M. Avena, and M. M. Boggiano, "Feeding and Reward: Perspectives from Three Rat Models of Binge Eating," *Physiology & Behaviour* 104 (2011): 87–97.

6. Traci Mann et al., "Medicare's Search for Effective Obesity Treatments: Diets Are Not the Answer," *American Psychologist* 62 (2007): 220–233; Dianne Neumark-Sztainer et al., "Obesity, Disordered Eating, and Eating Disorders in a Longitudinal Study of Adolescents: How Do Dieters Fare 5 Years Later?" *Journal of the American Dietetic Association* 106 (2006): 559–568; K. H. Pietiläinen et al., "Does Dieting Make You Fat? A Twin Study," *International Journal of Obesity* 36 (2012): 456–464.

7. Paul Ernsberger and Paul Haskew, "Health Implications of Obesity: An Alternative View," *Journal of Obesity and Weight Regulation* 6, no. 2 (1987): 55–137.

8. Marlene Cimons, "Five Diet Firms Charged with Deceptive Ads," *Los Angeles Times*, October 1, 1993.

9. Barbara Altman Bruno, "The HAES® Files: History of the Health at Every Size Movement—the Early 1990s," published on the Association for Size Diversity and Health blog, www.healthateverysizeblog .org/2013/07/16/the-haes-files-history-of-the-health-at-every-size-move ment-the-early-1990s/.

10. David M. Garner, "Ineffectiveness of Weight Loss and the Exaggeration of Health Risks Associated with Obesity," testimony before the Committee on Small Business Subcommittee on Regulation, Business Opportunities, and Energy, May 7, 1990.

11. David M. Garner and Susan C. Wooley, "Obesity Treatment: The High Cost of False Hope," *Journal of the American Dietetic Association* 91 (1991): 1248–1251.

12. K. H. Pietiläinen et al., "Does Dieting Make You Fat? A Twin Study," *International Journal of Obesity* 36 (2011): 456–464.

13. M. J. Müller, A. Bosy-Westphal, and S. B. Heymsfeld, "Is There Evidence for a Set Point That Regulates Human Body Weight?" *F1000 Medicine Reports* 2 (2010): 59.

14. Janet Tomiyama et al., "Low Calorie Dieting Increases Cortisol," *Psychosomatic Medicine* 72 (2010): 357–364.

15. Sendhil Mullainathan, "The Mental Strain of Making Do With Less," *New York Times,* September 21, 2013.

16. Janet Polivy, Julie Coleman, and C. Peter Herman, "The Effect of Deprivation on Food Cravings and Eating Behavior in Restrained and Unrestrained Eaters," *International Journal of Eating Disorders* 38, no. 4 (2005): 301–309.

17. Susmita Kaushik et al., "Autophagy in Hypothalamic AgRP Neurons Regulates Food Intake and Energy Balance," *Cell Metabolism* 14 (2011): 173–183.

18. Nancy Krebs et al., "Assessment of Child and Adolescent Overweight and Obesity," *Pediatrics* 120 (2007): S193–S228.

19. Paul Campos, "Childhood Shmobesity," *The New Republic*, February 11, 2010.

20. See www.cdc.gov/nchs/data/hestat/underweight_child_07_10 /underweight_child_07_10.htm for more details.

21. J. Norman and R. Reynolds, "The Consequences of Obesity and Excess Weight Gain in Pregnancy," *Proceedings of the Nutrition Society* 70 (2011): 450–456; and Matthew Gillman and David Ludwig, "How Early Should Obesity Prevention Start?" *New England Journal of Medicine* 369 (2013): 2173–2175.

22. Lindsey Murtagh and David S. Ludwig, "State Intervention in Life-Threatening Childhood Obesity," *JAMA* 306, no. 2 (2011): 206–207.

23. Mattias Öberg et al., "Worldwide Burden of Disease from Exposure to Second-Hand Smoke: A Retrospective Analysis of Data from 192 Countries," *The Lancet,* November 26, 2010.

24. Dianne Neumark-Sztainer et al., "Dieting and Disordered Eating Behaviors from Adolescence to Young Adulthood: Findings from a 10-Year Longitudinal Study," *Journal of the American Dietetic Association* 111 (2011): 1004–1011.

25. E. Enriquez, G. E. Duncan, and E. A. Schur, "Age at Dieting Onset, Body Mass Index, and Dieting Practices. A Twin Study," *Appetite* 71 (2013): 301–306.

26. Dianne Neumark-Sztainer, "Dieting and Unhealthy Weight Control Behaviors During Adolescence," *Journal of Adolescent Health* (2012): 80–86.

27. Dianne Neumark-Sztainer et al., "Obesity, Disordered Eating, and Eating Disorders in a Longitudinal Study of Adolescents: How Do Dieters Fare 5 Years Later?" *Journal of the American Dietetic Association* 106 (2006): 559–568.

28. Interview with Katie Loth, December 2013.

29. Lisa Belkin, "Dara-Lynn Weiss, Author of 'The Heavy,' Does Not Regret Putting her 7-Year-Old on a Diet," *Huffington Post*, January 15, 2013.

30. The campaign continues, however, at www.strong4life.com.

31. Daniel Callahan, "Obesity: Chasing an Elusive Epidemic," *Hastings Center Report*, 2013.

32. Leora Pinhas et al., "Trading Health for a Healthy Weight: The Uncharted Side of Healthy Weights Initiatives," *Eating Disorders* 21 (2013): 109–116; and Dianne Neumark-Sztainer, "Integrating Messages from the Eating Disorders Field into Obesity Prevention," *Adolescent Medicine* 23 (2012): 529–543.

33. You can read the full story in *Brave Girl Eating: A Family's Struggle with Anorexia* (New York: William Morrow, 2010).

34. Annemarie Olsen, Per Møller, and Helene Hausner, "Early Origins of Overeating: Early Habit Formation and Implications for Obesity in Later Life," *Current Obesity Reports* 2 (2013): 157–164.

35. M. L. Butryn and T. A. Wadden, "Treatment of Overweight in Children and Adolescents: Does Dieting Increase the Risk of Eating Disorders?" *International Journal of Eating Disorders* 37, no. 4 (2005): 285–293.

36. Comments made at the 2013 American Diabetes Association convention.

37. Per Wing's bio on the National Weight Control Registry page, www.nwcr.ws/people/Rena.htm.

38. Steven N. Blair et al., "Body Weight Change, All-Cause Mortality, and Cause-Specific Mortality in the Multiple Risk Factor Intervention Trial," *Annals of Internal Medicine* 119 (1993): 749–757; and Lauren Lissner et al., "Variability of Body Weight and Health Outcomes in the Framingham Population," *New England Journal of Medicine* 324 (1991): 1839–1844.

39. Emily K. Anderson et al., "Weight Cycling Increases T-cell Accumulation in Adipose Tissue and Impairs Systemic Glucose Tolerance," *Diabetes* 62, no. 9 (2013): 3180–3188; and Linda Nebeling et al., "Weight Cycling and Immunocompetence," *Journal of the American Dietetic Association* 104 (2004): 892–894.

40. Daniel P. Beavers et al., "Cardiometabolic Risk After Weight Loss and Subsequent Weight Regain in Overweight and Obese Postmenopausal Women," *Journal of Gerontology A Biol Sci Med Sci* 68 (2012): 691–698.

41. H. Yatsuya et al., "Association Between Weight Fluctuation and Fasting Insulin Concentration in Japanese Men," *International Journal of Obesity and Related Metabolic Disorders* 27 (2003): 478–483.

42. M. B. Olson et al., "Weight Cycling and High-Density Lipoprotein Cholesterol in Women: Evidence of an Adverse Effect: A Report from the NHLBI-Sponsored WISE Study," *Journal of the American College of Cardiology* 36 (2000): 1565–1571.

43. J.-P. Montani et al., "Weight Cycling During Growth and Beyond as a Risk Factor for Later Cardiovascular Diseases: The 'Repeated Overshoot' Theory," *International Journal of Obesity* 30 (2006): S58–S66.

44. Emanuele Cereda et al., "Weight Cycling Is Associated with Body Weight Excess and Abdominal Fat Accumulation: A Cross-Sectional Study," *Clinical Nutrition* 30 (2011): 718–723.

45. Taeko Kajioka et al., "Effects of Intentional Weight Cycling on Non-Obese Young Women," *Metabolism* 51, no. 2 (Feb 2002): 149–154.

46. Alison Field, Susan Malspeis, and Walter C. Willet, "Weight Cycling and Mortality Among Middle-Aged or Older Women," *JAMA Internal Medicine* 169 (2009): 881–886; and Victoria Stevens et al., "Weight Cycling and Mortality in a Large Prospective U.S. Study," *American Journal of Epidemiology* 175 (2012): 785–792.

47. Alison Field et al., "Weight Cycling and the Risk of Developing Type 2 Diabetes Among Adult Women in the United States," *Obesity Research* 12, no. 2 (2004): 267–274; Gary Foster, D. B. Sarwer, and T. A. Wadden, "Psychological Effects of Weight Cycling in Obese Persons: A Review and Research Agenda," *Obesity Research* 5 (1997): 474–488; and Lauren R. Simkin-Silverman et al., "Lifetime Weight Cycling and Psychological Health in Normal-Weight and Overweight Women," *International Journal of Eating Disorders* 24 (1998): 175–183.

48. Robyn L. Osborn et al., "Yo-Yo Dieting in African American Women: Weight Cycling and Health," *Ethnicity and Disease* 21 (2011): 274–280.

49. J. P. Foreyt et al., "Psychological Correlates of Weight Fluctuation," *International Journal of Eating Disorders* 17 (1995): 263–275.

50. C. A. Geissler, D. S. Miller, and M. Shah, "The Daily Metabolic Rate of the Post-Obese and the Lean," *American Journal of Clinical Nutrition* 45 (1987): 914–920.

51. Asheley C. Skinner, Michael J. Steiner, and Eliana M. Perrin, "Self-Reported Energy Intake by Age in Overweight and Healthy-Weight Children in NHANES, 2001–2008," *Pediatrics* 130 (2012): e936–e942.

Chapter 3: Good Food, Bad Food

1. Alisha Coleman-Jensen, Mark Nord, and Anita Singh, "Household Food Security in the United States in 2012," a report from the Economic Research Service of the US Department of Agriculture, September 2013.

2. Per the US Department of Agriculture's Economic Research Service, accessed October 24, 2014, www.ers.usda.gov/data-products/

food-expenditures.aspx#.U9WXlo1dVrg. I have seen lower estimates from other sources, but this one seems the most reliable.

3. Shan Guisinger, "Adapted to Flee Famine: Adding an Evolutionary Perspective on Anorexia Nervosa," *Psychological Review* 110, no. 4 (1993): 745–761.

4. R. M. Puhl, J. Luedicke, and J. A. Depierre, "Parental Concerns About Weight-Based Victimization in Youth," *Childhood Obesity* 9 (2013): 540–548.

5. Excerpts from the first edition of "Dietary Goals for the United States," February, 1977, www.zerodisease.com/archive/Dietary_Goals _For_The_United_States.pdf.

6. "Interview with Arthur Agatston," *Frontline*, January 7, 2004, www .pbs.org/wgbh/pages/frontline/shows/diet/interviews/agatston.html.

7. See www.choosemyplate.gov/food-groups/ for more information.

8. Jason Andrade et al., "Ancel Keys and the Lipid Hypothesis: From Early Breakthroughs to Current Management of Dyslipidemia," *British Columbia Medical Journal* 51, no 2 (2009): 66–72.

9. Nina Teicholz, *The Big Fat Surprise: Why Butter, Meat, and Cheese Belong in a Healthy Diet* (New York: Simon & Schuster, 2014).

10. "Diet Wars," *Frontline*, first aired April 2004.

11. Michael Gard and Jan Wright, *The Obesity Epidemic: Science, Morality, and Ideology* (Oxon: Routledge, 2005), 114–115; and Julie Guthman, *Weighing In: Obesity, Food Justice, and the Limits of Capitalism* (Berkeley and Los Angeles: University of California Press, 2011), 93–95.

12. M. F. Rolland-Cachera, F. Bellisle, and M. Deheeger, "Nutritional Status and Food Intake in Adolescents Living in Western Europe," *European Journal of Clinical Nutrition* 54 (2000): S41–S46.

13. Jeffrey Sobal and Albert J. Stunkard, "Socioeconomic Status and Obesity: A Review of the Literature," *Psychological Bulletin* 105 (1989): 260–275.

14. L. Hallberg et al., "Iron Absorption from Southeast Asian Diets," *American Journal of Clinical Nutrition* 30 (1977): 539–548.

15. David Ludwig and Mark Friedman, "Always Hungry? Here's Why," *New York Times*, May 16, 2014.

16. Roland Sturm and An Ruopeng, "Obesity and Economic Environments," *CA: A Cancer Journal for Clinicians* 64 (2014): 337–350.

17. See *Scientific American*'s entertaining "Processed Food: A 2-Million-Year History" in its September 2013 issue.

18. "Rise and Fall of Trans Fat: A History of Partially Hydrogenated Oil," *Los Angeles Times*, November 7, 2013, www.latimes.com/food /dailydish/la-dd-rise-and-fall-of-trans-fat-20131107-story.html.

19. Miriam E. Bocarsly et al., "High Fructose Corn Syrup Causes Characteristics of Obesity in Rats," *Pharmacology, Biochemistry, and Behavior* 97 (2010): 101–106.

20. H. Bart Van der Worp et al., "Can Animal Models of Disease Reliably Inform Human Studies?" *PLOS Medicine*, March 30, 2010.

21. Iris Higgins, "An Open Apology to All My Weight Loss Clients," *Huffington Post*, August 16, 2013, www.huffingtonpost.com/iris -higgins/an-open-apology-to-all-of_b_3762714.html.

4: Money, Motivation, and the Medical Machine

1. Andrew Newman, "Enticing Doctors to Endorse a Weight-Loss Program," *New York Times*, December 27, 2011.

2. Michael Gard and Jan Wright, *The Obesity Epidemic: Science, Morality, and Ideology* (Oxon: Routledge, 2005), 179.

3. Robert Pool, *Fat: Fighting the Obesity Epidemic* (Oxford: Oxford University Press, 2001), 189.

4. Jeffery Sobal, "The Medicalization and Demedicalization of Obesity," in *Eating Agendas: Food and Nutrition as Social Problems*, ed. Donna Maurer and Jeffery Sobal (New York: Aldine de Gruyter, 1955), 70.

5. Norman Jolliffe, "Some Basic Considerations of Obesity as a Public Health Problem," *American Journal of Public Health* 43 (1953): 989–992.

6. Paul E. Craig, "Obesity: A Practical Guide to Its Treatment Based on a Controlled Study of 821 Cases," *Medical Times* 83, no. 2 (1955): 156–164.

7. From "Ideal Weight/Ideal Women: Society Constructs the Female," in *Weighty Issues: Fatness and Thinness as Social Problems,* ed. Jeffery Sobal and Donna Maurer (New York: Aldine de Gruyter, 1999): 97–116.

8. Flemming Quadde, "Stereotaxy for Obesity," *The Lancet* 303 (1974): 267.

9. Ted Rothstein, "The Dental Professionals Role in the Treatment of Morbid Obesity—None!" January 14, 2013, accessed October 24, 2014, www.drted.com/OJW%20NYSDJ%20articles%20Dec04.html.

10. Maaike Kruseman et al., "Dietary, Weight, and Psychological Changes Among Patients with Obesity, 8 Years After Gastric Bypass," *Journal of the American Dietetic Association* 110 (2010): 527–534; N. V. Christou, D. Look, and L. D. Maclean, "Weight Gain After Short- and Long-Limb Gastric Bypass in Patients Followed for Longer Than 10 Years," *Annals of Surgery* 244 (2006): 734–740; and Daniela O. Magro et al., "Long-Term Weight Regain After Gastric Bypass: A 5-Year Prospective Study," *Obesity Surgery* 18 (2008): 648–651.

11. Jonathan P. Weiner et al., "Impact of Bariatric Surgery on Health Care Costs of Obese Persons," *JAMA* 148 (2013): 555–562.

12. Jean Mitchell and Tim Roger Sass, "Physician Ownership of Ancillary Services: Indirect Demand Inducement or Quality Assurance?" *Journal of Health Economics* 14 (1995): 263–289.

13. Susan Coyle, "Physician-Industry Relations. Part 1: Individual Physicians," *Annals of Internal Medicine* 136 (2002): 396–402.

14. "Conflict-of-Interest Policies for Academic Medical Centers," a report from the Pew Charitable Trusts, December 2013.

15. Bernard Lo and Marilyn J. Field, eds., *Conflict of Interest in Medical Research, Education, and Practice* (Washington, DC: National Academies Press, 2009).

16. "An Epidemic of Obesity Myths," Center for Consumer Freedom, accessed October 24, 2014, www.obesitymyths.com.

17. Per ProPublica's "Dollars for Docs" website http://projects.propublica.org/docdollars; Michael F. Jacobson et al., Unpublished letter to Donald Kennedy, editor-in-chief of *Science*, August 21, 2003;

Xavier Pi-Sunyer, "The Medical Risks of Obesity," *Postgrad Med* 121 (2009): 21–33, www.ncbi.nlm.nih.gov/pmc/articles/PMC2879283/; and Xavier Pi-Sunyer, "The Role of the Endocannabinoid System in Contributing to Obesity," *Medscape*, online slides with audio www.medscape.org/viewarticle/567417; click on "Faculty and Disclosures."

18. Michael Oldani, "Thick Prescriptions: Toward an Interpretation of Pharmaceutical Sales Practices," *Medical Anthropology Quarterly* 18, no. 3 (2004): 325–356.

19. Eric Quiñones, "A Prescription for Change," *Princeton Weekly Bulletin* 92, no. 25 (2003).

20. Mark Friedberg et al., "Evaluation of Conflict of Interest in Economic Analyses of New Drugs Used in Oncology," *JAMA* 282 (1999): 1453–1457; Justin Bekelman, Yan Li, and Cary P. Gross, "Scope and Impact of Financial Conflicts of Interest in Biomedical Research: A Systematic Review," *JAMA* 289 (2003): 454–465; Thomas Bodenheimer, "Uneasy Alliance: Clinical Investigators and the Pharmaceutical Industry," *New England Journal of Medicine* 342, no. 20 (2000): 1539–1544; and Richard A. Davidson, "Source of Funding and Outcome of Clinical Trials," *Journal of General Internal Medicine* 1 (1986): 155–158.

21. Dana Katz, Arthur L. Caplan, and Jon F. Merz, "All Gifts Large and Small: Toward an Understanding of the Ethics of Pharmaceutical Industry Gift-Giving," *American Journal of Bioethics* 3 (2003): 39–46.

22. Jason Dana and George Loewenstein, "A Social Science Perspective on Gifts to Physicians from Industry," *JAMA* 290 (2003): 252–255.

23. Jason Dana, "How Psychological Research Can Inform Policies for Dealing with Conflicts of Interest in Medicine," in *Conflict of Interest in Medical Research, Education, and Practice* (Washington, DC: National Academies Press, 2009).

24. George A. Bray, "Why Do We Need Drugs to Treat the Patient with Obesity?" *Obesity* 21, no. 5 (2013): 893–899.

25. Per COI information in the *International Journal of Obesity*, www.nature.com/ijo/journal/v32/n7s/full/ijo2008230a.html.

26. Kevin Lomangino, "Conflicted Obesity Mythbusting," *Clinical Nutrition Insight* 39 (2013): 8–9.

27. George Budwell, "The Paradox of Obesity Drugs," *The Motley Fool,* November 25, 2013.

28. Benjamin Djulbegovic, "The Uncertainty Principle and Industry-Sponsored Research," *The Lancet* 356 (2000): 635–638; Howard Mann and Benjamin Djulbegovic, "Comparator Bias: Why Comparisons Must Address Genuine Uncertainties," *Journal of the Royal Society of Medicine* 106 (2013): 30–33; and Benjamin Djulbegovic et al., "Medical Research: Trial Unpredictability Yields Predictable Therapy Gains," *Nature* 500 (2013): 395–396.

29. Paula Rochon et al., "A Study of Manufacturer-Supported Trials of Nonsteroidal Anti-Inflammatory Drugs in the Treatment of Arthritis," *Archives of Internal Medicine* 154 (1994): 157–163.

30. Bodenheimer, "Uneasy Alliance," 2000.

31. Ibid.

32. Helena W. Rodbard et al., "Statement by an American Association of Clinical Endocrinologists/American College of Endocrinology Consensus Panel on Type 2 Diabetes Mellitus: An Algorithm for Glycemic Control," *Endocrine Practice* 6 (2009): 540–559, www.project inform.org/pdf/diabetes_aace.pdf.

33. John Fauber and Ellen Gabler, "Doctors with Links to Drug Companies Influence Treatment Guidelines," *Milwaukee Journal Sentinel,* December 18, 2012.

34. Amanda Sainsbury and Phillipa Hay, "Call for an Urgent Rethink of the 'Health at Every Size' Concept," *Journal of Eating Disorders* 2 (2014): 8.

35. Rebecca Puhl and Chelsea A. Heuer, "The Stigma of Obesity: A Review and Update," *Obesity* 17, no. 5 (2009): 941–964.

36. M. R. Hebl and J. Xu, "Weighing the Care: Physicians' Reactions to the Size of a Patient," *International Journal of Obesity and Related Metabolic Disorders* 25 (2001): 1246–1252.

37. Rebecca Puhl and Kelly Brownell, "Bias, Discrimination, and Obesity," *Obesity Research* 9 (2001): 788–805.

38. Peggy Ward-Smith, in a poster presentation at the 2014 meeting of the American Association of Nurse Practitioners.

39. K. Davis-Coelho, J. Waltz, and B. Davis-Coelho, "Awareness and Prevention of Bias Against Fat Clients in Psychotherapy," *Professional Psychology: Research and Practice* 31 (2000): 682–684; and e-mailed notes from Rebecca Puhl.

40. Delese Wear et al., "Making Fun of Patients: Medical Students' Perceptions and Use of Derogatory and Cynical Humor in Clinical Settings," *Academic Medicine* 81, no. 5 (2006): 454–462.

41. Marlene Schwartz et al., "Weight Bias Among Health Professionals Specializing in Obesity," *Obesity Research* 11 (2003): 1033–1039.

42. George Blackburn, "Medicalizing Obesity: Individual, Economic, and Medical Consequences," *Virtual Mentor* 13 (2011): 890–895.

43. There's an entire website devoted to personal stories of encounters with biased medical professionals, called First, Do No Harm, at http://fathealth.wordpress.com.

44. C. L. Olson, H. D. Schumaker, and B. P. Yawn, "Overweight Women Delay Medical Care," *Archives of Family Medicine* 3 (1994): 888–892.

45. N. K. Amy et al., "Barriers to Routine Gynecological Cancer Screening for White and African-American Obese Women," *International Journal of Obesity* 30 (2006): 147–155.

46. Eugenia Calle et al., "Body-Mass Index and Mortality in a Prospective Cohort of U.S. Adults," *New England Journal of Medicine* 341 (1999): 1097–1105.

47. Kortni Jones, "Weight Stigma Among Providers Decreases the Quality of Care Received by Obese Patients," unpublished dissertation, 2010.

48. R. M. Puhl, T. Andreyeva, and K. D. Brownell, "Perceptions of Weight Discrimination: Prevalence and Comparison to Race and Gender Discrimination in America," *International Journal of Obesity* 32 (2008): 992–1000.

49. Puhl and Heuer, "The Stigma of Obesity."

50. "National Diabetes Statistics Report, 2014," Centers for Disease Control and Prevention, accessed October 24, 2014, www.cdc.gov/diabetes/pubs/estimates14.htm.

51. Albert Samaha, "Type Miscast: An Elmhurst Doctor's Type 2 Diabetes Misdiagnosis Results in the Death of a Six-Year-Old Girl," *The Village Voice,* October 2, 2013.

52. See "Statistics About Diabetes: Overall Numbers, Diabetes and Prediabetes," American Diabetes Association, accessed October 24, 2014, www.diabetes.org/diabetes-basics/statistics/.

Chapter 5: The Truth About Beauty

1. Patricia Owen and Erika Laurel-Seller, "Weight and Shape Ideals: Thin Is Dangerously In," *Journal of Applied Social Psychology* 30, no. 5 (2000): 979–990.

2. Dennis Hummel et al., "Visual Adaptation to Thin and Fat Bodies Transfers Across Identity," *PLOS One* 7, no. 8 (2012).

3. Nancy Etcoff, *Survival of the Prettiest* (New York: Doubleday, 1999), 70.

4. Karl Grammar and Randy Thornhill, "Human (*Homo sapiens*) Facial Attractiveness and Sexual Selection: The Role of Symmetry and Averageness," *Journal of Comparative Psychology* 108, no. 3 (1994): 233–242.

5. Deborah L. Rhode, *The Beauty Bias: The Injustice of Appearance in Life and Law* (Oxford: Oxford University Press, 2010); and Judith H. Langlois et al., "Maxims or Myths of Beauty: A Meta-Analytic and Theoretical Review," *Psychological Bulletin* 126, no. 3 (2000): 390–423.

6. Laura Fraser, "The Inner Corset: A Brief History of Fat in the United States," in *The Fat Studies Reader*, ed. Esther Rothblum and Sandra Solovay (New York: New York University Press, 2009), 11–14.

7. Jeanne Martin, "The Development of Ideal Body Image Perceptions in the U.S.," *Nutrition Today* 45 (2010): 98–110.

8. Ibid.

9. According to a June 22, 2009, story on Jezebel.com, which quotes Monroe's dressmaker.

10. Ian D. Stephen and A. Treshi-Marie Perera, "Judging the Difference Between Attractiveness and Health: Does Exposure to Model Images Influence the Judgments Made by Men and Women?" *PLOS One*, January 20, 2014.

11. Henri Tajfel et al., "Social Categorization and Intergroup Behaviour," *European Journal of Social Psychology* 1 (1971): 149–178.

12. Henri Tajfel and J. C. Turner, "An Integrative Theory of Intergroup Conflict," in *The Social Psychology of Intergroup Relations,* ed. W. G. Austin and S. Worchel (Brooks/Cole, 1979).

13. Seth Stephens-Davidowicz, "Google, Tell Me. Is My Son a Genius?" *New York Times,* January 18, 2014.

14. Lenny Vartanian and Meghan Hopkinson, "Social Connectedness, Conformity, and Internalization of Societal Standards of Attractiveness," *Body Image* 7 (2010): 86–89.

15. You can track the progress of the Truth in Advertising Act of 2014 online at www.congress.gov/bill/113th-congress/house-bill/4341.

16. Rheanna N. Ata, J. Kevin Thompson, and Brent J. Small, "Effects of Exposure to Thin-Ideal Media Images on Body Dissatisfaction: Testing the Inclusion of a Disclaimer Versus Warning Label," *Body Image* 10 (2013): 472–480.

17. Marika Tiggemann, Amy Slater, and Veronica Smyth, "'Retouch Free': The Effect of Labeling Media Images as Not Digitally Altered on Women's Body Dissatisfaction," *Body Image* 11 (2013): 85–88.

18. N. Micali et al., "Frequency and Patterns of Eating Disorder Symptoms in Early Adolescence," *Journal of Adolescent Health* 54 (2014): 574–581.

19. Michaela Bucchianeri et al., "Body Dissatisfaction from Adolescence to Young Adulthood: Findings from a 10-Year Longitudinal Study," *Body Image* 10 (2013): 1–7.

20. Eve Wiseman, "Uncomfortable in Our Skin: The Body-Image Report," *The Guardian,* June 9, 2012.

21. Donna Maurer and Jeffery Sobal, *Eating Agendas: Food and Nutrition as Social Problems* (New York: Aldine de Gruyter, 1995).

22. According to research from the American Association of Advertising Agencies. See "How Many Advertisements Is a Person Exposed to in a Day?," ams.aaaa.org/eweb/upload/faqs/adexposures.pdf.

23. Viren Swami et al., "The Attractive Female Body Weight and Female Body Dissatisfaction in 26 Countries Across 10 World Regions: Results of the International Body Project I," *Personality and Social Psychology Bulletin* 36 (2010): 309–325.

24. Anne Becker et al., "Eating Behaviours and Attitudes Following Prolonged Exposure to Television Among Ethnic Fijian Adolescent Girls," *British Journal of Psychiatry* 180 (2002): 509–514.

25. According to Facebook, as reported by *Bloomberg BusinessWeek,* July 23, 2014.

26. Per *Business Insider*'s report on Social Media Engagement, September 2014; www.businessinsider.com/social-media-engagement-statistics-2013–12.

27. Patti M. Valkenburg, Jochen Peter, and Alexander P. Schouten, "Friend Networking Sites and Their Relationship to Adolescents' Well-Being and Social Self-Esteem," *CyberPsychology & Behavior* 9 (2006): 584–590; Corey Neira and Bonnie Barber, "Social Networking Site Use: Linked to Adolescents' Social Self-Concept, Self-Esteem, and Depressed Mood," *Australian Journal of Psychology* 66 (2014): 56–64; Michael Chan, "Multimodal Connectedness and Quality of Life: Examining the Influences of Technology Adoption and Interpersonal Communication on Well-Being Across the Life Span," *Journal of Computer-Mediated Communication* (2014): 1–16; and Moira Burke, Cameron Marlow, and Thomas Lento, "Social Network Activity and Social Well-Being," *Proceedings of the SIGCHI Conference on Human Factors in Computing Systems* CHI 10 (2010): 1909–1912.

28. Wen-ying Silvia Chou, Abby Prestin, and Stephen Kunath, "Obesity in Social Media: A Mixed Methods Analysis," *Translational Behavioral Medicine* 4 (2014): 314–323.

29. Anna North, "Shamed, Flamed, Harassed: What It's Like to Be Called Fat Online," *New York Times*, October 3, 2014.

30. Sumitra, "Rest at Your Own Risk: Moscow Benches to Publicly Display Sitters' Weight," Oddity Central, September 23, 2014, accessed October 24, 2104, www.odditycentral.com/news/rest-at-your-own-risk -moscow-benches-to-publicly-display-sitters-weight.html

31. Jason D. Seacat, Sarah Dougal, and Dooti Roy, "A Daily Diary Assessment of Female Weight Stigmatization," *Journal of Health Psychology* (2014): 1–13.

32. Evolutionary psychologist Glenn Geher wrote an interesting blog post on how social comparison can help us. See www.evostudies. org/2013/06/social-comparison-evolutionary-psychology-and-the-best -job-in-the-world/.

33. Laura Turner Garrison, "Who Lives Like That? The Most Absurd Aspirational Ads Out There," SplitSider, July 31, 2012, accessed October 24, 2014, www.splitsider.com/2012/07/newcastle-who-lives -like-that/.

34. Julie Guthman, *Weighing In: Obesity, Food Justice, and the Limits of Capitalism*, (Berkeley and Los Angeles: University of California Press, 2011), 52.

35. "New Beauty Study Reveals Days, Times and Occasions When U.S. Women Feel Least Attractive," PRNews Media, accessed October 24, 2014, www.prnewswire.com/news-releases/new-beauty-study-reveals-days-times-and-occasions-when-us-women-feel-least-attrac tive-226131921.html.

36. Michelle Yeomans, "Global Beauty Market to Reach $265 Billion in 2017 Due to an Increase in GDP," CosmeticsDesign.com, November 7, 2012, accessed October 24, 2014, www.cosmeticsdesign.com /Market-Trends/Global-beauty-market-to-reach-265-billion-in-2017 -due-to-an-increase-in-GDP.

37. According to psychologist Charlotte Markey, puberty is a risk factor for body dissatisfaction, and body image is a crucial developmental issue. Charlotte Markey, "Why Body Image Is Important to Adolescent Development," *Journal of Youth and Adolescence* 39 (2010): 1387–1391.

38. Line Tremblay et al., "Perceptions of Self in 3–5-Year-Old Children: A Preliminary Investigation into the Early Emergence of Body Dissatisfaction," *Body Image* 8 (2011): 287–292.

39. John Worobey and Harriet Worobey, "Body-Size Stigmatization by Preschool Girls: In a Doll's World, It Is Good to Be 'Barbie,'" *Body Image* 11, no. 2 (2014): 171–174.

40. Sarah Harrison et al., "No Fat Friend of Mine: Very Young Children's Responses to Overweight and Disability," European Congress on Obesity (2013). The Leeds research actually reprised a study done in the 1960s with ten- to twelve-year-olds, who showed greater liking for the obese characters though they still rejected them.

41. Christine E. Blake et al., "Adults with Greater Weight Satisfaction Report More Positive Health Behaviors and Have Better Health Status Regardless of BMI," *Journal of Obesity* (2013).

42. Patricia van den Berg and Dianne Neumark-Sztainer, "Fat 'n Happy 5 Years Later: Is It Bad for Overweight Girls to Like Their Bodies?" *Journal of Adolescent Health* 41 (2007): 415–417.

43. Sharon Hayes and Stacey Tantleff-Dunn, "Am I Too Fat to Be a Princess? Examining the Effects of Popular Children's Media on Young Girls' Body Image," *British Journal of Developmental Psychology* 28 (2010): 413–426.

44. N. R. Kelly, C. M. Bulik, and S. E. Mazzeo, "An Exploration of Body Dissatisfaction and Perceptions of Black and White Girls Enrolled in an Intervention for Overweight Children," *Body Image* 8 (2011): 379–384.

45. Sarah Kate Bearman et al., "The Skinny on Body Dissatisfaction: A Longitudinal Study of Adolescent Girls and Boys," *Journal of Youth and Adolescence* 35 (2006): 217–229.

46. Ann Frisén and Kristina Holmqvist, "What Characterizes Early Adolescents with a Positive Body Image? A Qualitative Investigation of Swedish Girls and Boys," *Body Image* 7 (2010): 205–212; and Kristina Holmqvist and Ann Frisén, "'I Bet They Aren't That Perfect in Reality': Appearance Ideals Viewed from the Perspective of Adolescents with a Positive Body Image," *Body Image* 9 (2012): 388–395.

47. "Women in the Labor Force in 2010," US Department of Labor, accessed October 24, 2104, www.dol.gov/wb/factsheets/Qf--laborforce-10.htm.

48. "Why Do Women Outnumber Men in College?," National Bureau of Economic Research, accessed October 24, 2014, www.nber.org/digest/jan07/w12139.html.

49. Marika Tiggemann and Jessica E. Lynch, "Body Image Across the Life Span in Adult Women: The Role of Self-Objectification," *Developmental Psychology* 37 (2001): 243–253.

50. Megan Gannon, "Americans Feel Most Attractive at This Age," LiveScience, July 10, 2014, accessed October 24, 2014, www.livescience.com/46741-older-americans-feel-best-about-their-looks.html.

51. Kate Coyne, "Melissa McCarthy In Her Own Words," *People,* July 7, 2014.

Chapter 6: It's All In How You Look at It

1. R. H. Salk and R. Engeln-Maddox, "'If You're Fat, Then I'm Humongous!' Frequency, Content, and Impact of Fat Talk Among College Women," *Psychology of Women Quarterly* 35 (2011): 18–28.

2. Lauren E. Britton et al., "Fat Talk and Self-Presentation of Body Image: Is There a Social Norm for Women to Self-Degrade?" *Body Image* 3 (2006): 247–254.

3. Helen Sharpe, Ulrike Naumann, and Janet Treasure, "Is Fat Talking a Causal Risk Factor for Body Dissatisfaction? A Systematic Review and Meta-Analysis," *International Journal of Eating Disorders* 46, no. 7 (2013): 643–652.

4. Christine E. Blake et al., "Adults with Greater Weight Satisfaction Report More Positive Health Behaviors and Have Better Health Status Regardless of BMI," *Journal of Obesity* (2013).

5. Michael D. Wirth et al., "Chronic Weight Dissatisfaction Predicts Type 2 Diabetes Risk," *Health Psychology* 33 (2014): 912–919.

6. Charlotte Markey, "Why Body Image Is Important to Adolescent Development," *Journal of Youth and Adolescence* 39 (2010): 1387–1391.

7. Adam B. Cohen and Ilana J. Tannenbaum, "Lesbian and Bisexual Women's Judgments of the Attractiveness of Different Body Types," *Journal of Sex Research* 38, no. 3 (2001): 226–232.

8. G. Staines, C. Tavris, and T. E. Jayaratne, "The Queen Bee Syndrome," in *The Female Experience,* ed. C. Tavris (Del Mare, CA: Communications Research Machines, 1973).

9. Rachel Fox, "Too Fat to Be a Scientist?" *Chronicle of Higher Education*, June 17, 2014.

10. Georgie Silvarole, "Fat Acceptance Movement Prioritizes Comfort Over Healthy Lifestyle," *The Daily Orange,* September 24, 2014.

11. "Chronic Stress Puts Your Health at Risk," Mayo Clinic, accessed October 24, 2014, www.mayoclinic.org/healthy-living/stress-management /in-depth/stress/art-20046037.

12. Peter Muennig, "The Body Politic: The Relationship Between Stigma and Obesity-Associated Disease," *BMC Public Health* 8 (2008).

13. Ibid.; and Peter Muennig, "I Think Therefore I Am: Perceived Ideal Weight as a Determinant of Health," *American Journal of Public Health* 98 (2007): 501–506.

14. Julie Lumeng, "Weight Status as a Predictor of Being Bullied in Third Through Sixth Grades," *Pediatrics* 125 (2010): e1301–e1307.

15. Rebecca M. Puhl and Joerg Luedicke, "Weight-Based Victimization Among Adolescents in the School Setting: Emotional Reactions and Coping Behaviors," *Journal of Youth and Adolescence* 41 (2011): 27–40.

16. Rebecca M. Puhl, Jamie Lee Peterson, and Joerg Luedicke, "Weight-Based Victimization: Bullying Experiences of Weight Loss Treatment-Seeking Youth," *Pediatrics* 131 (2013): e1–e9.

17. Janet Latner et al., "Residual Obesity Stigma: An Experimental Investigation of Bias Against Obese and Lean Targets Differing in Weight-Loss History," *Obesity* 20 (2012): 2035–2038.

18. R. M. Puhl, T. Andreyeva, and K. D. Brownell, "Perceptions of Weight Discrimination: Prevalence and Comparison to Race and Gender Discrimination in America," *International Journal of Obesity* 32 (2008): 992–1000.

19. Marlene Schwartz et al., "The Influence of One's Own Body Weight on Implicit and Explicit Anti-Fat Bias," *Obesity* 14 (2006): 440–447.

20. These comments were drawn from two personal interviews with Majdan and from his essay "Memoirs of an Obese Physician," *Annals of Internal Medicine* 153 (2010): 686–687.

Chapter 7: Now What?

1. Jen Christensen and Jacque Wilson, "Congressional Hearing Investigates Dr. Oz 'Miracle' Weight Loss Claims," CNN, June 19, 2014, www.cnn.com/2014/06/17/health/senate-grills-dr-oz/.

2. The youngest child known to have had bariatric surgery was a two-year-old boy from Saudi Arabia.

3. Stephen R. Daniels and Aaron S. Kelly, "Pediatric Severe Obesity: Time to Establish Serious Treatments for a Serious Disease," *Childhood Obesity* 10 (2014): 283–284.

4. After getting pushback, Obama changed the campaign's rhetoric from fighting childhood obesity to raising healthier kids; the White House later credited Let's Move! with plateauing rates of childhood obesity, though those rates had actually plateaued several years earlier.

5. Tricia L. Psota, Barbara Lohse, and Sheila G. West, "Associations Between Eating Competence and Cardiovascular Disease Biomarkers," *Journal of Nutrition Education Behaviors* 39 (2007): S171–S178; and Barbara Lohse et al., "Eating Competence of Elderly Spanish Adults Is Associated with a Healthy Diet and a Favorable Cardiovascular Risk Profile," *Journal of Nutrition* 140 (2010): 1322–1327.

6. For more information, see ellynsatterinstitute.org/hte/whatis normaleating.php.

7. Burgard maintains a website called Body Positive, www.body positive.com.

8. Evelyn Tribole and Elyse Resch, *Intuitive Eating: A Revolutionary Program That Works*, 3rd ed. (New York: St. Martin's Press, 2012).

9. Marcia Wood, "Health at Every Size: New Hope for Obese Americans?" USDA website, March 2006, accessed October 24, 2014, www.ars.usda.gov/is/ar/archive/mar06/health0306.htm.

10. Amanda Sainsbury-Salis and Phillipa Hay, "Call for an Urgent Rethink of the 'Health at Every Size' Concept," *Journal of Eating Disorders* 2, no. 8 (2014).

11. Christopher Freind, "Solve America's Obesity Problem with Shame," PhillyMag.com, October 12, 2012.

12. Leon Festinger, "A Theory of Social Comparison Processes," *Human Relations* 7 (1954): 117–140.

13. Sara B. Cohen, "Media Exposure and the Subsequent Effects on Body Dissatisfaction, Disordered Eating, and Drive for Thinness: A Review of the Current Research," *Mind Matters: The Wesleyan Journal of Psychology* 1 (2006): 57–71.

14. Jill A. Cattarin et al., "Body Image, Mood, and Televised Images of Attractiveness: The Role of Social Comparison," *Journal of Social and Clinical Psychology* 19 (2000): 220–239.

15. Anna Campbell and Heather A. Hausenblas, "Effects of Exercise Interventions on Body Image: A Meta-Analysis," *Journal of Health Psychology* 14 (2009): 780–793; and Katherine M. Appleton, "6 x 40 Mins Exercise Improves Body Image, Even Though Body Weight and Shape Do Not Change," *Journal of Health Psychology* 18, no. 1 (2012): 110–120.

16. T. Smith-Jackson, J. J. Reel, and R. Thackeray, "Coping with 'Bad Body Image Days': Strategies from First-Year Young Adult College Women," *Body Image* 8 (2011): 335–342. That last item on the list was the least-used strategy, maybe because body acceptance is a process rather than a decision.

SELECTED BIBLIOGRAPHY

Here's a very heavily edited selection of the books and articles that were useful in researching this book.

Books

Bacon, Linda. *Health at Every Size: The Surprising Truth About Your Weight*. Dallas, TX: Benbella Books, 2008.

Campos, Paul. *The Obesity Myth: Why America's Obsession with Weight Is Hazardous to Your Health*. New York: Gotham Books, 2004.

Ensler, Eve. *The Good Body*. New York: Villard, 2005.

Etcoff, Nancy. *Survival of the Prettiest: The Science of Beauty*. New York: Anchor Books, 1999.

Fraser, Laura. *Losing It: America's Obsession with Weight and the Industry That Feeds on It*. New York: Dutton, 1997.

Gaesser, Glenn A. *Big Fat Lies: The Truth About Your Weight and Your Health*. New York: Fawcett Columbine, 1996.

Gard, Michael, and Jan Wright. *The Obesity Epidemic: Science, Morality and Ideology*. Oxon: Routledge, 2005.

Guthman, Julie. *Weighing In: Obesity, Food Justice, and the Limits of Capitalism*. Berkeley: University of California Press, 2011.

Harding, Kate, and Marianne Kirby. *Lessons from the Fat-O-Sphere: Quit Dieting and Declare a Truce with Your Body*. New York: Perigee, 2009.

Kater, Kathy J. *Healthy Bodies: Teaching Kids What They Need to Know.* St. Paul, MN: Body Image Health, 2012.

Kolata, Gina. *Rethinking Thin: The New Science of Weight Loss—and the Myths and Realities of Dieting.* New York: Farrar, Straus & Giroux, 2007.

Kulick, Don, and Anne Meneley, eds. *Fat: The Anthropology of an Obsession.* New York: Penguin, 2005.

Orbach, Susie. *Fat Is a Feminist Issue.* New York: BBS Publishing, 1997.

Rhode, Deborah L. *The Beauty Bias: The Injustice of Appearance in Life and Law.* Oxford: Oxford University Press, 2010.

Rothblum, Esther, and Sondra Solovay, eds. *The Fat Studies Reader.* New York: New York University Press, 2009.

Russell, Sharman Apt. *Hunger: An Unnatural History.* New York: Basic Books, 2005.

Saguy, Abigail. *What's Wrong with Fat?* Oxford: Oxford University Press, 2013.

Satter, Ellyn. *Secrets of Feeding a Healthy Family: How to Eat, How to Raise Good Eaters, How to Cook.* Madison, WI: Kelcy Press, 2008.

Sobal, Jeffery, and Donna Maurer, eds. *Eating Agendas: Food and Nutrition as Social Problems.* New York: Aldine de Gruyter, 1995.

———. *Weighty Issues: Fatness and Thinness as Social Problems.* New York: Aldine de Gruyter, 1999.

Tucker, Todd. *The Great Starvation Experiment: The Heroic Men Who Starved So That Millions Could Live.* New York: Free Press, 2006.

Wann, Marilyn. *Fat!So? Because You Don't Have to Apologize for Your Size!* Berkeley: Ten Speed Press, 1998.

Whelan, Charles. *Naked Statistics: Stripping the Dread from the Data.* New York: W. W. Norton & Company, 2013.

Wolf, Naomi. *The Beauty Myth: How Images of Beauty Are Used Against Women.* New York: Harper Perennial, 1991.

Zilberberg, Marya. *Between the Lines: Finding the Truth in Medical Literature.* Goshen, MA: EviMed Research Press, 2012.

Articles

Albert, M., and D. R. Williams. "Invited Commentary: Discrimination—An Emerging Target for Reducing Risk of Cardiovascular Disease?" *American Journal of Epidemiology* 173, no. 11 (2011): 1240–1243.

Allison, David B., et al. "Annual Deaths Attributable to Obesity in the United States." *JAMA* 282 (1999): 1530–1538.

Anderson, Emily K., et al. "Weight Cycling Increases T-Cell Accumulation in Adipose Tissue and Impairs Systemic Glucose Tolerance." *Diabetes* 62, no. 9 (2013): 3180–3188.

Angerås, Oskar, et al. "Evidence for Obesity Paradox in Patients with Acute Coronary Syndromes: A Report from the Swedish Coronary Angiography and Angioplasty Registry." *European Heart Journal* 34 (2013): 345–353.

Aphramor, Lucy. "Validity of Claims Made in Weight Management Research: A Narrative Review of Dietetic Articles." *Nutrition Journal* 9 (2010): 30.

Appleton, Katherine. "6 x 40 Mins Exercise Improves Body Image, Even Though Body Weight and Shape Do Not Change." *Journal of Health Psychology* 18, no. 1 (2012): 110–120.

Ata, Rheanna N., J. Kevin Thompson, and Brent J. Small. "Effects of Exposure to Thin-Ideal Media Images on Body Dissatisfaction: Testing the Inclusion of a Disclaimer Versus Warning Label." *Body Image* 10 (2013): 472–480.

Barry, Vaughn, et al. "Fitness vs. Fatness on All-Cause Mortality: A Meta-Analysis." *Progress in Cardiovascular Diseases* 56 (2014): 382–390.

Beavers, Daniel, et al. "Cardiometabolic Risk After Weight Loss and Subsequent Weight Regain in Overweight and Obese Postmenopausal Women." *Journal of Gerontology* 68 (2013): 691–698.

Becker, Anne, et al. "Eating Behaviours and Attitudes Following Prolonged Exposure to Television Among Ethnic Fijian Adolescent Girls." *British Journal of Psychiatry* 180 (2002): 509–514.

Bekelman, Justin, Yan Li, and Cary P. Gross. "Scope and Impact of Financial Conflicts of Interest in Biomedical Research: A Systematic Review." *JAMA* 289 (2003): 454–465.

Blake, Christine E., et al. "Adults with Greater Weight Satisfaction Report More Positive Health Behaviors and Have Better Health Status Regardless of BMI." *Journal of Obesity* (2013).

Bocarsley, Miriam E., et al. "High-Fructose Corn Syrup Causes Characteristics of Obesity in Rats." *Pharmacology, Biochemistry and Behaviour* 97 (2010): 101–106.

Bodenheimer, Thomas. "Uneasy Alliance: Clinical Investigators and the Pharmaceutical Industry." *New England Journal of Medicine* 342, no. 20 (2000): 1539–1544.

Bucchianeri, Michaela, et al. "Body Dissatisfaction from Adolescence to Young Adulthood: Findings from a 10-Year Longitudinal Study." *Body Image* 10 (2013): 1–7.

Callahan, Daniel. "Obesity: Chasing an Elusive Epidemic." *The Hastings Center Report* 43, no. 1 (2013): 34–40.

Calle, Eugenia, et al. "Body-Mass Index and Mortality in a Prospective Cohort of U.S. Adults." *New England Journal of Medicine* 341 (1999): 1097–1105.

Carnethon, Mercedes, et al. "Association of Weight Status with Mortality in Adults with Incident Diabetes." *JAMA* 308, no. 6 (2012): 581–590.

Casazza, Krista, et al. "Myths, Presumptions, and Facts About Obesity." *New England Journal of Medicine* 368, no. 5 (2013): 446–454.

Corwin, R. L., N. M. Avena, and M. M. Boggiano. "Feeding and Reward: Perspectives from Three Rat Models of Binge Eating." *Physiology & Behavior* 104 (2011): 87–97.

Coyle, Susan L. "Physician-Industry Relations, Parts 1 and 2." *Annals of Internal Medicine* 136 (2002): 396–406.

Dana, Jason, and George Lowenstein. "A Social Science Perspective on Gifts to Physicians from Industry." *JAMA* 290 (2003): 252–255.

De Gonzalez, Amy, et al. "Body-Mass Index and Mortality Among 1.46 Million White Adults." *New England Journal of Medicine* 363 (2010): 2211–2219.

Drewnowski, A., et al. "Food Environment and Socioeconomic Status Influence Obesity Rates in Seattle and in Paris." *International Journal of Obesity* 38 (2014): 306–314.

Enriquez, E., G. E. Duncan, and E. A. Schur. "Age at Dieting Onset, Body Mass Index, and Dieting Practices: A Twin Study." *Appetite* 71 (2013): 301–306.

Ernsberger, Paul, and Paul Askew. "Health Implications of Obesity: An Alternative View." *Journal of Obesity and Weight Regulation* 6, no. 2 (1987): 55–137.

Faber, John, and Ellen Gabbler. "Doctors with Links to Drug Companies Influence Treatment Guidelines." *Milwaukee Journal Sentinel,* December 18, 2012.

Festinger, Leon. "A Theory of Social Comparison Processes." *Human Relations* 7 (1954): 117–140.

Field, Alison, et al. "Weight Cycling and the Risk of Developing Type 2 Diabetes Among Adult Women in the United States." *Obesity Research* 12, no. 2 (2004): 267–274.

Flegal, Katherine, et al. "Association of All-Cause Mortality with Overweight and Obesity Using Standard Body Mass Index Categories: A Systematic Review and Meta-Analysis." *JAMA* 309, no. 1 (2013): 71–82.

Flegal, Katherine, and Kampar Kalantar-Zadeh. "Overweight, Mortality, and Survival." *Obesity* 21 (2013): 1744–1745.

Flegal, Katherine, et al. "Sources of Differences in Estimates of Obesity-Associated Deaths from First NHANES 1 Hazard Ratios." *American Journal of Clinical Nutrition* 91 (2010): 519–527.

Fox, Bradley, et al. "Fat Equals Sick: Is This About the Money?" *Medscape,* July 15, 2013.

Fox, Rachel. "Too Fat to Be a Scientist?" *Chronicle of Higher Education,* June 17, 2014.

Frisen, Ann, and Kristina Holmqvist. "What Characterizes Early Adolescents with a Positive Body Image? A Qualitative Investigation of Swedish Girls and Boys." *Body Image* 7 (2010): 205–212.

Fugh-Berman, Adriane, and Sunita Sah. "Physicians Under the Influence: Social Psychology and Industry Marketing Strategies." *Journal of Law, Medicine & Ethics* 41 (2013): 665–672.

Fugh-Berman, Adriane, and Shahram Ahari. "Following the Script: How Drug Reps Make Friends and Influence Doctors." *PLOS Medicine* (2007).

Garner, David M., and Susan C. Wooley. "Obesity Treatment: The High Cost of False Hope." *Journal of the American Dietetic Association* 91 (1991): 1248–1251.

Gillman, Matthew, and David Ludwig. "How Early Should Obesity Prevention Start?" *New England Journal of Medicine* 369 (2013): 2173–2175.

Hallberg, L., et al. "Iron Absorption from Southeast Asian Diets." *American Journal of Clinical Nutrition* 30 (1977): 539–538.

Harriger, Jennifer, et al. "Body Size Stereotyping and Internalization of the Thin Ideal in Preschool Girls." *Sex Roles* 63 (2010): 609–620.

Hatzenbuehler, M. L., J. C. Phelan, and B. G. Link. "Stigma as a Fundamental Cause of Population Health Inequalities." *American Journal of Public Health* 103, no. 5 (2013): 813–821.

Holmqvist, Kristina, and Ann Frisen. "'I Bet They Aren't That Perfect in Reality': Appearance Ideals Viewed from the Perspective of Adolescents with a Positive Body Image." *Body Image* 9 (2012): 388–395.

Hummel, Dennis, et al. "Visual Adaptation to Thin and Fat Bodies Transfers Across Identity." *PLOS One* 7, no. 8 (2012).

Jerant, Anthony, and Peter Franks. "Body Mass Index, Diabetes, Hypertension, and Short-Term Mortality: A Population-Based Observational Study, 2000–2006." *Journal of the American Board of Family Medicine* 25, no. 4 (2012): 422–431.

Joliffe, Norman. "Some Basic Considerations of Obesity as a Public Health Problem." *American Journal of Public Health* 43 (1953): 998–992.

Kabat, Geoffrey. "Why Labeling Obesity as a Disease Is a Big Mistake." Forbes.com, October 2013.

Kajioka, Taeko, et al. "Effects of Intentional Weight Cycling on Non-Obese Young Women." *Metabolism* 51, no. 2 (2002): 149–154.

Katz, Dana, Arthur L. Caplan, and Jon F. Merz. "All Gifts Large and Small: Toward an Understanding of the Ethics of Pharmaceutical Industry Gift-Giving." *American Journal of Bioethics* 3 (2003): 39–46.

Katz, David, et al. "Exploring Effectiveness of Messaging in Childhood Obesity Campaigns." *Childhood Obesity* 8 (2012): 97–105.

Kaushik, Susmita, et al. "Autophagy in Hypothalamic AgRP Neurons Regulates Food Intake and Energy Balance." *Cell Metabolism* 14 (2011): 173–183.

Klimentidis, Yann, et al. "Canaries in the Coal Mine: A Cross-Species Analysis of the Plurality of Obesity Epidemics." *Proceeding of the Royal Society B* 278 (2011): 1626–1632.

Kramer, Caroline, Bernard Zinman, and Ravi Retnakaran. "Are Metabolically Healthy Overweight and Obesity Benign Conditions? A Systematic Review and Meta-Analysis." *Annals of Internal Medicine* 159 (2013): 758–769.

Latner, Janet, Laura Durso, and Jonathan Mond. "Health and Health-Related Quality of Life Among Treatment-Seeking Overweight and Obese Adults: Associations with Internalized Weight Bias." *Journal of Eating Disorders* 1, no. 3 (2013).

Lavie, Carl, et al. "Body Composition and Survival in Stable Coronary Heart Disease—Impact of Lean Mass Index and Body Fat in the 'Obesity Paradox.'" *Journal of the American College of Cardiology* 60 (2012): 1374–1380.

Lee, Timothy C., et al. "Socioeconomic Status and Incident Type 2 Diabetes Mellitus: Data from the Women's Health Study." *PLOS One* (2011).

Liebel, Rudolph, and Jules Hirsch. "Diminished Energy Requirements in Reduced-Obese Patients." *Metabolism* 33, no. 2 (February 1984): 164–170.

Lissner, Lauren, et al. "Variability of Body Weight and Health Outcomes in the Framingham Population." *New England Journal of Medicine* 324 (1991): 1839–1944.

Look AHEAD Research Group. "Cardiovascular Effects of Intensive Lifestyle Intervention in Type 2 Diabetes." *New England Journal of Medicine* 369 (2013): 145–154.

Lustig, Robert H. "Which Comes First? The Obesity or the Insulin? The Behavior or the Biochemistry?" *Journal of Pediatrics* 152 (2008): 601–602.

Majdan, Joseph. "Memoirs of an Obese Physician." *Annals of Internal Medicine* 153 (2010): 686–687.

Mann, Traci, et al. "Medicare's Search for Effective Obesity Treatments: Diets Are Not the Answer." *American Psychologist* 62 (2007): 220–233.

Markey, Charlotte. "Why Body Image Is Important to Adolescent Development." *Journal of Youth and Adolescence* 39 (2010): 1387–1391.

Masters, Ryan, et al. "The Impact of Obesity on U.S. Mortality Levels: The Importance of Age and Cohort Factors in Population Estimates." *American Journal of Public Health* 103 (2013): 1895–1901.

McAllister, E. J., et al. "Ten Putative Contributors to the Obesity Epidemic." *Critical Reviews in Food Science & Nutrition* 49 (2009): 868–913.

McAuley, Paul, et al. "Fitness, Fatness, and Survival in Adults with Pre-diabetes." *Diabetes Care* 37 (2014): 529–536.

McAuley, Paul. "Obesity and Mortality: The Missing Link." *British Medical Journal* 342 (2011).

Menachemi, N., et al. "Overstatement of Results in the Nutrition and Obesity Peer-Reviewed Literature." *American Journal of Preventive Medicine* 45 (2013): 615–621.

Miller, Wayne C. "How Effective Are Traditional Dietary and Exercise Interventions for Weight Loss?" *Clinical Sciences* 31, no. 8 (1999): 1129–1134.

Montani, J.-P., et al. "Weight Cycling During Growth and Beyond as a Risk Factor for Later Cardiovascular Diseases: The 'Repeated

Overshoot' Theory." *International Journal of Obesity* 30 (2006): S58–S66.

Muennig, Peter. "I Think Therefore I Am: Perceived Ideal Weight as a Determinant of Health." *American Journal of Public Health* 98 (2008): 501–506.

———. "The Body Politic: The Relationship Between Stigma and Obesity-Associated Disease." *BMC Public Health* 8 (2008).

Müller, M. J., A. Bosy-Westphal, and S. B. Heymsfield. "Is There Evidence for a Set Point that Regulates Human Body Weight?" *F1000 Medicine Reports* 2 (2010): 59.

Murtagh, Lindsay, and David S. Ludwig. "State Intervention in Life-Threatening Obesity." *JAMA* 306, no. 2 (2011): 206–207.

Nebeling, Linda, et al. "Weight Cycling and Immunocompetence." *Journal of the American Dietetic Association* 104 (2004): 892–894.

Neumark-Sztainer, Dianne, et al. "Obesity, Disordered Eating, and Eating Disorders in a Longitudinal Study of Adolescents: How Do Dieters Fare 5 Years Later?" *Journal of the American Dietetic Association* 106 (2006): 559–568.

———. "Dieting and Disordered Eating Behaviors from Adolescence to Young Adulthood: Findings from a 10-Year Longitudinal Study." *Journal of the American Dietetic Association* 111 (2011): 1004–1011.

Oldani, Michael. "Thick Prescriptions: Toward an Interpretation of Pharmaceutical Sales Practices." *Medical Anthropology Quarterly* 18, no. 3 (2004): 325–356.

Olshansky, S. Jay, et al. "A Potential Decline in Life Expectancy in the United States in the 21st Century." *New England Journal of Medicine* 352 (2005): 1138–1145.

Orpana, Heather, et al. "BMI and Mortality: Results from a National Longitudinal Study of Canadian Adults." *Obesity* 18 (2009): 214–218.

Padwal, R., et al. "Bariatric Surgery: A Systematic Review and Network Meta-Analysis of Randomized Trials." *Obesity Reviews* 12 (2011): 602–621.

Peretti, Jacques. "Fat Profits: How the Food Industry Cashed In on Obesity." *The Guardian,* August 7, 2013.

Pew Research Center. "Conflict-of-Interest Policies for Academic Medical Centers." *Pew Research Center Report,* December 2013.

Pham-Kanter, Genevieve. "Revisiting Financial Conflicts of Interest in FDA Advisory Committees." *The Milbank Quarterly* 92 (2014): 446–470.

Phelan, Suzanne, et al. "Recovery from Relapse Among Successful Weight Maintainers." *American Journal of Clinical Nutrition* 78 (2003): 1079–1084.

Pietiläinen, K. H., et al. "Does Dieting Make You Fat? A Twin Study." *International Journal of Obesity* 36 (2012): 456–464.

Pinhas, Leora, et al. "Trading Health for a Healthy Weight: The Uncharted Side of Healthy Weight Initiatives." *Eating Disorders* 21 (2013): 109–116.

Polivy, Janet, and C. Peter Herman. "Distress and Eating: Why Do Dieters Overeat?" *International Journal of Eating Disorders* 26, no. 2 (1999): 153–164.

Polivy, Janet, Julie Coleman, and C. Peter Herman. "The Effect of Deprivation on Food Cravings and Eating Behavior in Restrained and Unrestrained Eaters." *International Journal of Eating Disorders* 38, no. 4 (2005): 301–309.

Psota, Tricia L., Barbara Lohse, and Sheila G. West. "Associations Between Eating Competence and Cardiovascular Disease Biomarkers." *Journal of Nutrition Education and Behavior* 39 (2007): S171–S178.

Schvey, N. A., R. Puhl, and K. D. Brownell. "The Stress of Stigma: Exploring the Effect of Weight Stigma on Cortisol Reactivity." *Psychosomatic Medicine* 76 (2014): 156–162.

Puhl, Rebecca, and Chelsea Heuer. "Obesity Stigma: Important Considerations for Public Health." *American Journal of Public Health* 100 (2010): 1019–1028.

Puhl, Rebecca, and Chelsea Heuer. "The Stigma of Obesity: A Review and Update." *Obesity* 17, no. 5 (May 2009): 941–964.

Puhl, Rebecca, and Kelly Brownell. "Bias, Discrimination, and Obesity." *Obesity Research* 9, no. 12 (2001): 788–805.

Raeburn, Paul. "The Real Truth About Weight Loss? Follow the Money." Knight Science Journalism at MIT, blog post February 11, 2013.

Robbins, Jessica, et al. "Socioeconomic Status and Diagnosed Diabetes Incidence." *Diabetes Research and Clinical Practice* 68 (2004): 230–236.

Romero-Corral, Abel, et al. "Association of Bodyweight with Total Mortality and with Cardiovascular Events in Coronary Artery Disease: A Systematic Review of Cohort Studies." *The Lancet* 368 (2006): 666–678.

Satter, Ellyn. "Eating Competence: Definition and Evidence for the Satter Eating Competence Model." *Journal of Nutrition Education and Behavior* 39 (2007): S142–S153.

Schwartz, Marlene, et al. "The Influence of One's Own Body Weight on Implicit and Explicit Anti-Fat Bias." *Obesity* 14 (March 2006): 440–447.

Seacat, Jason, Sarah Dougal, and Dooti Roy. "A Daily Diary Assessment of Female Weight Stigmatization." *Journal of Health Psychology* (2014): 1–13.

Sharpe, Helen, Ulrike Naumann, and Janet Treasure. "Is Fat Talking a Causal Risk Factor for Body Dissatisfaction? A Systematic Review and Meta-Analysis." *International Journal of Eating Disorders* 46, no. 7 (2013): 643–652.

Sismondo, Sergio. "How Pharmaceutical Industry Funding Affects Trial Outcomes: Causal Structures and Responses." *Social Sciences & Medicine* 66 (2008): 1909–1914.

Smith-Jackson, T., J. J. Reel, and R. Thackeray. "Coping with 'Bad Body Image Days': Strategies from First-Year Young Adult College Women." *Body Image* 8 (2011): 335–342.

Sobal, Jeffery, and Albert J. Stunkard. "Socioeconomic Status and Obesity: A Review of the Literature." *Psychological Bulletin* 105 (1989): 260–275.

Stephen, Ian, and A. Treshi-Marie Perera. "Judging the Difference Between Attractiveness and Health: Does Exposure to Model Images Influence the Judgments Made by Men and Women?" *PLOS One,* January 20, 2014.

Sumithran, Priya, and Joseph Proietto. "The Defence of Body Weight: A Physiological Basis for Weight Regain After Weight Loss." *Clinical Science* 124 (2013): 231–241.

Swami, Viren, et al. "The Attractive Female Body Weight and Female Body Dissatisfaction in 26 Countries Across 10 World Regions: Results of the International Body Project I." *Personality and Social Psychology Bulletin* 36 (2010): 309–325.

Tiggemann, Marika, Amy Slater, and Veronica Smyth. "'Retouch Free': The Effect of Labeling Media Images as Not Digitally Altered on Women's Body Dissatisfaction." *Body Image* 11 (2013): 85–88.

Tomiyama, A. Janet, Britt Ahlstrom, and Traci Mann. "Long-Term Effects of Dieting: Is Weight Loss Related to Health?" *Social and Personality Psychology Compass* 7 (2013): 861–877.

Tomiyama, A. Janet, et al. "Low Calorie Dieting Increases Cortisol." *Psychosomatic Medicine* 72 (2010): 357–364.

Tylka, Tracy, et al. "The Weight-Inclusive Versus Weight-Normative Approach to Health: Evaluating the Evidence for Prioritizing Well-Being over Weight Loss." *Journal of Obesity* (2014).

van den Berg, Patricia, and Dianne Neumark-Sztainer. "Fat 'n Happy 5 Years Later: Is It Bad for Overweight Girls to Like Their Bodies?" *Journal of Adolescent Health* 41 (2007): 415–417.

Van Wye, G., et al. "Weight Cycling and 6-Year Weight Change in Healthy Adults: The Aerobics Center Longitudinal Study." *Obesity* 15, no. 3 (2007): 731–739.

Vartanian, Lenny, and Joshua Smyth. "Primum Non Nocere: Obesity Stigma and Public Health." *Bioethical Inquiry* 10 (2013): 49–57.

Wazana, Ashley. "Physicians and the Pharmaceutical Industry: Is a Gift Ever Just a Gift?" *JAMA* 283 (2000): 373–380.

Wear, Delese, et al. "Making Fun of Patients: Medical Students' Perceptions and Use of Derogatory and Cynical Humor in Clinical Settings." *Academic Medicine* 81, no. 5 (May 2006): 454–462.

Wirth, Michael D., et al. "Chronic Weight Dissatisfaction Predicts Type 2 Diabetes Risk: Aerobic Center Longitudinal Study." *Health Psychology* 33 (2014): 912–919.

Wood, Marcia. "Health at Every Size: New Hope for Obese Americans?" *Agricultural Research Magazine*, USDA (2006).

INDEX

American Medical Association
(AMA)
Committee on Science and
Public Health, 102–103
obesity classified as disease by,
102–103
American Psychological
Association, 45
American Public Health
Association, 98
Amylin Pharmaceuticals, 109
"An Epidemic of Obesity Myths,"
45n
"An Open Apology to All of
My Weight Loss Clients"
(Higgins), 90–91
Andres, Reubin, 15
Aniston, Jennifer, xxii
Anorexia, 4, 51–54, 81–82, 130,
135, 170–171
anxiety, eating disorders, and,
6
changing language around,
170n
fat and, 92–93
fear of food and, 92–94
genetics and, 6
overweight/obese and, 5
perfectionism and, 6
as physiological and
psychological disease, 81
recovery from, 4–6
recovery from, social aspects of
food and, 74

recovery from, story of, 4–5
school-based health eating
initiatives and, 54
theory of why some people
develop, 74–75
Anxiety
eating disorders, anorexia and,
6
See also Body anxiety
Anxiety disorder, 8
Anxiety drugs, 13
Appetite
hunger and, neurobiology of,
5–6
internal sense of, reconnecting
with, 188
Aristotle, 17
Armstrong, Lance, xxi
Artificial sweeteners, 13
Astrup, Arne, 110
Attia, Peter, 25–26
Avena, Nicole, 114
Averill, Lindsey, 164–165

Babies
appetite of, mothers' fear of,
75–76
instinctive eating and, 183
Bacon, Linda, 14, 189–190,
196–197
Baker, Sarah, 156
Bariatric doctors, weight bias
among, 116
Bariatric surgeons, 95–96, 101

ABOUT THE AUTHOR

HARRIET BROWN began her writing life as a poet. She has written about subjects ranging from Alzheimer's to job discrimination to eating disorders for the *New York Times, Ms., Prevention, Health, O Magazine,* and many other publications. She has edited two anthologies and published a number of nonfiction books, including *Brave Girl Eating: A Family's Struggle with Anorexia,* which combined science journalism with memoir to call for a new approach to treating eating disorders. Brown grew up near Camden, New Jersey, and has since lived in New York City; Madison, Wisconsin; and now Syracuse, New York, where she's an associate professor of magazine journalism at the S. I. Newhouse School of Public Communications at Syracuse University.